A DARKLING PLAIN: STORIES OF CONFLICT AND HUMANITY DURING WAR

How do people maintain their humanity during wars? Despite its importance, this question receives scant scholarly attention, perhaps because of the over-whelming aspect of war. "The enormity of it all tended to reduce everything else in life to a kind of footnote," one soldier said of World War II. The gener-ally accepted wisdom is that wars bring out the worst in us, pitting us against one another. "War is hell," William Tecumseh Sherman famously noted, and even wars clearly designated "just" nonetheless inflict massive destruction and cruelty. Since ethics is concerned with discovering what takes us to a morally superior place, one conducive to human flourishing and happiness, studying what helps people survive wartime trauma becomes an extremely valuable enterprise. *A Darkling Plain* thus fills an important scholarly void, analyzing wartime stories that reveal much about our capacity to process trauma, heal wounds, reclaim lost spirits, and derive meaning and purpose from the most hor-rific of personal events.

Kristen Renwick Monroe is Chancellor's Professor of Political Science at the Uni-versity of California at Irvine, where she founded and directs the UCI Inter-disciplinary Center for the Scientific Study of Ethics and Morality and is Asso-ciate Director of the Program in Political Psychology. Past President of the International Society of Political Psychology and Vice President of the Ameri-can Political Science Association, Monroe is the author or editor of more than 15 books and 100 articles, including the award-winning *The Heart of Altruism* (1996), *The Hand of Compassion* (2004), and *Ethics in an Age of Terror and Genocide* (2012). Her co-authors were interns at the UCI Ethics Center when they worked on this book with Monroe. They now are undergraduates, Chloe Lampros-Monroe at Bryn Mawr College and Jonah Robnett Pellecchia at Cornell University.

A DARKLING PLAIN

Stories of Conflict and Humanity during War

KRISTEN RENWICK MONROE
University of California, Irvine

WITH

CHLOE LAMPROS-MONROE
Bryn Mawr College

JONAH ROBNETT PELLECCHIA
Cornell University

CAMBRIDGE
UNIVERSITY PRESS

CAMBRIDGE
UNIVERSITY PRESS

32 Avenue of the Americas, New York, NY 10013-2473, USA

Cambridge University Press is part of the University of Cambridge.

It furthers the University's mission by disseminating knowledge in the pursuit of education, learning, and research at the highest international levels of excellence.

www.cambridge.org
Information on this title: www.cambridge.org/9781107690172

First published 2015

Printed in the United States of America

A catalog record for this publication is available from the British Library.

Library of Congress Cataloging in Publication Data
Monroe, Kristen R., 1946–
A darkling plain : stories of conflict and humanity during war / Kristen Monroe, University of California-Irvine; Chloe Lampros-Monroe, University of California-Irvine; Jonah Pellecchia, University of California-Irvine.
   pages cm
Includes bibliographical references and index.
ISBN 978-1-107-03499-0 (hardback) – ISBN 978-1-107-69017-2 (paperback)
1. War – Moral and ethical aspects.   2. War – Psychological aspects.
3. Humanity – Philosophy.   I. Lampros-Monroe, Chloe.   II. Pellecchia, Jonah.
III. Title.
U22.M57   2014
303.6'6 – dc23   2014002475

ISBN 978-1-107-03499-0 Hardback
ISBN 978-1-107-69017-2 Paperback

The sea is calm to-night.
The tide is full, the moon lies fair
Upon the straits; on the French coast the light
Gleams and is gone; the cliffs of England stand;
Glimmering and vast, out in the tranquil bay.
Come to the window, sweet is the night-air!

Only, from the long line of spray
Where the sea meets the moon-blanched land,
Listen! you hear the grating roar
Of pebbles which the waves draw back, and fling,
At their return, up the high strand,
Begin, and cease, and then again begin,
With tremulous cadence slow, and bring
The eternal note of sadness in.

Sophocles long ago
Heard it on the Agaean, and it brought
Into his mind the turbid ebb and flow
Of human misery; we
Find also in the sound a thought,
Hearing it by this distant northern sea.

The Sea of Faith
Was once, too, at the full, and round earth's shore
Lay like the folds of a bright girdle furled.
But now I only hear
Its melancholy, long, withdrawing roar,
Retreating, to the breath
Of the night-wind, down the vast edges drear
And naked shingles of the world.

Ah, love, let us be true
To one another! for the world, which seems
To lie before us like a land of dreams,
So various, so beautiful, so new,
Hath really neither joy, nor love, nor light,
Nor certitude, nor peace, nor help for pain;
And we are here as on a darkling plain
Swept with confused alarms of struggle and flight,
Where ignorant armies clash by night.

Matthew Arnold, "Dover Beach," 1867

CONTENTS

PREFACE

It's not glamorous. It was a very messy thing.

Frank was at Stanford when the Japanese bombed Pearl Harbor. An Irish Catholic with a father in the Navy, Frank enlisted and spent two years in the Pacific in the Army Air Corps, assigned to the Navy. Frank took part in the invasion of the Marianas, Iwo Jima, and Palau,[1] and was scheduled to go in as part of the home island invasion of Japan. Frequently in battle areas as a support soldier dealing with technical aspects that drew on his engineering background, Frank quickly learned the "terrible impact of war."

> *It's not glamorous. You've got to realize there was a lot of propaganda in World War II to develop patriotism and support. You found out that was an awful lot of baloney! It was a very messy thing. . . . When you think in terms of the destruction . . . you learn to hate. The tendency for all of us in the Pacific was to hate the Japanese. We hated them for [what] they did on the Bataan Death March.[2] To them, if you were willing to become a prisoner then you ceased to be a human. You were no better than an animal, maybe not even that good. . . . The samurai code caused them to be very brutal. If you look at the history of the Japanese in China and what they did to American prisoners, that leads to the ability to hate. It led to the view that the only good Japanese was a dead one. Ask and give no quarter. . . . I get a bit cynical when I hear all these things about the Geneva Convention. You fought the war the same way the enemy fought it. . . . Like for like. You only go to war to win. It's not a game, and you don't win by scoring a certain amount of points.*

After the war, Frank simply closed a door.

> *We just didn't talk about it. It was one of those things you repress. That's how you cope with things. . . . I never talked about the war. I've probably*

talked about it more tonight than I ever have. To me it was a chapter and when the chapter was over, you closed it and put it behind you.

Frank came home and returned to Stanford, where he met and married his wife – college roommate to Sandra Day O'Connor – and made a life as a successful engineer in the aerospace industry, settling in Southern California and becoming President and Chief Operating Officer of the Northrop Corporation. After Frank retired, he went back to school.

I didn't have any problems leaving that [business] world completely. I just went off and felt like doing different things. That's what got me to UCI. Most of my friends, they retire, they golf. Travel a lot. Stuff retired folks do. My reaction was that it was not very satisfying to do that. I came back to school.

Frank ended up in one of my courses at the University of California, Irvine, and our conversations after class in time led to a friendship. We were an unlikely pair in many ways. Frank was a Republican who ranked Calvin Coolidge our greatest president. I argued for Franklin Roosevelt. He supported John McCain and bought von Hayek's arguments on government as the enemy of freedom. I was a Hillary (Clinton) girl who distrusted politicians but thought government could be a tool for good if used wisely. We debated politics, frequently differing but always respecting the other's arguments even when we disagreed vehemently with the conclusions.

Over the fifteen-some years of our friendship, I came to respect Frank as a sensitive, thoughtful individual, a decent man of integrity and honesty. I recognized him as a humane person, even if I could not define that term precisely. As we discussed Frank's wartime participation, I asked Frank how he managed to survive the war emotionally unscathed.

It's an attitude you develop. Everybody, to maintain their sensibilities in such a situation, that's generally the way they cope with it. It was fatalism. It was, "If something's going to get you, it'll get you. If it's not, it'll not." That was the basic thing. A lot of men in the war thought that way. They used to joke about who's going to get it next, that type of thing. I guess I still am fatalistic. That is to say, I don't believe I have a predestined direction or that somebody has got a plan for me, that I am fulfilling this plan. My reaction is that you live in a world where all sorts of things are happening. Events occur, and it's how you react to them. But you don't control events. You don't control the world around you.

Was this the answer? Were Frank's experiences and his reaction to World War II typical of others' experiences with wars? What made Frank the way he was? What kept him from continuing to hate the Japanese, an enemy Frank openly acknowledged he once detested but whose country he later visited frequently, whom he did business with successfully, and whose language he even mastered? What factors helped Frank – and many people like him – lay to rest the negative feelings, to keep and maintain humanity during a bloody war, and what helped these people create a life afterwards that was meaningful and ethical in its treatment of others?

Answering these questions is the topic of this book.

NOTES

1. Iwo Jima is perhaps the most famous of the battles in which Frank participated. Fought from February 19th to March 26th, 1945, the Battle of Iwo Jima is memorialized in Joe Rosenthal's photograph of five marines and one navy corpsman raising the U.S. flag on the fifth day of the 35-day battle. Frank's description of the Japanese desire to never surrender seems justified by the facts of Iwo Jima. The Japanese army was heavily fortified and fought stubbornly to rebuff what was the first American attack on the Japanese home islands. Out of an estimated 18,000+ Japanese soldiers at the beginning of the battle of Iwo Jima, only 216 remained alive to be taken prisoner. This statistic is all the more remarkable since an American victory seemed assured from the start, given American superiority in arms and numbers and the impossibility of a Japanese retreat or reinforcement.

   The battle of the Marianas that Frank refers to – also called the Battle of the Philippine Sea – was a decisive naval battle, involving the largest aircraft carrier battle in history. Between June 19th and 20th, 1944, the United States Navy's Fifth Fleet and the Imperial Japanese Navy's Combined Fleet fought near the Mariana Islands, in a battle in which superior American air power and skilled carrier aircrew were decisive. The Mariana and Palau Islands campaign was a U.S. offensive against Imperial Japanese forces in the Mariana Islands and Palau between June and November 1944, under the command of Admiral Chester Nimitz. The campaign was designed to neutralize Japanese bases and support the Allied drive to retake the Philippines, deemed critical to the Allied advance because the Philippines would provide bases for the strategic bombing of Japan. In all three of these important campaigns, air power and support of the kind provided by Frank would prove crucial.

2. The Bataan Death March refers to the Japanese Army's forcible transfer of 75,000 American and Filipino prisoners of war. Coming immediately after the three-month Battle of Bataan in the Philippines in 1942, this 60-mile march included extensive killing, starvation, and physical abuse of thousands of American POWs and civilians. An Allied military commission later judged the Bataan Death March a Japanese war crime. All quotes from Frank's interview come from Chapter 2. I have condensed the conversation for clarity of presentation. Full transcripts are available at www.ethicscenter.uci.edu.

INTRODUCTION
The human aspect of living through a war

An opportunity to think more systematically about how people keep their humanity during war occurred in the fall of 2010 when I taught a course on psychology and international politics. I had just finished a book on the psychology of genocide and was interested in seeing how the book manuscript played when I taught it. But I also wanted to explore a slightly different aspect of the problem, wanted to understand and show students how people keep their humanity during genocide and war and how they reclaim it later in life. Uncertain what to call this course, in a rash moment I dubbed it "Ethics in a time of terror and genocide," ordered the books, and promptly forgot about the course until the late summer, when I wandered into the Department office and asked the Departmental Secretary if any of the books had arrived.

"Sure. They're over there."

"Thanks," I said, as I turned to the shelf where desk copies were stored.

"Do you want to get the books for your TA, too?" Natalie asked.

I was surprised. "There's no TA for the course. It's a small course, and very specialized. I've never taught it before and no one knows about it so it probably won't have more than twenty students."

"Kristi!" she exclaimed. "There are eighty students in the course and a waiting list a mile long."

"Really?" I was taken aback. "I can't imagine why."

"They might not know about the course," Natalie explained, "but it's a great title."

Natalie was right. The course was fully booked and my plans for a small seminar with lots of student interaction seemed to fly out the window, as I sadly envisioned a large lecture room filled with students

I would never get to know well and lectures that might capture the basic ideas but would not permit the feedback necessary to determine whether the ideas really were going in or were just hovering out there in the room, untouched and unclaimed by any student.

Always somewhat sedulous and ornery concerning rules, I had taught long enough to chuck traditional norms. "Well, I'm going to teach the kind of course I want to teach anyway. I don't care if there are eighty students in the class. I'm going to run a seminar and have some fun," I said to myself. And that's exactly what I did.

I found surprisingly little of interest in the political science literature on the subject so the course drew heavily on documentary films and autobiographies from people who had lived through a war, genocide, or another of the political disasters that can befall human beings. We focused on the human element, on how ordinary people – people like Frank (Chapter 2) – responded to these political upheavals, asking what kept them sane, whole, and psychologically intact during their trials and during the rest of their lives as they struggled to assimilate what had happened to them, tried to make sense of events that perhaps carried none.[1] Despite the class size, the last two weeks of the course were devoted to student projects. Each class member had to find someone who had lived through a period of political upheaval: a war, genocide or ethnic cleansing, an oppressive and cruel political regime, a revolution, and so on. Students could work in groups of up to five and, although the interview exercise was primarily pedagogical, students nonetheless were taught about Institutional Review Board procedures, which they had to follow when doing interviews. The interviews themselves were kept simple. Students were cautioned to treat individual interviewees with respect and care, viewing them as human beings, not research subjects. Students were to ask speakers to talk about the war, genocide, ethnic cleansing, or political upheaval[2] they lived through in whatever manner speakers felt most comfortable, with students asking questions of clarification only if speakers seemed at ease with further questions. Beyond that, students posed only three simple questions as prompts. (1) What was the political event you lived through? (2) What were the moral dilemmas you confronted? And (3) what enabled you to keep your humanity during that time? Interviews were taped – occasionally filmed – and transcribed, with the transcriptions to be shown to speakers for approval before the interviews were analyzed or shared with others.

Here's why I begin the book with the poem by Matthew Arnold. This classroom, which looked so ordinary, filled with lovely young people, fresh and bubbly and light, illustrating the southern California stereotype – in shorts and sandals and hurrying from one class to another as they shifted their backpacks and chatted happily with friends – produced some of the most amazing student papers I've ever seen. The experience reminded me of Arnold's "tranquil bay" filled with "the sweet night air." But underneath, the sea was restive. Each of these happy-go-lucky-looking teenagers carried the story of a friend or family member who had been through hell. Each student listened to their friend or loved one's story of loss, tragedy, and endurance and, in doing so, effectively communed with Sophocles who "long ago / Heard it on the Agaean, and it brought / Into his mind the turbid ebb and flow / Of human misery," as Arnold wrote.

One student's great grandmother must be one of the few living survivors of the Armenian genocide. A father told his daughter, for the first time, how he had survived Idi Amin's time of terror. (His daughter never understood why he sent so much money to people in Uganda instead of giving it to her. Now, she said, it made sense.) Several Japanese-American grandmothers had been interned by the Americans during World War II, part of a shameful policy only acknowledged as such in the 1980s. There were soldiers, of course – friends of the students, occasionally fathers, brothers, or boyfriends – fighting in wars from Vietnam to Afghanistan. One young man interviewed his half-uncle Gunther, chosen because Gunther was a refugee from Vienna. Before the interview, the student never knew Gunther's father had been SS, or that the student's own grandfather was so abusive that Gunther moved out at 14, living on the streets of Chicago, breaking into Frank Lloyd Wright's Robie House during the harsh winters to spend the night before the staff returned in the morning. Uneducated and living by his wits, Gunther ran afoul of the Chicago mob and, after enlisting in the U.S. Army, later endured his own "One Flew over the Cuckoo's Nest" experience.

Other students had parents who had fought in Vietnam: Americans and South Vietnamese soldiers who knew their civil war meant they might have to kill a relative fighting for the North, or be killed themselves by that same relative. After the war, one Vietnamese student's father told her the worst trauma was being incarcerated in a re-education camp. He spoke of the torment of having to decide to escape by boat, leaving his wife and child behind while he lived as a refugee in Indonesia and the United States, alone until he could bring his family to a new land, where my student would be conceived and born. So it went. Story after story. Moral choices, yes, and difficulty assimilating it all. Anguish and varying degrees of success in making sense of what had happened to them. But exquisitely moving personal stories that reveal the myriad parts of the moral complexity and nuance of the human aspect of living through a war.

We deliberately include *all* participants caught up in wars; we do not restrict analysis to stories of soldiers in the field. Although we do include such soldiers (Tuan, Sebastian, Doc), we also hear from support troops who cleaned up the carnage (Frank). We listen to refugees displaced by wars (Gunther, Reza), and noncombatants in resistance movements (Mafalda, Ngugi).[3] Our intent is to present not just the battlefield experience – as important as that is – but also war's crippling aftermath and the panic of confronting death up close. What is it like for a young girl to smell burning corpses (Fabiola)? How does it feel to never know when you might be killed by a stray bullet (Marie) or turned in by neighbors (Herb, Laura)? To know you have absolutely no control over the most fundamental aspects of your life (Kimberly, Sara, and Leyla)? How do people – such as Rose – assimilate wartime trauma and construct a meaningful life afterwards? These questions engage all of us. They connect us with "the turbid ebb and flow / Of human misery." They remind us that our own lives often lack the light, the certitude, the peace, and the help for pain that we all hunger for as part of being human, and that we have much to learn from those who have gone before us.

This book thus embraces the full wartime experience. By adding stories collected by the 2010 summer interns at the UCI Ethics Center,[4] the book reflects my efforts – in formal classes and via the Ethics Center internship program – to talk about ethics with young people in a process that draws on both their intellectual and emotional intelligence. Indeed, one of my goals here is to provide a concrete illustration of how ethics can be taught in ways that move students beyond the mere accumulation of intellectual knowledge and on to a deeper understanding of ethics and moral psychology.

The research serves a more traditional scholarly purpose as well. In particular, it asks: What helps people maintain their humanity during wars, genocides, revolutions, and other traumatic political conflicts? Despite the seemingly obvious importance of the topic, we find remarkably little scholarly work on how people respond to wars and other searing political tragedies in a manner that retains their humanity. Perhaps the overwhelming aspect of war accounts for this scholarly neglect. "The enormity of it all tended to reduce everything else in life to a kind of footnote," one American G.I. said after surviving the Battle of the Bulge. Analyzing wars' human impact thus is a daunting task.

The generally accepted wisdom – probably because it is the norm – is that wars and genocides bring out the worst in humankind, destroying us and pitting us against each other. William Tecumseh Sherman famously noted: "You don't know the horrible aspects of war. I've been through two wars and I know. I've seen cities and homes in ashes. I've seen thousands of men lying on the ground, their dead faces looking up at the skies. I tell you, war is hell!"[5] Scholars find even the wars most clearly designated *worthy* or *just* suffer from massive cruelty and inhumanity.[6] Since part of what drives scholarship in ethics, however, is a concern to discover what takes people to a morally superior place – one conducive to human flourishing and happiness – studying what helps people survive the trauma of war and genocide thus becomes an extremely valuable, if not urgent, enterprise.[7] This is the topic of this book.

The book proceeds in five parts. Part One sets our research in the context of the literature on wars and humanity. Given the paucity of social science literature on this topic, we draw heavily on research on post-traumatic stress disorder syndrome and on literary works about war, including memoirs, biographies, and autobiographies. Part One thus reviews the scholarly literature, condenses it into propositions to be examined, and describes our method of analysis. Part Two contains narrative interview data from World War II. These data take the form of life story interviews with six individuals: Frank, an American soldier who fought in the South Pacific; Laura Hillman, a Holocaust survivor saved by Oskar Schindler; Gunther, a displaced person whose father was Gestapo, killed on the Eastern front, and who fled the Russians in Yugoslavia to come to Austria and the United States after the war; Mafalda, code name for a Portuguese princess with the Resistance, arrested and tortured by the Gestapo as part of their interrogation of participants in the July 20th plot to kill Hitler; Herb, an Austrian Jewish émigré who fled the Third Reich shortly before the war began; and Grace, a Japanese-American teenager living in California and interned during the war. Part Three presents stories from five speakers from other wars: Tuan, a South Vietnamese soldier who survived re-education camp, being a boat person and refugee in Indonesia and the United States; Kimberly and Sara, both of whom survived the Khmer Rouge in Cambodia; and Sebastian and Doc, who were American soldiers in Iraq. Part Four contains interviews with people who lived through civil wars and genocides. Rose must be one of the last survivors of the Armenian genocide, who nonetheless remembers, as a six-year-old, seeing her grandfather beheaded because he would not give up his Bible; Ngũgĩ wa Thiong'o lived through Kenya's Mau Mau rebellion, with brothers on both sides of the conflict. An Amnesty International prisoner of conscience, Ngũgĩ finds language a form of colonial domination and used prison toilet paper to write the first book published in Gĩkũyũ. Fabiola lived through the civil war in Nicaragua and Marie in Lebanon. Reza escaped from Afghanistan during the Russian occupation and Okello fled from Idi Amin's Uganda. Finally, Leyla was a college professor married to a highly placed official under the Shah of Iran; Leyla hid students in her home, without her husband's knowledge, and fled the Islamic Republic so her daughter could be educated and her sons would not have to fight against Iraq.[8]

All these interviews are analyzed in Part Five, where we find surviving war with one's humanity intact both a complex and a fragile psychological process, equal elements of chance and personal psychology. We nonetheless find six psychological dimensions exert critical influences, albeit in ways that are often counterintuitive: identity and belonging to a larger group, such as family or political entity; the ability to establish self continuity; fatalism and hope; cognitive stretching; the conceptualization of happiness; and the particular assignment of blame and guilt.

Our conclusion asks what an analysis of people who lived "as on a darkling plain, / Swept with confused alarms of struggle and flight, / Where ignorant armies clash by night" can teach the rest of us about living in a world that "seems / To lie before us like a land of dreams, / So various, so beautiful, so new, [yet] / Hath really neither joy, nor love, nor light, / Nor certitude, nor peace, nor help for pain."

What did these people hold fast to in the dark of night? What can we find?

NOTES

1. A focus on the human element reflects my desire to go beyond traditional political science literature in this field to provide a text that supplements standard works in international relations and appeals to a broader, more general audience, many of whom will be interested in the stories as much as, and perhaps more than, the political science analysis.
2. When we use the term "war" we include all these events.
3. Mafalda's story has historical interest, and documents the role of neutral countries during war. Ngũgĩ illustrates the wide range of resistance to wartime injustice.
4. The full title is the Interdisciplinary Center for the Scientific Study of Ethics and Morality. Each summer the Ethics Center runs an intern program for students. In 2010 we focused on how ordinary people made moral choices; those interviews deemed relevant for this book are included here. Interviews with Herb and Mafalda were conducted as part of another research project. Most interviews were

conducted by students in Political Science 149, taught at UCI during the fall term of 2010, as a pedagogical exercise.

5. Slightly varying accounts of Sherman's speech to the Michigan Military Academy on June 19, 1879 have been quoted. This version comes from Dr. Charles O. Brown in the Battle Creek *Enquirer and News* (November 18, 1933).

6. See the *New York Times Book Review*, Sunday, May 29, 2011, p. 1, for summary.

7. Defining ethics is a noble task but not one to be attempted here. It seems accurate to say, however, that much of ethics in the post-Christian/post-Kantian era conceptualizes ethics as a series of obligations and duties. An earlier Greek tradition emphasizes the concept of human flourishing and asks what people need to thrive and be happy, and then makes the pursuit of such a life central to ethics.

8. We adopt pseudonyms unless specifically asked by speakers to use their full names. Critical details and identifiers have been modified to protect privacy and safety of relatives who might still be in some danger. We apologize if our desire to protect privacy means we have not publicly acknowledged anyone's life story.

PART ONE

WAR IS A TERRIBLE THING!

You people speak so lightly of war; you don't know what you're talking about. War is a terrible thing!
– William Tecumseh Sherman,
in Shelby Foote, *The Civil War: A Narrative*
(1986), p. 58

1 CONSTRUCTING AN ANALYSIS OF THE UNSPEAKABLE

Literature, Methodology, and Data

INTRODUCTION

There is little doubt about the negative impact of war on the human psyche.[1] But what do we know about the ability to recover from the trauma of war, to heal wounds and flourish as we construct a meaningful life? Playwrights, poets, biographers, and writers of fiction often provide revealing insights into war, asking how to best protect and draw forth humanity during war, and suggesting what does this best. Indeed, how people deal with the moral choices such catastrophes present and how people manage to cling to their humanity – if they do – constitutes a familiar theme in great literature. Sophocles' *Antigone*[2] and the updated version presented in Nazi-occupied France during World War II by Jean Anouilh,[3] the eighth-century BCE *Iliad* and the *Odyssey*, Leo Tolstoy's *War and Peace*,[4] John Steinbeck's *The Moon is Down*,[5] Arthur Koestler's *Arrival and Departure*,[6] and Steven Galloway's *The Cellist of Sarajevo*[7] are but a few illustrations of literary treatments touching on this issue. Biographies and autobiographies abound with such themes. Christabel Bielenburg's *Once I Was a German*,[8] Albert Speer's autobiography and Gitta Sereny's counterbiography,[9] as well as fictionalized biographies, such as Elie Wiesel's *Night*[10] or Tom Keneally's *Schindler's List*,[11] all illustrate this genre's recent treatment of moral choice during war, in this instance World War II. Hollywood, too, frequently features issues of moral choice and humanity during war, in films such as *Casablanca, Life is Beautiful, The Deerhunter, Coming Home*, and *The Hurt Locker*, to mention just a few.

Surprisingly, it is the political science literature that is lacking, with philosophical literature equally sparse. Psychologists address the topic in a variety of ways. Social psychologists note the importance of both personality and the environment. Researchers on post-traumatic stress disorder highlight factors from positive beliefs about the world[12] and control[13] to a sense of agency, and the hardiness literature[14] emphasizes the importance of not remaining isolated and the desire to participate in and learn from new experiences.

Literature on narrative therapy documents how writing memoirs or talk therapy can teach survivors of wars – and other traumas – how to cope with and eventually control memories that intrude in the present, causing problems in current lives and relationships.[15] Much of this literature overlaps with or falls into the category of work on post-traumatic stress disorder (hereafter PTSD); most PTSD literature either analyzes traumatic stress or emphasizes therapeutic, even pharmaceutical ways to deal with inhumane and debilitating responses to conflict.[16] Post-traumatic stress disorder treatment usually encourages patients to work through feelings of guilt, self-blame, and mistrust of others, and to explore their thoughts and feelings about the trauma.[17] These focused therapeutic attempts are designed to help the person exist better in the present. Within the PTSD literature, assumptions about the resilience of human beings vary, with many mental health professionals and media commentators portraying individuals as victims of stressful events and emotions. Indeed, this victim approach is evident in the very terms "disorder" and "syndrome." In contrast, we find a sturdier view of humankind in the hardiness literature[18] and the positive psychology approach.[19] One of our questions concerns how adaptive, resilient, and untraumatized human beings can remain, even in the face of the most devastating situations and experiences. A second is to assess the human ability to recover from stress, loss, and grief. In asking about the human ability to cope as a typical human reaction to adversity, we assess work on coping mechanisms related to political trauma[20] and ask how people's attempts to make sense of negative experiences helps them escape the distress caused by these events.

This chapter summarizes critical findings in these diverse literatures, literatures not often discussed together, to explain how people retain and reclaim their humanity during war. To contribute to the debates revealed by a close examination of this literature, we begin by contrasting theories emphasizing the importance of situation and luck (Adler, Bettelheim) with those stressing the importance of personality (Freud, Adler, and Frankl). We next review relevant recent literature from social psychology, PTSD, and narrative therapy. Finally, we describe how we structure our empirical analysis to assess and lend additional insight to prior findings in the literature. We intend our analysis to fill gaps in the general theoretical models and link our research to the growing literature on the psychology of coping and recovering from politically induced trauma.[21] Our goals thus are two-fold: (1) determining what helps people survive emotionally intact during traumatic political conflicts and (2) discovering how people move beyond the harrowing aspect of these conflicts to fashion meaningful post-war lives.

LITERATURE REVIEW

GENERAL THEORETICAL APPROACHES. Sigmund Freud, Alfred Adler, Viktor Frankl, and Bruno Bettelheim all discussed the extent to which human flourishing depends on psychological factors centering on identity. Two of these writers are psychiatrists[22] who survived Nazi incarceration, and both acknowledged developing their theories as part of a coping response to this incarceration. Adler, Frankl and Bettelheim lived in an intellectual world dominated by Sigmund Freud, and we cannot fully understand their works without a short consideration of Freud and the general context of psychoanalysis in mid-twentieth-century Vienna. Freud's influence is so immeasurable it seems unnecessary to note that the following provides only the briefest of discussions as a point of reference.[23]

Sigmund Freud was a neurologist whose work on hysteria led him to develop the "talking cure," a treatment where patients talked through their problems. The goal of talk therapy was to locate and release powerful pent-up emotions imprisoned in the unconscious mind. Freud called these pent-up emotions "repression" and argued that repression formed an impediment to normal functioning of the psyche.[24] The "talking cure" is widely seen as the basis of psychoanalysis. Freud simultaneously developed a theory of the human mind and how it is organized and a theory that human behavior both reflects and conditions this mental organization. Freud's approach emphasizes certain clinical techniques for treating mental illness and makes human personality strongly shaped by childhood experiences. Among these, Freud made sexual drives a primary motivational force of human life, arguing that the raw will to survive – as expressed in sexual urges – is part of our human nature.

Alfred Adler was one of the members of the first psychoanalytic circle organized in Vienna by Freud. Adler left the group in 1911 over personal and intellectual differences with Freud, whom Adler nonetheless credited with providing a scientific foundation for psychoanalysis.

Perhaps because Adler began working with circus people, his ideas emphasize the importance of strength and overcompensation for perceived inferiorities. Adler's own theory centered on critical differences between Adler and Freud and focused on Adler's contention that the social realm (exteriority) is as important to psychology as the internal realm (interiority). For Adler, dynamics of power and compensation extend far beyond sexuality and, Adler claimed, gender and politics can be as important to well-being as libido. Adler thus was more sympathetic to power dynamics and emphasized the importance of equality for preventing psychopathology.[25] Adler's emphasis on the inferiority complex and self-esteem – and its negative effects on human health – and his emphasis on power dynamics reflect Nietzsche's influence. But Adler's conceptualization of the "will to power" focuses on the individual's creative power to change for the better and made Adler among the first in psychology to make the case that power dynamics between men and women are critical in understanding human psychology.[26]

Frankl developed a theory directly relevant for understanding how people retain and reclaim humanity during war. Frankl's experience as a clinical psychoanalyst incarcerated by the Nazis led to his development of an existential analysis called *logotherapy*,[27] in which Frankl addresses a concern central to this book: how to find meaning in all forms of existence, even those as sordid as the genocidal conditions of concentration camps.[28] (Frankl's wife and parents were killed in the camps; only his sister escaped. Frankl himself was liberated on April 27, 1945.) Frankl's personal wartime experiences led him to conclude that life has potential meaning, even in the midst of the most tragic, absurd, and dehumanizing situations.[29] This realization served as the basis for Frankl's theory, which argues that the lack of meaning is the paramount existential crisis. Frankl expanded this view to argue that "existential frustration" is a common phenomenon and one accompanied by boredom, apathy and emptiness.[30]

Often referred to as the third Viennese School of psychotherapy,[31] after Freud's psychoanalysis and Adler's individual psychology, logotherapy focuses on a *will to find meaning* as opposed to Freud's emphasis on the *pleasure principle* or Adler's more Nietzschean emphasis on the *desire for power*. Essentially, logotherapy claims it is the striving to find meaning in one's life that is the primary and certainly the most powerful motivating force driving human behavior. If logotherapy is correct, we would expect individuals who experience wars and genocides to (1) talk about how they were able to find some kind of meaning in their circumstances, even the most miserable ones; (2) locate as a motivation for their survival their ability to find meaning in life; and (3) speak of their lives after the war as ones in which they found meaning in what they did and experienced, if only in the stand they took when faced with conditions – such as wars – that entailed unchangeable and unbearable suffering.[32] In contrast, Freudian thought would suggest people simply want to survive, and Adler's theory submits people will survive best when they retain self-esteem and a sense of control over their environment.

Bruno Bettelheim also was Viennese and, like Frankl, Bettelheim used his wartime camp experience[33] to develop his version of *milieu therapy*.[34] In existence since the late 1800s, milieu therapy involves treating psychiatric problems in residential, inpatient settings and, more recently, in day treatment or partial hospitalization. The critical assumption underlying Bettelheim's theory is the belief that the environment plays a critical role in psychic well-being. Emotional health thus is a combination of individual dynamics and the social system, which can be manipulated to change both behavior and relationships. Like Frankl's, Bettelheim's work reflects Bettelheim's personal experience with both Nazism and psychoanalysis. Bettelheim breaks with Freudian analysts, however, by agreeing with Adler and weighting the critical importance of social systems on individuals. *Individual and Mass Behavior in Extreme Situations* (1943) reflects Bettelheim's observations of the extreme environment's impact on inmates, camp guards, and even himself as self-designated participant observer. Bettelheim drew on psychoanalytic concepts, such as Anna Freud's concept of identification with the aggressor, to explain why so many inmates adopted the perpetrator's values in order to survive. He also drew on the concept of victim guilt, defined as a feeling that victims somehow deserved their destiny. *The Informed Heart: Autonomy in a Mass Age* (1960), Bettelheim's intellectual autobiography, further elaborated Bettelheim's ideas about the relationship between mental disorder and the external environment. This work reflects Bettelheim's views on why Freudian principles failed to explain why some individuals survived the Nazi camps when others did not.

Bettelheim's was one of the first attempts to explain the Nazi system not as evil incarnate or psychopathology run amuck but rather as a comprehensive, carefully constructed system to control people through breaking their identity and their links to their pre-camp selves. The fearful possibility of midnight raids, the nonsensical beatings, and the humiliation camp inmates endured, all were designed systematically, Bettelheim argued, to break ties to previous identities. The break with prior identities effectively created a new self, an inmate self that would do anything to survive. Bettelheim claimed the environment can greatly determine one's sanity, and that people who managed to maintain some link with their prewar selves would be more likely to survive.[35] In *The Informed Heart*, Bettelheim extended his wartime experiences to critique modern society. He compared his experiences in concentration camps – his attempts to preserve his autonomy, integrity, and personal freedom – with life in modern, mass society, which he also judged dehumanizing and depersonalizing in forcing people to behave in certain ways, even when doing so involved their loss of humanity. Bettelheim noted that all people must struggle to maintain their sanity, much like inmates in the camps.

Our interest in Bettelheim arises from his emphasis on the environment and on individuals forging links with prewar identities. If Bettelheim is correct, we should expect survivors of war to be as much affected by the environment as by their individual personality traits, and we would expect those who can maintain a link between pre- and post-war selves to be more likely to flourish.

The interplay between the environment and the individual personality, so central for Bettelheim and key in Adler, also exists in social psychology. In particular, consider two of the most famous experiments concerning man's inhumanity to man: the Milgram and the Stanford prison experiments. In Stanley Milgram's (1963) classic study of obedience to authority, subjects were instructed to administer what were described as electric shocks to a fellow subject. In fact, there were no shocks and the "subject" supposedly receiving shocks actually was a confederate of the experimenter. The real subjects were told they were participating in an experiment on how people learned. Their role – so they were told – was to administer shocks as part of this experiment to encourage learning by punishing wrong answers. Nearly two-thirds of Milgram's subjects continued to administer shocks of increasing intensity to the "victim" when instructed to do so by the experimenter, even when the victim cried out in apparent agony and begged to be released. The study is interpreted as a classic demonstration of the power of authority to compel ordinary people to perform inhumane acts of violence. It clearly applies to situations of war or genocide in which a common defense, after the fact, is that one was "just following orders."

Nonetheless, some participants (35%) defied the experimenter, refusing to administer higher levels of electric shock.[36] Most refused politely, even apologetically. Although many demonstrated nervousness, a few made stronger statements protesting the inhumanity of the experiment. This raises interesting questions. What might cause people to hold fast to their moral principles even when faced with an authority figure demanding the contrary? Do situational or personality factors encourage individuals to obey or defy the experimenter? Milgram's original study did not address these questions; subsequent studies replicating his experiment have done so, finding important both situational factors and the interaction of situation and personality.[37] For instance, subjects were less likely to obey the experimenter when physically separated from him, when another subject (an accomplice) also refused to obey, when the experimenter did not seem professional or authoritative, when the "victim" was placed in closer proximity to the subject, when the authority figure had less prestige, and so on.[38] More important for our purposes, personality and worldview factors also seemed relevant. Subjects who defied the experimenter tended to score lower on the F-Scale measure of authoritarianism than did subjects who obeyed.[39] Similarly, participants higher in right-wing authoritarianism, after viewing a video of the Milgram study, were less likely to hold the experimental subjects morally accountable for shocking the victim.[40] And in a recent replication of the experiment using a computer screen, obedience was associated with higher scores on both right-wing authoritarianism and a measure of anger.[41] Other correlates of disobedience were a higher stage of moral development as assessed by the Kohlberg scale,[42] greater social intelligence, and lower levels of hostility.[43] A subject's locus of control[44] may interact with situational factors to bear an influence on obedience. (Subjects with an internal locus of control were better able to resist the experimenter than were those with an external locus of control, at least under some circumstances.[45]) Greater religiosity also correlates with increased tendency to obey.[46] Finally, participants' comments during a replication of the study suggest disobedience was associated with a greater sense of personal responsibility for the victim's suffering on the part of the subject.[47] In short, while situational variables play a strong role in determining whether an individual will obey an authority, personality traits and factors such as authoritarianism, locus of control, and religiosity also may exert an influence.

Another classic study in the same vein is the Stanford prison experiment.[48] Here, a group of normal, psychologically healthy undergraduate men were randomly assigned to play the role of either prisoner or guard in a mock prison constructed in the basement of Stanford's psychology building. Phil Zimbardo and his colleagues found students assigned to play guards quickly internalized the role, subjecting the "prisoners" – their fellow students – to a shocking degree of humiliation, abuse, and brutality. The prisoners, in turn, became docile, submissive, and despondent; several suffered emotional breakdowns and had to be released. The experiment itself was curtailed after only six days.[49]

The Stanford prison experiment is typically used to illustrate the power of the situation and group processes to trump individual notions of right and wrong. Zimbardo (2007) reported that while there were a few "good" guards who did not harm the prisoners, these "good" guards did not intervene to prevent "bad" guards from inflicting abuse; instead, they acted as bystanders. Results from a recent partial replication (the BBC prison study)[50] were somewhat more hopeful. There were fewer instances of abuse by guards and less depression and helplessness on the part of prisoners, who rallied to oppose the guards' regime. Inmates even attempted – albeit unsuccessfully – to institute an egalitarian "commune." The designers of the BBC prison study attribute their different findings, at least partly, to a strong sense of collective identity among prisoners, a sense missing in the original Zimbardo study. They "contest the premise that group behavior is necessarily uncontrolled, mindless and antisocial."[51]

RECOVERING FROM POST-TRAUMATIC STRESS DISORDER. Some of the best literature on reclaiming humanity after war comes from medical work on post-traumatic stress disorder (PTSD).[52] PTSD is traditionally defined as an anxiety disorder that occurs after seeing or undergoing an event so unsettling and harrowing that it is experienced as life-threatening. While natural disasters, terrorist incidents, sexual attacks, physical assaults, or even serious accidents can trigger PTSD symptoms,[53] interpersonal events involving human intent – such as combat and assault during wars – are far more likely to result in PTSD than are impersonal events such as natural disasters and accidents.[54] Medication is a common treatment, but recovering from PTSD also is aided by emotional and social support, such as connecting/talking with friends and family; relaxing; exercising; sufficient rest; keeping a journal; avoiding drugs, caffeine, and alcohol; reconnecting with the community by volunteering, especially via activities that increase social networks; and avoiding disturbing news. Positive social support before and following a traumatic event is associated with lower risk of, and faster recovery from, PTSD. Negative social environments that foster blame and stigma may exacerbate it.[55] Joining a treatment group and sharing stories with others who suffered similar traumas can ameliorate PTSD. In addition, successful recovery from PTSD has been linked to a number of individual psychological factors: emotional engagement with one's traumatic memories rather than avoidance or suppression; active processing of those memories into organized narratives; and maintaining positive beliefs about the self and the world.[56] While at first glance it may seem counterintuitive that recounting and reliving one's traumatic memories (exposure treatment) would facilitate recovery from PTSD, many studies find this is precisely the case.[57] In addition, traumatic events often lead to "shattered assumptions" about the self and the world, such as the belief that the world is a good, meaningful, and safe place; the sense that the self is worthy; and the belief that one has control over events in his or her life.[58] Individuals who endure traumatic events with their previous worldviews intact are less likely to develop PTSD. Among those whose existing belief systems are shattered by war, cognitive-behavioral therapy aids individuals in reestablishing these beliefs. Attribution of responsibility may play a role, at least in some kinds of traumatic events. (Those who attribute responsibility to themselves following motor vehicle accidents, for example, are both less likely to develop PTSD and more likely to recover than those who blame someone else,[59] perhaps because of a reduced sense of victimization and vulnerability.[60]) On the other hand, unrealistic and irrational attributions of self-blame for traumatic events – such as a sexual assault – may lead to guilt and shame, and part of the individual's healing process may include overcoming such feelings.[61]

Research on hardiness – also called existential courage – relates to PTSD and seems directly relevant to our analysis. Hardiness refers to an individual's ability to cope successfully with the stress and anxiety arising when one is confronted with new experiences and unfamiliar situations.[62] The concept of hardiness involves three components: (1) commitment, or the desire to remain actively involved in the situation at hand rather than to isolate oneself; (2) control, or the perception that one can influence one's circumstances rather than feeling powerless; and (3) challenge, or the desire to participate in and learn from new experiences, rather than shying away and sticking to the tried-and-true. An integral aspect of hardiness is the ability to find or create meaning out of otherwise stressful and challenging situations, an aspect that links hardiness to Frankl's theory. Much of the literature on hardiness attempts to predict physical and mental health following stressful life events among corporate executives, college students, and other populations.[63] A number of studies have asked how hardiness contributes to mental health among military personnel. For instance, Army reservists high in hardiness reported fewer symptoms of ill health after deployment in the Gulf War than did reservists low in hardiness.[64] The healthful effect of hardiness was especially pronounced among reservists exposed to high levels of combat-related stress. Similarly, both hardiness and social support were associated with fewer PTSD symptoms among Vietnam veterans. Finally, hardiness, along with attachment style, was associated with fewer symptoms of PTSD and mental illness among victims of natural and political disasters.[65]

This review summarizes the relevant literature. How might we test what it suggests about retaining humanity during war? We answer this via a methodological discussion of specific propositions to be tested. We then describe how we conducted such empirical tests.

METHODOLOGY, PROPOSITIONS, AND DATA

NARRATIVE METHODOLOGY AND WAR. Essentially, we scrutinized our wartime stories to detect common themes and patterns in handling the trauma and recovery from war. Ironically, a similar narrative methodology is used as a therapeutic treatment for wartime stress.[66] Clinicians and medical anthropologists[67] interested in the psychological process of coping with painful events find recounting harrowing experiences metaphorically restores a semblance of order and continuity in peoples' lives. Both social and emotional support play a critical role in the positive construction of such narratives.[68] Research on illness, infertility, and refugees finds people rework their ideas about themselves, trying to interpret past events and experiences to make sense of what happened to them and where they are now.[69] Establishing a sense of connection to ordinary routines of daily life, even repetitive and mundane acts – such as coffee with the morning newspaper – can provide a structure and logic that comforts. The chaos, shock, and suffering of war often trigger inner confusion and anxiety about the future. "Restoring order to life necessitates reworking understandings of the self and the world, redefining the disruption and life itself."[70] This process is especially acute when cultural expectations about life are disrupted.

While continuity comprises a universal expectation that cuts across cultures, we did not attempt to disentangle cultural variations in responses to war. Our main goal is simply to utilize narratives of war to discover how people respond when things go terribly wrong and how they cope when events fall outside their experiences of life and their expectations about it.[71] What narratives do they construct to make sense of it all?[72]

PROPOSITIONS. Taken as a whole, the literature suggested the following as fruitful propositions.[73]

Will to survive (Freud). An innate human instinctual drive to survive will surface during wars and related political conflict. This raw desire to live may work against people maintaining their humanity, however, reducing them to creatures who will do anything to survive.

Repression (Freud, Becker). Repression of difficult memories will inhibit constructing a happy life after war. Those who can emotionally engage their traumatic memories will fare better than those who do not.

Control over one's fate (Adler, Bettelheim, Maddi, Janoff-Bulman). When environment and personality combine to provide a sense of control over one's destiny, surviving with one's humanity intact will be more likely. Similarly, work on the importance of agency (described as follows) suggests control matters for survival and well-being.

Locus of control/agency (Maddi, Rotter, Bettelheim, Gallagher). Agency refers to the mover of events and to the subjective awareness that one can initiate, execute, and control one's volitional actions. An agent can be an individual or an external force, such as the winds of history, or a dialectical force, such as Marx's emphasis on economic systems as determinants of history. Those who see themselves as weak and helpless (low on agency) will fare less well than those who see themselves as people who can take charge of their lives and the situation and effect change. The locus of control[74] refers to the extent to which people believe they control themselves and their situations. Individuals with external locus of control tend to believe outside forces determine what happens to them; individuals with internal locus of control believe they exert the strongest influence on their own fate. Internal locus of control is associated with a lower incidence of post-traumatic stress disorder following trauma, including sexual assault, war, and combat-related stress.[75] This suggests an intriguing question/proposition to test: Do individuals high on agency, with a strong internal locus of control, fare better during the fog of war, or do those who lack such a sense of agency fare better, finding their lack of control less of a shock?[76]

Link with former selves (Bettelheim, Becker, Butler, Zimbardo). Individuals who maintain their humanity will be those who establish a link between prewar selves and their selves during the wartime experience. Indeed, one of the findings[77] in the Stanford prison study was that prisoners seldom spoke with one another about their lives before the experiment; nearly all their communications emphasized the ongoing prison situation. Zimbardo hypothesized such discontinuity constituted part of prisoners' loss of identity – in other words loss of a link to their previous selves – and contributed to their submissiveness and helplessness.

> *We expected to hear them talk about their college lives, majors, vocations, girlfriends, favorite teams, music preferences, hobbies, what they would do for the remainder of the summer once the experiment was over, or maybe what they would do with the money they would earn. Not at all!... The prisoner role dominated all expressions of individual character.*   (Zimbardo 2007: 204)

Environment/situation/luck (Adler, Bettelheim, Zimbardo, Milgram). In the psychological process of forging a link to the prior self, the environment will represent as critical a factor as does underlying personality strength, since the social environment constitutes a crucial influence on moral action.[78]

Meaning in suffering (Frankl, Maddi). People who can find meaning in their suffering will be more likely to keep their humanity. In responding well to the trauma of war and genocide, the successful search to find meaning in the wartime experience will be more important than the raw drive to survive (Freud) or the need to enjoy power and control over one's life (Adler). Thus, the ability to feel some sense of control by learning from new experiences – both hallmarks of the existential energy central to hardiness – may affect how one keeps in touch with one's humanity.

Self-esteem and continuity (Adler, Frankl, Bettelheim, Becker, PTSD literature).[79] People with high self-esteem will be more likely to both withstand and recover from the shocks of war. Doing so may require a number of psychological mechanisms, from denial and psychologically focusing on family and friends to reestablishing a post-trauma routine that recreates a semblance of the order and community felt in the prior life.

Blame (PTSD literature). Those who manage to address their sense of survivor guilt will avoid being consumed by the feeling that they did something wrong by living. This will aid in their leading productive, happy lives after the war.[80]

Emotional support (PTSD literature). High levels of emotional support – provided by family, political, or religious groups, for example – will help survivors cope with loss and reestablish or maintain their humanity.[81]

Data. This project grew out of an instructional class project in which students were asked to interview people who had lived through a war, genocide, or similarly searing political conflict, such as Idi Amin's reign of terror. This book thus documents stories of ordinary people caught up in political events beyond their control. It asks how speakers managed the moral choices these events forced upon them and how speakers maintained their humanity during these dark times.[82] In addition to the student interviews, additional wartime stories – such as Frank's – were collected by the 2010–11 summer interns at the UCI Ethics Center, as part of an ongoing project in which ordinary people talk about their moral choices.[83] These interviews are more extensive than the interviews collected by students in the class project and deal with issues other than wartime experiences. We thus include only critical sections of these more extensive Ethics Center interviews; full interviews are available at www.ethicscenter.uci.edu.

All the stories analyzed are free-format narrative interviews with little prompting, other than the initial request to tell us about themselves and then to ask the speaker about (1) the specifics of the political conflict endured, (2) the moral choices the conflict presented, and (3) the mechanisms a speaker utilized to retain his or her humanity throughout the conflict, its resolution, and the aftermath. A narrative interpretive analysis of over fifty taped and transcribed interviews is supplemented with more detailed narrative interpretive analysis, by five independent coders, of a smaller subset of eighteen interviews. These interviews make up the central part of the book; most are printed here in their entirety so the reader can enjoy them and form an independent opinion about what forces most influenced the speakers.[84] Only after these interviews have been presented do we offer our analysis of them. We also briefly describe the war or genocide through which the speaker lived, to provide historical context for the more subjective and personal experience. These factual overviews appear at the beginning of stories of a particular conflict.

The eighteen interviews featured here include life stories of the following speakers, grouped into three separate parts. We begin (Part Two) with World War II, since individuals from that period will not long be with us and since the war encompassed such a wide range of survivors. These include:

- Frank, an American soldier who fought in the South Pacific;
- Laura, a Jewish survivor saved by Oskar Schindler;
- Gunther, a refugee from Vienna whose father was an SS officer;
- Mafalda, sister of the pretender to the Portuguese throne, known as the "Red Princess," who worked in the Resistance and was associated with the July 20th plot to kill Hitler;
- Herb, a Jewish émigré from the Third Reich; and
- Grace, a Japanese-American woman interned in the United States.

In Part Three, we hear from speakers from other wars, from Indochina to Iraq, and including:

- Tuan, a South Vietnamese student, drafted to fight in the army, who later endured a re-education camp under the North Vietnamese and escaped via a boat, coming to Indonesia and the United States;
- Kimberly and Sara, Khmer Rouge survivors; and
- Doc and Sebastian, American soldiers who fought in Iraq.

Finally, we conclude (Part Four) with stories from genocides and civil wars or, according to the participant, fights for freedom. These speakers include:

- Rose, one of the last survivors of the Armenian genocide;
- Ngũgĩ, a writer with brothers on different sides during the Mau Mau rebellion and later a prisoner because of his opposition to the neo-colonial Kenyan government;
- Fabiola, whose father was a Somoza Cabinet member, and who escaped the Nicaraguan civil war with the help of a mysterious San-dinista;
- Marie, who lived through the civil war in Lebanon;
- Okello, a survivor of Idi Amin's Uganda;
- Reza, an Afghani who fled during the Russian occupation; and
- Leyla, college professor and wife of a high official in the regime of the Shah of Iran, who fled Khomeini's Islamic Republic.[85]

Although we conceptualized the interviews only as pedagogical tools for a class, all interviewers underwent IRB training and were instructed to ask if speakers were willing to have their stories made available for analysis. Only those speakers who agreed had their stories analyzed. Unless specifically requested by the speakers, we adopt pseudonyms and, when necessary, modify details to protect safety of friends/family members still in a dangerous situation in home countries. While we occasionally quote other speakers from our broader sample, we try to concentrate on the eighteen speakers whose stories are presented in full here since the nature of narrative interpretation makes it useful to have the space to present the entire story, thus allowing readers the opportunity to judge for themselves whether we have interpreted the narrative in a correct manner. Because of this, we place the stories first so readers may make independent assessment of the stories before turning to our interpretation of them.

NARRATIVE ANALYSIS

Each story was read and interpreted by (1) the student who interviewed the particular speaker and (2) five independent coders. Readers were asked to focus on only a few major themes. (1) What helped the individual speakers get through the war? (2) What guided them in the moral choices they confronted? (3) What helped them retain their humanity after their wartime experiences? This analysis revealed the following eleven topics as central themes, closely related to whether or not the speaker was able to keep or retain a sense of humanity during and after the war. Each of the stories was identified by the independent coders, central themes were given names and assigned to nodes in the N-Vivo computer program, used to code large pieces of narrative data. Each item is called a node. As coders read the transcript, they highlight a quotation that seems to capture a particular node. For example, if a speaker says, "I just knew I had to survive. Just keeping alive was what kept me going." That phrase would be classified as "survival," placed in a node designed for such comments, and would be interpreted as lending support for Freud's emphasis on survival. If a speaker said, "I kept thinking of my family. I knew I had to stay alive for my family, to get back to see my parents," that node would be classified as "family" and placed in a category of quotes that might be interpreted as providing support for theories emphasizing the importance of close ties to families. If a speaker said it was just luck that kept her alive, that would be classified as "luck" and would be interpreted as support for Bettelheim's theory emphasizing the environment. And so on. While we could create more specific nodes of this nature, we relied on the following broad general theme categories as nodes:

- **VIEW OF SELF.** *Individual identity.* What constitutes the individual as a person and how an individual sees him/herself – for example, not as a victim but rather as a survivor – constitutes an extremely important part of one's ability to retain humanity during war. An individual's identity is constructed of various elements, from religion and family to education and upbringing. It is this identity that individuals draw on when they make crucial moral decisions in times of war, terror, or genocide. This identity can constrain their choices, as many individuals insist they could not possibly imagine themselves taking an action that does not fall into line with their identity. Many of the individuals interviewed, for example, saw themselves as mothers and protectors of their families, and credited this factor as leading to acts of bravery.
- **IDENTITY.** *Group identity.* The sense of belonging to a group broader than one's self can provide an important buffer during situations in which human beings are exposed to war, terror, or genocide. This larger identity can be drawn on to protect against the emotional trauma of the war, providing a sense of solidarity with others in the group. Critical group identities can be provided by movements (Zionism, anticolonialism), a religion, or even family, as long as these provide an overarching identity that inoculates against the personalized stings of war.
- **FATALISM.** *Sense of fatalism.* This category includes statements indicating that speakers have lost their sense of agency and now believe the situation they are in is fatal. It encompasses the idea that the locus of control has passed from them and that there is little they can do to alter their fate. They have become passive actors in the sequence of events.
- **HOPE.** *Hope of better future.* The psychology surrounding hope is complex and related to fatalism. We initially thought that in order to retain humanity during war, some hopeful light at the end of the tunnel would be necessary. We hypothesized that hope could influence people during the war in a variety of ways. Literature[86] on the psychology of hope finds worldview and goal-directed thinking critical in helping the individual utilize both pathways thinking (the perceived capacity to find routes to meet desired goals) and agency thinking (the requisite motivations to use these routes). Our findings, however, suggest another entirely different avenue through which hope entered the psychological equation for some speakers.

- **LOSS.** *Nothing to lose versus extensive loss.* Does having more to lose materially make you angrier and more spiteful toward people who took away these things you held dear? We found interesting correlations between how much an individual had to lose (material goods and wealth) and the victims' forgiveness of those responsible for this loss.
- **COGNITIVE STRETCHING.** *Anticipation.* To be forewarned is to be prepared, or so we assume. Presumably, mental preparation helps us deal with disaster more calmly if and when the worst does occur. How does this phenomenon parse during war? Does seeing death as inevitable cause panic or acceptance? What impact does the ability to mentally prepare one's self for and anticipate the worst wartime events have on the ability to retain humanity?
- **LINK TO PREVIOUS LIFE.** *Stability.* Stability should exert a significant influence on the maintenance of humanity. We expected family to be key here but also asked about elements of continuity, such as contact with old friends or familiar communities, perhaps even old routines or mementos, and their impact on retaining humanity.
- **COPING.** *Coping mechanisms.* Speakers can cope with wartime trauma in two main ways. (1) Ignore what happened to them, through denial or repression of the event, and refuse to discuss their experiences, even with their children, perhaps because it is too difficult emotionally to expound on their experience. (2) Talk openly about their experiences, often at great length. How the past was dealt with – letting go versus not letting go of the past – had an interesting and complex relationship with moving on and achieving forgiveness and closure.
- **HAPPINESS.** *Idea of happiness.* We explored whether individuals' ideas of happiness would prove critical in dictating what speakers considered to be humane or inhumane.
- **GUILT.** We expected most survivors to experience guilt, because of those who died or the plight of others who survived but endured worse experiences than the speaker. We expected how people resolved guilt would be critical in moving on emotionally after the war.
- **WHO'S TO BLAME?** Blame was another major theme, touching on guilt as well as on an individual's hate toward the government and especially the government's inability to protect them from war. In fact, we found blame's influence to be far more complex.

• **LIVING WELL.** *Dealing with regret.* The final node included statements about regrets. We expected that speakers who had no regrets
or felt their mission was accomplished would be better able to let go
of their past. Speakers who had clear goals – such as getting one's
family safely to the United States or having children who received
education and became established in the new land – illustrate key
aspects of this node.

N-Vivo. We utilized a computer program called N-Vivo, designed to
handle large amounts of qualitative data in a systematic manner. N-Vivo
facilitates examining texts by topic to enable rigorous and systematic
searching for patterns. It also facilitates comparing coding by different
analysts, and aids in testing theories or explanations grounded in the
data. This system was used for all the interviews analyzed.

In addition to my own close reading of these transcribed interviews,
four independent coders read each interview, noting the factors they
found influential in explaining the subject's wartime behavior.[87] This
made five coders in addition to the student who initially conducted
and analyzed the interview. Independent coders were asked to focus
on background characteristics and on the nodes listed earlier: view of
self, group identity, sense of fatalism, hope, sense of loss, cognitive
stretching, coping mechanisms, idea of happiness, link to prior life,
guilt, blame, and living well/dealing with regret. Coders highlighted all
phrases relating to these key concepts and entered these into the N-Vivo
computer program for coding qualitative data. (For example, a speaker
might say: "I realized then there was no hope for me, that the world was
just a miserable place where horrible things happened and you had no
control over them." This statement would be coded for both fatalism
and hope. To do this, the phrase would be highlighted and then placed in
the analytical categories for "hope" and "fatalism." A statement such as:
"I wasn't the kind of person who could let this happen to me" would be
designated as relevant for "self-image" and "agency" and so on. Quotes
were stored under every category for which they were deemed relevant.)
Once all texts were analyzed, the N-Vivo program then can list all quotes
classified under each category. Each analytical category contains all the
separate quotes and their speakers' names, to facilitate analysis. Only
quotes on which there was uniform coder agreement are considered in
the analysis.

Let us now turn to fuller consideration of the data underlying our
analysis and told in the form of stories.

NOTES

1. General estimates suggest twentieth-century wartime dead topped 160 million, with millions more injured, displaced, or wounded. See Scaruffi 2009, Kohn 1999, Marley 2002, and Banks 2004. Even determining the number of wars just in the twentieth century becomes complex. We can count the Boer, Korean, and Vietnamese wars, plus World Wars I and II, certainly, but then we have the Indochinese wars, the Russo-Japanese wars, Yugoslavian/Balkan wars, including Kosovo and Bosnia, and wars in the Indian subcontinent, from Indian independence to ongoing fighting in Kashmir. Civil wars in Burma, Lebanon, at least 22 in East Africa (the Mau Mau uprising, the Ugandan war, Somalia, and Eritrea); northern African wars of independence, from Algeria to Libya; Latin American civil wars (Mexican); and Indian wars (Yaqui); as well as wars between countries (Ecuador and Peru), and Africa and the Mideast provide examples of wars enduring for years. To begin to give some reality to these abstract numbers, consider just one group: children. UNICEF reports that "millions of children have been present at events far beyond the worst nightmares of most adults." Again, we note just two cases. (1) Almost one in four children was wounded during the 1990s Bosnian ethnic cleansing. A UNICEF survey of 1,505 children in the summer of 1993 found 97% of the children had experienced nearby shelling, 29% described feeling "unbearable sorrow," 20% had horrific nightmares, 55% had been shot at by snipers, and 66% had been in a situation where they thought they would die. (United Nations Children's Fund, "Psychosocial programmed," Emergency Operations in former Yugoslavia kit, UNICEF; reference to data collected in Sarajevo in June and July 1993.) (2) A 1995 survey found 66% of children in Angola had seen people being murdered, 91% had seen dead bodies, and 67% had seen people being tortured, beaten, or hurt. UNICEF concluded that more than two thirds of Angolan children had lived through events in which they had defied death. (United Nations Children's Fund, "Angola: Alliance for life," *op. cit.*, pp. 3–4.) There is some evidence that trauma is worse for adolescents than for younger children, and that women are especially vulnerable due to the incidence of rape as a tool of war and genocide.

2. Written in or before 442 BCE, during a time of national fervor, *Antigone* touches on themes such as personal loyalty, duty, obligation, family love, and, at least in Sophocles' version of the myth, ends in disaster for everyone involved.

3. 1943. Anouilh's play was first performed in Paris on February 6, 1944, during the Nazi occupation. Antigone represented the French Resistance and Creon the role of the Vichy Government. The play put Anouilh in a dangerous position and Anouilh purposefully was ambiguous concerning the rejection and acceptance of authority.

4. 1869.

5. *The Moon Is Down* was sponsored by the OSS and published in 1942 by both Viking Press and Les Editions de Minuit, a Resistance press working clandestinely in Nazi-occupied France.

6. *Arrival and Departure* (1943) is part of Koestler's trilogy on conflicts between morality and expediency.

7. Galloway's novel is based on the life of Vedran Smailović, a musician from Bosnia/Herzegovina who played the cello in orchestras in Sarajevo. Throughout

the siege of Sarajevo Smailović often played his cello – frequently Albinoni's *Adagio in G Minor* – in ruined buildings in the city. His actions inspired many artists, including Galloway, whose fictionalized version has the cellist arriving every day at 4 o'clock to play in honor of the 22 people killed by a bomb while they were lined up for bread. The book itself has been criticized, with Smailović publicly noting his anger that his name and identity had been stolen. Smailović himself played at funerals throughout the war, despite the fact that snipers targeted funerals. He escaped from Sarajevo in 1993 and now works in Northern Ireland.

8. Issued as (1) *The Past is Myself,* (2) *When I was a German,* and (3) *Ride Out the Dark,* Christabel Bielenberg's 1971 book tells of life inside Nazi Germany as an Englishwoman married to one of the July 20th plotters.

9. *Albert Speer: His Battle with Truth* 1995. Speer's book appeared in 1970/97.

10. 1958/1960.

11. Initially published as *Schindler's Ark* (1982), the book won the Booker Prize.

12. Foa 1997, Ehlers and Clark 2002.

13. Janoff-Bulman 1992.

14. Maddi and Kobassa 1984, Maddi 2004.

15. Becker 1997, Butler et al. 2009, and Holmes et al. 2007.

16. Resilience is the outcome of protective factors that help an individual cope with risk and stress. Interesting work exists on perpetrator trauma and the psychological and physiological aftereffects of killing exhibited through the body's response to having perpetrated the death of another human being. Findings suggest the highest form of post-traumatic stress disorder may occur in those who have actually caused death; those who have killed – even if they and their society believe their cause just – exhibit worse psychological outcomes. Work on post-traumatic stress disorder suggests a variety of things help survivors function, from journaling to social support (Butler et al. 2009, McDermott et al. 2011).

17. Specific treatments for post-traumatic stress disorder can be divided into four general categories. (1) Trauma-focused cognitive-behavioral therapy gradually helps patients expose themselves to thoughts and feelings, even situations, which remind them of the trauma. (2) Family therapy focuses on patients learning how to communicate with members of the sufferer's family. (3) Medication – especially antidepressants such as Prozac or Zoloft – is designed to remove the edge from sad emotions. Finally, (4) EMDR (Eye Movement Desensitization and Reprocessing) draws on aspects of cognitive-behavioral therapy with eye movements or even other forms of rhythmic, left-right stimulation, such as hand taps or sounds. These sounds – for example – are designed to "unfreeze" the brain's information processing system, which gets interrupted when the person is under extreme stress, leaving only frozen emotional fragments that retain their original intensity. The theory is that EMDR can free these fragments of the trauma and assemble and process them into a more integrated memory.

18. Maddi 2004.

19. Suedfeld 1997a,b; Suedfeld et al. 1998.

20. Butler et al. 2009, Holmes et al. 2007, Joseph and Linley 2008, Tedeschi and Calhoun 1995, Kross and Ayduk 2011, and Triplett et al. 2011.

21. Koopman 1997, McDermott et al. 2011.

22. Frankl was trained as a psychoanalyst before he was incarcerated. Bettelheim was not a trained psychoanalyst when incarcerated but worked as a

psychologist for most of the rest of his life. His original academic training was in art, which required the study of Jungian archetypes.

23. See Freud 1999; Adler 1927a,b, 1931; Bettelheim 1943, 1950, 1985, 1983; and Frankl 1977, 2004.

24. Supposedly the term "talking cure" was coined by a patient known as Anna O., treated by Freud's colleague Josef Breuer.

25. Adler advocated developing social interest and more democratic family structures in raising children.

26. Connell 2012.

27. Logotherapy itself comes from the Greek word for reason (Logos, λόγος) and therapy (Θεραπεύω, meaning *I heal*). With over 2 million copies sold, the best-selling *Man's Search for Meaning* was first published in 1959 as *From Death-Camp to Existentialism*; its original 1946 title was *Trotzdem Ja zum Leben sagen: Ein Psychologe erlebt das Konzentrationslager*.

28. Sent to Theresienstadt on September 25, 1942, Frankl established a special unit to help inmates address their shock and grief. This eventually grew into a suicide watch unit. For whatever reasons of his own, Frankl would often walk in the open air, delivering lectures to imaginary audiences about the psychotherapeutic experiences in camp. Even in the incredible conditions of a concentration camp, Frankl tried to cure his fellow prisoners of their despondency and to prevent them from committing suicide. We make no comment on this response.

29. Frankl describes a forced march during his time in the concentration camp, where the only thing that kept him going was thinking of his wife. "A thought transfixed me: for the first time in my life I saw the truth as it is set into song by so many poets, proclaimed as the final wisdom by so many thinkers. The truth – that love is the ultimate and the highest goal to which man can aspire. Then I grasped the meaning of the greatest secret that human poetry and human thought and belief have to impart: *The salvation of man is through love and in love.* I understood how a man who has nothing left in this world still may know bliss, be it only for a brief moment, in the contemplation of his beloved. In a position of utter desolation, when man cannot express himself in positive action, when his only achievement may consist in enduring his sufferings in the right way – an honorable way – in such a position man can, through loving contemplation of the image he carries of his beloved, achieve fulfillment. For the first time in my life I was able to understand the meaning of the words, 'The angels are lost in perpetual contemplation of an infinite glory.'" Frankl 2004: pp. 56–7.

30. Frankl developed this into a broader theory, including one that suggests people who work too hard often suffer from Sunday neurosis, a kind of depression that comes with realizing the emptiness of life once the work week ends.

31. The claim is made by Gordon W. Allport in the Preface to *Man's Search for Meaning*, p. xiv.

32. It seems important that Frankl uses the term spirit not in a religious sense but rather to refer to spirit as the will of the human being. See Seidner 2009.

33. Bettelheim studied philosophy and art in Vienna, which involved him in considerations of Jungian archetypes in art and Freud's work on art as an expression of the subconscious. His first wife was a disciple of Anna Freud and Bettelheim eventually studied to become a psychiatrist. Like Frankl, Bettelheim was arrested because he was Jewish and placed as a camp doctor to overview prisoners' mental

health. Bettelheim was allowed to have his freedom purchased as part of an amnesty for Hitler's birthday in 1939, and he resettled in Australia and eventually the United States in 1943. He worked at the University of Chicago as professor of psychology from 1944 until 1973. Bettelheim suffered from depression after his second wife died in 1984 and, increasingly infirm as a result of a stroke, killed himself on March 13, 1990, the 52nd anniversary of the Nazi annexation of Austria.

34. Early practitioners include August Aichorn, Fritz Redl, and David Wineman, who pioneered the use of milieu therapy to treat "impulse-ridden and ego-impaired" children in both school and residential settings, such as the Orthogenic School at the University of Chicago. Bettelheim's work at this school is highly controversial, with some former patients saying he used his position to abuse and terrorize children subjected to harsh treatment and others saying his treatment saved them. Despite Bettelheim's personal faults, the general consensus is that milieu therapy can be a powerful therapeutic tool when individual dynamics and the social system can be combined in a planned and meaningful way to manage and change behavior and relationships.

35. Bettelheim's interest in this psychological process was driven, at least in part, by a desire to understand how the process could be reversed and how a more positive environment could serve to remedy mental disorder. Based on his camp experiences, Bettelheim's "milieu therapy" at the Orthogenic School was designed to create a therapeutic environment that would support needs of severely disturbed children. The physical environment was clean and orderly, and patients could move from place to place as they liked, with the staff unconditionally accepting all the children's behavior. For personal assessments of Bettelheim's highly controversial work, see Tom Lyons' novel, *The Pelican and After* (1983), or Stephen Eliot's memoir, *Not the Thing I Was* (2003). Both authors were patients at the Orthogenics School.

36. In the original experiment, 26 out of 40 participants continued. Tests by other analysts find 61–66% of participants comply, despite culture or context.

37. See Blass 1991 for a review.

38. Milgram 1974.

39. See Elms and Milgram 1966 on revisions of the original Milgram findings and Adorno et al. 1950 for details on testing for authoritarianism.

40. Blass 1993.

41. Dambrun and Vatiné 2010.

42. Milgram 1974.

43. Haas 1966.

44. Rotter 1966.

45. Blass 1991.

46. Bock and Warren 1972.

47. Burger et al. 2011. See also Monroe 2012 on the importance of moral salience for moral choice.

48. Haney and Zimbardo 1973.

49. Zimbardo 2007.

50. Reicher and Haslam 2006.

51. Ibid., 33.

52. See, among other cites, the National Center for PTSD, U.S. Department of Veterans Affairs, "What is posttraumatic stress disorder (PTSD)?" at

http://www.ncptsd.va.gov/ncmain/ncdocs/factshts/fs_what_is_ptsd.html. The National Institute of Mental Health, "Anxiety Disorders," http://www.nimh.nih .gov/publicat/anxiety.cfm#1. The National Center for PTSD, U.S. Department of Veterans Affairs, "Treatment of PTSD," http://www.ncptsd.va.gov/facts/ treatment/fs_treatment.html.

53. Symptoms include fixating on the trauma; becoming easily startled and angered; being irritable, anxious, and preoccupied with staying safe; having difficulty sleeping and other physical problems, such as rapid breathing, quick heart rate, constipation, and diarrhea; panic attacks; feelings of mistrust; depression; thoughts of suicide; and difficulties with relationships.

54. Charuvastra and Cloitre 2008.

55. Ibid. for a review.

56. Ehlers and Clark 2000, Foa 1997.

57. Foa and Kozak 1986, Foa et al. 1995, and Foa et al. 1991. An alternative to exposure therapy, cognitive therapy involves talking with a therapist about the meaning and emotional affect of a traumatic event, without necessarily intensively recounting or reliving it.

58. Janoff-Bulman 1992.

59. Delahanty et al. 1997, Carll 2007.

60. See Suedfeld 1997a,b and Suedfeld et al. 1998 *inter alia.*

61. Cites for post-traumatic stress disorder include: Charuvastra and Cloitre 2008, Delahanty et al. 1997, Foa 1997, Foa and Kozak 1986, Foa et al. 1991, Foa et al. 1995, Ehlers and Clark 2000, Janoff-Bulman 1992.

62. Maddi and Kobasa 1984.

63. Maddi 2007 for a review.

64. Bartone 1999.

65. Neria et al. 2009.

66. See McDermott et al. 2011 on the challenges of applying lessons learned from psychology to international events such as wars; Holmes et al. 2007 on the therapeutic value of journaling; Andrews 2007 on political narrative; Langer 1991 on reliability of oral versus written testimony; and Monroe 2004, 2012 for details on narrative as a tool for political analysis.

67. Becker 1997.

68. Butler et al. 2009.

69. Butler 1997.

70. Becker 1997, 4.

71. Ibid., 5.

72. Medical anthropologists (Becker) underline the importance of how people attempt to deal with the discontinuity in their lives in the aftermath of political conflicts. They underscore the need to consider the significance of possible cultural variation in this process, suggesting those who construct linear narratives may have more difficulty assimilating the wartime experience and that linear thinking is more associated with Western cultures. We did not test this idea here.

73. We initially thought in terms of deriving hypotheses to test. This was premature. So although both *hypothesis* and *proposition* are terms frequently used interchangeably to refer to the formulation of a possible answer to a specific scientific question, we distinguish between them, arguing that a proposition

addresses the connection between existing concepts while a hypothesis must be testable, measurable, and falsifiable. Given the existing state of knowledge in this area and the nature of the data available, it thus seems more accurate to think in terms of propositions that deal with pure concepts for which no laboratory tests are currently available. The search for loose links between war and certain categories of responses to war thus reflects the level of social scientific work in this area. Modest aims are further dictated by concerns about any sample of wartime victims/participants one can analyze. Obviously we cannot know if the people interviewed here are typical of any larger group of wartime survivors, or even exactly what that larger group might look like. Further, the level of ability to make sense of the wartime experience – let alone speak thoughtfully and with social scientific insight about the wartime experience with others – is quite varied. (We omitted one fascinating interview with a highly educated, successful federal judge because he still cannot bear to discuss Vietnam, even with his daughter.) So it is perhaps too much to ask to find causal inferences. Nonetheless, it remains important to search for general patterns, to attempt to make initial determinations of the diverse ways with which wartime trauma can be coped. It is precisely because people are complex and cannot easily be pigeonholed, that there is value simply in presenting the full range of ways in which presumably ordinary people somehow cope with disasters that might reasonably be expected to crush the human spirit.

74. Rotter 1966.
75. Frye and Stockton 1982; Regehr et al. 1999; Zahava 1988.
76. The term "fog of war" comes from the smoke of musket fire, which made it almost impossible for soldiers to see whom they were shooting. The term acquired new meaning in the twentieth century, suggesting the overall confusion of war.
77. Zimbardo 2007.
78. Zimbardo 2007, Milgram 1974, or Monroe 2012 for a summary.
79. Innovative clinical work on PTSD is going on in many parts of the world, from Ervin Staub's work (Staub et al. 2005) with Rwanda-Burundi survivors to work in the United States and Europe with refugees, 85% of whom suffer some PTSD symptoms (Livingubunta.org or Psychology Beyond Borders). Much innovative work is done in Israel, where scholars such as Rony Berger (Ben-Gurion University and the Natal Trauma Center) and Sami Hamdan (Tel Aviv-Jaffa College) address their own local conflict, as well as conflict in other parts of the world.
80. Kelman 1999; Suedfeld et al. 1998.
81. See the literature on PTSD.
82. Most of the stories were collected by students in a course taught at the University of California, Irvine, during the fall of 2010, Political Science 149C. My deep thanks to these students for the educational experience they afforded me. Two students – Sif Heide-Ottosen and Shant Setrak Meguerditchian – had the time, interest, and energy to participate in the formal analysis of these stories. They are listed as co-authors of a paper presented at the Annual Meetings of the American Political Science Association in Seattle, September 2011. Two students from the Ethics Center summer intern program of 2011 did further analysis and are the co-authors of this book. I regret that we cannot acknowledge individual students in connection with the interviews they conducted but that might reveal the identities

of the speakers interviewed. We respect the students' work and thank the UCI Ethics Center for storing these interviews in the Vaughen Archives.

83. The Hillman interview grew out of a chance meeting with Laura Hillman, a Jewish survivor of the Holocaust on Schindler's List. My daughter, Chloe and I had gone to a performance of *The Diary of Anne Frank* by the Long Beach Opera, a rather avant-garde, funky local opera company whose next performance was Orpheus, performed in a swimming pool. The show we attended was good, most professionally presented and performed and with music I found interesting if a bit unconventional and modern for my traditional and untrained ear. There was only one singer but she was accompanied by an older woman who would occasionally read excerpts from her diary. The woman was Laura Hillman, a Holocaust survivor who was roughly the same age Anne Frank would be had Anne lived. After the opera ended, Chloe and I attended the cast party and I made sure Chloe met Hillman. I knew neither Hillman nor I would last forever and I wanted Chloe to be able to bear witness, to tell pernicious deniers of the Holocaust that she had met someone who had survived it. Hillman was an incredibly gracious, beautiful woman and Chloe was quite taken with her, asking if Hillman could come to the Ethics Center that summer so others could meet her and hear her story. Laura agreed to come and her story appears as Chapter 3.

84. These particular interviews were chosen to convey the full range of the wartime experience, and include soldiers who engaged in combat fighting (Tuan, Sebastian, Doc); refugees whose lives were up-ended (Tuan, Gunther, Leyla, Okello, Reza); those who fled neighbors who wanted to kill them (Laura, Herb, Sara, Kimberly); and those who engaged in resistance movements (Mafalda, Ngũgĩ).

85. We are grateful to the students at UCI who participated in this project. We are creating an archive of these interviews, accessible at the website for the UCI Ethics Center at www.ethicscenter.uci.edu. The archive will be put up during the fall of 2014 and will be available to anyone who wishes to access it.

86. Snyder 1994, 2000.

87. These include two co-authors of a conference paper and the two co-authors for the book. Beyond this, each class interview was analyzed initially by the student who conducted the interview. Since not all the interviews were conducted for class, however, we do not count class coders in our count.

PART TWO

GUARDING ONE'S HUMANITY DURING WAR: WORLD WAR II

Raging from 1939 to 1945, World War II was the deadliest, most widespread war in human history, involving more than 100 million military personnel from over thirty nations throughout the world. The war also resulted in the mass deaths of civilians, including deaths from the Holocaust and the first use of nuclear weapons. Estimates range from 50 to 75 million deaths, with countless injuries and untold human suffering.

Most agree WWII grew naturally from World War I and its punitive Versailles Peace Treaty. WWI killed an entire generation of young men and radically altered the political map, erasing the German, Austro-Hungarian, and Ottoman empires, indirectly putting the Bolsheviks in power in the USSR, and establishing many new, weak, small states throughout Central and Eastern Europe. Political instability was exacerbated by the Great Depression of the 1930s, which, along with the reparations from WWI, hit central Europe especially hard. Germany's response turned militaristic with the coming to power of the Nazis (National Socialist Party) in 1933. The Nazis immediately instituted a series of racist and anti-Semitic laws and over the following years led Germany in campaigns of territorial expansion in Austria and Czechoslovakia. In August 1939, Germany and Russia signed a nonaggression pact, effectively dividing Poland. Now free to invade Poland without Russian interference, Germany did so on September 1, 1939. The violation of Poland's sovereignty, which Great Britain had sworn to protect, led both Great Britain and France to declare war on Germany. On September 3, 1939 World War II officially began.

The Holocaust – the systematic persecution of Roma/gypsies, homosexuals, and most aggressively and extensively the Jewish population – relocated people like Laura (Chapter 3) to death camps where they were executed by the millions in history's most horrific genocide. For a few Jews, salvation came when they were put on the famous Schindler's list, created by Oskar Schindler, a German war profiteer and member of the Nazi party who nonetheless saved over 1,000 Jews by bribing authorities to let him hire the Jews in his enamelware and ammunitions factories, thus removing them from the concentration camps and saving their lives. Other Jews – such as Herb (Chapter 6) – immigrated to the few countries willing to take them.

In Asia, World War II commenced with imperialist Japan's invasion of Manchurian China in 1931, culminating in a full-scale invasion of China in 1937. Beginning in the 1940s, Japan successfully invaded and occupied former European colonies in Southeast Asia. After the Japanese attack on Pearl Harbor on December 7, 1941, the United States became involved in the war. On February 19, 1942, President Franklin Roosevelt implemented Executive Order 9066, authorizing the Secretary of War to prescribe certain parts of the United States as military zones. Eventually, EO 9066 cleared the way for the deportation of all Japanese-Americans along the Pacific coast and Hawaii to internment camps, including people such as Grace (Chapter 7).

With U.S. involvement in both the European and Pacific theaters, the tide of the war began to turn as both German and Japanese forces were slowly defeated. By the summer of 1945, Germany was occupied by Allied forces and in August that same year, the United States dropped two atomic bombs on Hiroshima and Nagasaki, thus ending the conflict in the Pacific theater (Frank, Chapter 2). Six years and between 50 and 75 million deaths later, World War II was over. Then began the task of recovery for survivors such as Gunther (Chapter 4), Mafalda (Chapter 5), and all the others whose lives had been upended by the war.

2 IF SOMETHING'S GOING TO GET YOU, IT'LL GET YOU

Frank, American Soldier in the South Pacific

You should probably realize that I'm eighty-nine, so that gives you a perspective. When I grew up we didn't have television or a lot of other things that we all take for granted today. As a matter of fact, when I was growing up we still had horse carts delivering things in various neighborhoods. My father was a Navy Chief Petty Officer. That's like a Master Sergeant in the Army; it's the top-ranked enlisted man. He had been in the military pretty much all of his life. He ran away to the Spanish-American War when he was seventeen. He lied about his age and told them he was nineteen so they'd take him. He spent three years in the Philippines, during which time the Spanish were defeated at the Battle of Manila, which was a presage to what we have today. When the Americans threw the Spanish out, the Filipinos weren't all that interested in just trading them for Americans as colonial masters. They wanted to be independent so there was a Philippine insurrection led by a man named Aguinaldo.[1] My father was in the 13th Minnesota Regiment, along with the Dakota regiments. Many of the senior enlisted men and officers were old Indian fighters who had fought the Sioux on the plains in the 1870s and 1880s, so they had experience in, as they put it, "good old fighting."

Dad started out his life that way, then came back to the United States. My background is Irish, and at that time the Irish and the Chinese were the Coolies, the people at the bottom of the class system. They did the grunt work and were discriminated against. The Chinese had been imported from Asia to work on building the railroads from west to east. The Irish had come over during the potato famines in the 1840s, and they primarily built railroads from east to west. My grandfather worked on those railroads. They began work on the railroads as firemen and engineers. If you were in good shape, you got to be a conductor and didn't have to do the hard work. Dad came back and worked on the

Great Northern Railway, on the division between Fargo, North Dakota, and Missoula, Montana. In those days railroads were run by coal. There was a coal car and an engine and the fire box, and the fireman, which is where you started out, would shovel coal from the coal car or tender into the fire box, standing on a coupling that was going back and forth. It was forty degrees below on one side and on the other you had the heat of the fire box. Half of you was freezing and the other half was burning up. After a year of that he said, "If I have to shovel coal for a living I'll do it in comfort," and he joined the Navy.

He spent eight years in the China Station, as they called it, in the Asiatic fleet. When you signed up for the Navy, you signed up for four years, then you renewed your enlistment. So Dad did two enlistments out in the Asiatic fleet. At the end of World War I, the Navy sent him to San Francisco and so, courtesy of the United States Navy, that's where I was born – a great break. So many things in your life happen not because you plan them; it's just the way it happens. That was right after World War I, and at that time my dad was in destroyers. They were berthed out at Hunters Point, and the Navy didn't have much in the way of money to do anything so they had one cruise a year that went from San Francisco to San Diego and back. That was it. That was the way they kept the Navy up. There was no money for spare parts or things of that sort. One of the ways Dad learned to keep the ship running was to have the other chiefs play poker in the fire room of the Kennedy, which was his ship. While the poker game was going on, Dad had his firemen going round all of the other ships – they were all berthed together, about five across – picking up parts out of them so that they could make the Kennedy run. Scrounging, if you will. One of the things you learned in life was how to scrounge. As a result, the Kennedy was always in good shape.

Now, is that stealing? Where's the moral in this thing? You have a duty to keep your ship in first-class shape; then at the same time, "Thou shalt not steal." Is it stealing to just borrow? You haven't taken it away from the U.S. Navy. Who does the part belong to anyway? So there are little moral questions here. It seemed like the right thing to do was to keep your ship running. That was what you were there for. It was viewed as borrowing more than stealing. If they needed something you would let them have something of yours.

The reason I give that background is that I was brought up by my father not with all the modern ideas of self-esteem and the like. He viewed little boys as miniature sailors. I had two brothers, one a little older and one a little younger. My father's attitude was that you treated your sons like they were men, just smaller. You were expected to do your duty and shape up. No crying. It was a tough little life but it was a pretty good one because you learned a lot by being raised that way. I suppose there's a lot to say about modern educational methods but frankly I'm just as grateful I had a good, swift kick in the behind when I did something wrong. Physical punishment was not considered child abuse; it was part of teaching young men to shape up.

I grew up in San Francisco and went to public school there until my dad retired in 1931. We lived in what you'd call a ghetto. San Francisco in those days was divided up into ethnic neighborhoods. North Beach were the Italians, or the wops as we called them – we used language like that – and the Western section was all Irish. The Irish had a sort of monopoly on the civil service jobs. They always had a way of looking for soft, cushy things. They were the motormen and the conductors on the streetcars, the mailmen. My next door neighbor was a cop. We fit into this Irish neighborhood in San Francisco. Of course there were the very fancy neighborhoods like Knob Hill and the Pacific Beach and Saint Francis Woods, where the rich, white Protestants lived. But you've got to realize the Irish were Catholics so were considered one of those outsider groups.

One of the first ethical lessons I learned happened right there. Our next door neighbor, Mr. O'Brien, was a cop. Every year he had a beautiful new Graham-Paige automobile in his driveway, polishing it up. That was a little much for our neighborhood, so everybody figured Mr. O'Brien had another source of income, maybe from a legacy. As it turned out he did have an outside source of income: he shook down people on his beat. Along with a bunch of other cops, he was caught and fired from the police force for corruption. So my buddy Arty O'Brien and his family were in disgrace. That was the first time I came across a crime. It worked out in time because in the thirties they were building the Bay Bridge and the Golden Gate Bridge and Mr. O'Brien was able to get a job working on those. But it was interesting to watch what happened to someone who got involved in corruption and had to pay a price for it. That gave you a lesson not to get involved in corruption.

We then moved to the country. A Chief Petty Officer's retirement pay wasn't a great deal of money so we were living a self-sustained life. We grew our own veggies. We had two pairs of blue jeans and two chambray shirts; one set was washed each week and that was your entire wardrobe. We went to school five miles away in the little town of Boulder Creek, and the school bus was a Ford Model A truck. Like an Army truck with a canvas over the back and seats that folded down, not one of these nice big yellow buses you have today. We'd climb into it over the back. Old Man Harter drove it. He brought us to school in the morning then took the same truck down to Santa Cruz to get the mail for the Boulder Creek Post Office, brought that back and then took us home in the afternoon. Things you think of as necessities you can't live without today, we didn't necessarily have. But somehow things went along. As a matter of fact that was a lot of fun in that school bus. We had a riotous time in the back, separated from the driver with nobody overseeing us. We were in the fifth or sixth grade and rambunctious. The big kid Mario Piccone, who was probably 15, got to ride up front with Mr. Harter and then come back and open the back gates. Somehow we all survived it.

Q. There were no girls?

Oh, yeah, there were some girls. They had a terrible beating. They were teased and had their hair pulled, all the things little boys do to little girls. It was awful. Remember I said we were raised like little sailors, and sailors have a bad reputation for raising hell when they get into port! But Mr. O'Brien with the shakedowns and the Graham-Paige cars was the first example I remember of an ethical issue. People in power will oftentimes get to the stage of misusing that power in inappropriate ways, whether it's a cop or a boss in the office or so on. What do you do with them? How do you control them?

Anyway, I got through fifth and sixth grade. I even won a contest, for an essay on temperance. In those days we had prohibition; liquor was not allowed. I didn't really know anything about alcohol because we never had any around the house but I wrote an essay about the evils of alcohol and got a prize from the Women's Christian Temperance Union! I've lost the certificate some place. The high school years – you got through them. I'll skip the teenage years because they were terrible. Teenagers are in the worst stage of their lives. They're learning to become independent and they don't quite know where to draw lines. I certainly didn't.

I went off to college. I got a scholarship because I did have good grades in high school and I went to Stanford. My older brother had gone to San Jose State Teachers College. Up there you either went to Cal or Stanford, or San Jose State if you couldn't get into those. If you couldn't get into that you went to junior college. Very few of us were on the college prep course. Today everyone's supposed to go to college but then only a very few were expected to do so. Most of the kids out of Santa Cruz High School took a vocational course, training them to do something practical. Auto mechanic courses and for girls secretarial or home economics. But at that time I really wasn't all that interested in girls; I was more interested in sport. Doing things that made the other guys respect you, that was the most important thing. That brought up ethical questions. Where do you draw the line? There was always a tendency to be pushed to the point of doing something wrong, and you had to judge whether to do it to gain the respect of the other guys. I got caught sometimes. One of the wrong things that we did in my high school years was painting "Class of '39" on the smokestack of the high school, which of course was vandalism. But the other guys thought we were pretty neat. The authorities finally identified those of us who did it and it turned out we were all on the student council! We were punished with suspension. You had to make judgments whether it's worth doing something you know is not right just to get the respect of your peers. So I got through those kinds of things, learning there is a penalty, and where to start drawing the lines.

I went off to college. The war came along and I enlisted in the Army Air Corps. I spent four years in the service, two of them in the United States while they tried to make me into something useful. There was a lot of benefit in that military training, particularly the kind of training I got as an aviation cadet, because it was a lot of discipline. How do you make somebody do something when they don't want to? Maybe because there's some risk to themselves? How to get someone to the point where they obey the order *right now* as compared to arguing about it or wondering whether they should or shouldn't? In a military situation instant obedience is a requirement. It's a necessity. There was a great deal of that training.

I spent two years overseas out in the Pacific. You probably don't realize this but we had five wars in World War II. There's the one you hear about and read about in your history books, which was Eisenhower and the invasion through Normandy. There was another war in Europe, which was the southern war. It came across North Africa, through the boot of Italy and was a very hard war for those who fought it. The major resources all went to Normandy. Those guys in south Europe got what was left over. The idea in World War II was to defeat Hitler first and then deal with the Japanese, so in the Pacific the idea was to hold as best as we could with what limited resources we had left. That was where I went. We got very little in the way of support and equipment.

In the Pacific there were two wars. There was the MacArthur war, up from Australia back through the Philippines; and there was the Nimitz'[2] war, which went across the central Pacific, island hopping. There was a fifth war I may have already mentioned, the General Stilwell war in China. That was primarily to keep the Japanese occupied. It got the minimum amount of activity or support that could be given. The Nimitz war was a Navy and Marines war, and that was the one I was in. I was an Army Air Corps guy assigned to the Navy. That taught me about interservice politics. The Air Corps had been assigned all the radio navigational aids throughout the world. We were supposed to provide those for the Navy. The Navy didn't like that. You began to learn about the strategic things that went on at the top. These were the issues of interservice rivalries. I didn't understand this at the time. I just knew we were short of things in the Pacific, compared to what was going on in Europe.

I ended up being the operations officer for the 78th AACS group, based on the Marianas. I'd gone to the invasions of the Marianas and Iwo Jima and Palau. I was a First Lieutenant in a Lieutenant Colonel's berth. Here was I, twenty years old and the rank that was supposed to be doing my job was three ranks above me. That was how short the Army Air Corps was of qualified people. We were having a lot of trouble maintaining adequate communications, contacts, and equipment. We were all cast-offs and rejects, and my commanding officer was a drunk. We hardly saw him.

We got a call one day from the headquarters of Admiral Nimitz, Commander-in-Chief in the Pacific, CinCPac. They wanted the commanding officer to come down to headquarters to answer for why we were not supporting them adequately. There was nobody else available so I climbed into a Jeep and went down to CinCPac headquarters and met with Captain Shepherd, who was the Chief Communications Officer and worked directly for the Admiral. He was nonplussed that the Colonel hadn't shown up. He asked me, "What's the trouble up there, son?"

I explained that the Colonel was ill. He was in his cups, which was unfortunate. I told him all the things we didn't have and the problems we were facing and he said, "Let's see how we can fix that." Next thing I know I've got a bunch of Marines and sailors to fill in the empty spots. A Marine radio teletype repair man we needed showed up. We got some Navy TDQ transmitters because the ones the Air Force had furnished us were inadequate to stand up to the tropical heat and humidity. Soon we had everything humming. Everything was fine. The Captain was happy. I was happy.

Next thing I know, a message had gone back from Admiral Nimitz' headquarters, all the way to Washington, explaining what they had to do to fulfill the Air Corps' other mission and how inadequate it was.

Of course that also came all the way down the line the other way, to the Colonel in Hawaii, who got a reprimand. I thought we were fighting the Japanese. Turned out we were fighting each other! That's one of the things you learn about bureaucracies. You get people with different turfs and different goals or priorities. What are they trying to do together? Are they all caught up in little fights with each other? This was a classic case of that. Of course with Colonel Smith in Hawaii, it really wasn't his fault. It goes all the way back to the priorities that were given to the various theaters, and the shortage of resources. You can understand why he was upset. His career was ruined by something I had done, not knowing what the impact would be.

Q. Why did your actions hurt that Colonel so much?

Because the Navy complained to Washington. They had always fought the fact that they were reliant upon the Army Air Corps for support for things they felt they could do themselves, and do better. That was hurting their ability to pursue their part of the war. The real reasons were the shortage and reallocation of resources. Everything went to Normandy first, Italy second, MacArthur third, Nimitz fourth, and Stilwell fifth. There really weren't enough resources.

Q. Do you think this was because of a strategic decision that was rational?

Yes, the rational strategic decision in Washington was: defeat Hitler first. Once we have Hitler defeated, we can go after the Japanese. Until then we just hold them. Then on the Japanese side was a contest between the Navy and Marines going across the central Pacific, and MacArthur coming up the south Pacific, as to who was getting human resources. Just like how it was in Europe. In Europe there was a contest for who was going to race across Europe and get to the Rhine first. Those things are good and bad. It's good to have stimulation and competition to get the best out of people but on the other hand that can be somewhat destructive too.

So the Navy had gone back and complained to Washington about the inadequacy of the Air Force support. The Air Force had to admit to it, and then who's responsible? Well, sooner or later it's some poor guy in the middle. That guy was a guy in Hawaii named Colonel Smith, whose career was ruined by all of this. I had told the truth, and from that point I got what was called a "very satisfactory" proficiency rating – which is as good as saying "F"! And why? The Navy was now happy. Captain Shepherd and Admiral Nimitz were very pleased with what had occurred once we had the Navy and Marines helping us out doing our job. I thought it was wonderful too because I thought we were fighting the Japanese. No. We aren't! We're fighting each other. I was very naïve as to the politics of these interrelationships. I didn't mind but it made sure I was never going to be a military officer.

Q. Did the heightened awareness of the importance of the power of politics help you later in life?

Yes. What you began to understand is that things are not just straightforward. There are these other interrelationships. I didn't completely understand at the moment why these things went on, but when you became older and more mature you could look back and see what really had gone on and why these things occurred. There was always that contest in the Pacific between the Navy and the MacArthur forces. MacArthur had the greater political support so when the war was over he became what you might call the Shogun of Japan. That's a whole story by itself. He was a character! He finally got fired by Harry Truman for insubordination. So I went to war, and fortunately I came out of it with absolutely no scratches.

Q. Were you ever in battles?

I was in battle areas. I was not what you'd call a combat soldier; I was a support. My duties were to set up, maintain, and operate communication and navigation aids. We went in over the beaches right after the Marines with our portable equipment. We were bringing in airplanes to land on Iwo Jima and they were pushing the Japanese off the other end of the airfield, so you're in the middle of combat. I always carried a .45. With the Japanese you could never know when they'd pop up. There were a lot of banzai attacks and hidden traps, so you were always in a situation of having to be sure you were able to defend yourself.

Q. Did you have to kill anybody?

No.

Q. Did you see enough of combat that it had a significant effect on you mentally or emotionally? Did you see enough that it traumatized you?

I wouldn't call it "traumatized" but it made you very aware of the terrible impact of war, that it's not glamorous. You've got to realize there was a lot of propaganda in World War II to develop patriotism and support. You found out that was an awful lot of baloney! It was a very messy thing. When you think in terms of the destruction! You'd see one of those islands with all the palm trees leveled, and the natives on the island having to suffer through it all. The Japanese as a military culture had a position of never surrendering; they fought to the last man. If the Germans got themselves surrounded they'd put their hands up; Italians would run before then! But the Japanese were wholly different. It goes back to the culture of the samurai and the shoguns, and the whole nature of Japanese culture. They were a formidable fighting group because they never gave up.

Q. Did you feel – do you think your comrades felt – they were the enemy and you only felt hatred and hostility toward them? Or did you empathize with them and sympathize that they were going through similar things to you?

Well, you learn to hate. As far as I'm concerned the tendency for all of us in the Pacific was to hate the Japanese. We hated them for things they did, like on the Bataan Death March. To them, if you were willing to become a prisoner then you ceased to be a human. You were no better than an animal, maybe not even that good. It was against their culture and they wouldn't respect a person who would do something they considered beneath them. The samurai code caused them to be very brutal. If you look at the history of the Japanese in China and what they did to American prisoners, that leads to the ability to hate. It led to the view that the only good Japanese was a dead one. Ask and give no quarter. It was a whole different affair from the war in Europe thinking of ethical "rules of war." I get a bit cynical when I hear all these things about the Geneva Convention and stuff like that. You fought the war the same way the enemy fought it. We fought the Japanese like for like. You'd bring them out of the caves with flamethrowers. You only go to war to win. It's not a game, and you don't win by scoring a certain amount of points. To the Japanese it would have to be total destruction. You can view that attitude with disdain or pride, depending upon your direction and point of view.

Q. Do you still feel that hatred?

I did. I did for fifteen years.

Q. If you had the opportunity to meet someone who had fought against you on the Japanese side, would you shake his hand and talk with him?

Let's put it this way. I was involved with the early days of the occupation. I found I hated and detested the Japanese. It took a long time but finally after fifteen years it dissipated. In later years I did business with Japanese;

in fact I learned the language. The company I was with did business with them and we had good relationships.

Q. Did you learn Japanese during or after the war?

I learned it during the war because I had to be able to decode and understand intercepts. So I'd taken Japanese and had a moderately fluent capability in it during the war. I renewed it again later when we were doing business in Japan. Now I'm the same way I am with my French. *Très mal!* I've learned French, German, and Japanese, as well as several forms of English, one being British English.

Q. When we've spoken before you said the war was so horrific you did not want your parents to know what it was really like, that you protected them from that knowledge by what you wrote in your letters.

At first you couldn't write very long letters. V-mail, as they called it, could only be one page, and it was all "I'm okay." You didn't go into detail. I didn't need to because my father had been in war himself in the Philippines. He knew what it was like.

Q. Did your mother know what was going on or were you trying to protect her?

No. We just didn't talk about it. It was one of those things you repress. That's how you cope.

Q. Did any of it come out later in any way?

We didn't talk about it. I never talked about the war. I've probably talked about it more tonight than I ever have. To me it was a chapter and when the chapter was over you closed it and put it behind you.

Q. You said it took you fifteen years to stop hating the Japanese. Was there any one event that prompted that?

No. Just the simple fact that after about fifteen years I finally realized I'd reached the stage where I didn't hate them anymore. It had passed. I'd gotten over it. No particular event caused it. I think that's the way hatred oftentimes works.

Q. Did you ever want to get back at the Japanese?

We got back at them. They had Hiroshima and Nagasaki. They were going to get a couple more if they hadn't quit. On the other hand I have no regrets about dropping the bombs on them because they'd asked for it. There was lots of debate about dropping the bombs but it ended things.

Q. Did being in the war affect your feelings about war and make you see it as a last resort?

Well, yeah. Let's put it this way. You certainly don't go to war if there's any other reasonable way of solving the problems at hand. But you've got to be prepared to use force when it becomes evident there's no other reasonable solution. Most of us think of problems as linear things. Something that has a beginning, a period of solution, and an end, and then is completed. But the major problems of the world are not linear; they're circular. They have no beginning. They have no end and they don't disappear. They just get larger or smaller, and they're always going to be with us. With issues between countries and people, there are times when war becomes necessary but in general it's certainly not the first option. At the same time I think those who oppose you need to understand war's an option that's on the table.

Q. You said earlier that instant obedience is required in the military. Do you think it's okay to prosecute lower ranked soldiers for torture authorized by higher ranked officials?

No. What is the level of responsibility? A soldier is told to follow orders. That's how he's trained. At some point there's an authorization to do something. By the way, I'm not sure it's easy to define what torture is. We all have different views as to what is torture and what is acceptable pressure.

Q. You don't accept John Yoo's memos[3] then?

He's given a definition. I don't know whether I accept it or not. I'm just saying there are different views as to what constitutes actual torture. But whatever it is, the level of responsibility rests higher than the individual who is ordered to do it.

Q. If the soldier has a moral code that makes him feel he's not comfortable obeying an order, do you think he should speak up?

There is always the ability of the individual to refuse an order he or she feels is inappropriate, and to take the consequences of that, which could be a court-martial or discharge. No individual is compelled to do something they find totally repugnant or unacceptable. Yes, they're taught to obey, but sometimes you're given an order to do something that your self-programming, if you will, won't allow you to do. You can certainly refuse that order but you must take the consequences.

Q. So you're saying you have to do what is right for you, but you have to take the consequences. That's what you did during the war, by speaking up when you needed to, and you were prepared to take the consequence and felt no bitterness about it.

Yes, you accept that. You have your own moral compass that evolves over your life. You have to live with that as the primary guidance of your behavior. You will face conflicts at times over whether what you feel is morally acceptable. There are alternatives and consequences.

Q. When you're told to follow orders and you have a certain set of morals, do you think that because you know you're expected to follow orders and that not following them will have consequences, your morals eventually change a little bit to be able to fit in with those orders?

It can change your values. If you're asked to do something that's contrary to what you feel is what's morally right, and you do it, you have perhaps made an adjustment or a change to your values. You apparently didn't feel strongly enough about that particular issue.

Q. Has that happened to you?

I'm trying to think of an instance. I'm sure it has at some point. I might have had an aversion to doing something and did it even so; and having once done it, I guess you could say I found it acceptable.

Q. You've spent most of your professional life in the defense industry, is that right?

Yes, except for two years.

Q. Did you feel being in that industry posed its own ethical questions, if you're making a living making weapons that kill people?

No. Let's put it this way: I believe that whether or not we appreciate or like it, one needs a strong military. While I was growing up we went through a great period – between the wars – of isolationism, disarmament, and appeasement. That was considered the proper way to deal with conflict. In our country and Europe the issue was of negotiation and appeasement. It didn't solve the problems; it merely encouraged the fascists and the Nazis. If you didn't have a military force you were basically toothless and unable to cope with that situation.

Q. So did our country approach the Cold War in the right way?

Yes. Whether or not you agree with the strategy, over the years we didn't have a war. We basically had peace through all that time, from World War II to today. We've had conflicts around the edges but we didn't have a nuclear world war. If it had been approached with the tactic of stripping ourselves of all force and military capability, would it have gone the same way? I don't know, because we didn't do it. We rather chose to match force with force. You have to remember that power is not just force; it's force and will. Force without will gives you no power whatsoever, as does will without force. What is power but the ability to cause someone else to act in a fashion that's adverse to his interests and more in line with yours?

Q. Do you think if we had not engaged in the Cold War there would have been nuclear attacks?

I honestly don't know, and I don't think anybody can, because that's not what we did. You make a judgment, or a judgment gets made. The alternative doesn't get explored.

* * *

Q. Let's resume our conversation. You've taken us through the war. Can you tell us where you were and what happened when the war ended?

In Guam, preparing for the invasion of Japan. The war ended in late August. Before that, we were planning the invasion of the main islands of Japan, late that fall. All those who were to participate were getting whatever we needed to be prepared and ready for that invasion.

Q. Were you scared? Were you frightened?

No. The one time I got frightened was when the war was over. I realized "It's actually over and I'm still here. Nothing has happened." Then I began to get nervous. I was frightened that at that point something might happen.

Q. Frightened they would just keep you there?

No, no. It was that here we were, the war's over, and we were still among the living. Fear that something might happen to me now. That was the one time I got nervous. You go to these things like invasions, you can't afford to get frightened. You put all that behind you. You have to take a fatalistic attitude.

Q. You're saying that sometimes when you are in a stressful situation of one kind or another – obviously, war being such a situation, but it can be a job interview or another kind of stress – after you are out of the stress, then the adrenaline drops back. Or whatever it is that constitutes the psychological mechanism that lets you get through it, after it's over is when you experience the fear and anxiety. It's ironic, isn't it?

That's basically right. You take a major stress, the only way you can handle a major stressful thing like war is to become fatalistic. In other words, if anything is going to happen to you, it'll happen. The way that it's put by a lot of soldiers is that if it's got your name on it, you'll get hit; if it doesn't, it won't.

Q. Do you think people adopted that way of looking at things because it was the most healthy psychologically?

It was the way to survive it. To get through it. In other words, it was pure chance. I do what I have to. It's my turn, I'll get it, and if it's not . . . [Frank shrugged]. It's an attitude you develop. Everybody, to maintain their sensibilities in such a situation, that's generally the way they cope with it. It was fatalism. It was . . . if something's going to get you, it'll get you. If it's not, it'll not. That was the basic thing.

Q. Is fatalism a general pattern for you?

A lot of men in the war thought that way. They used to joke about who's going to get it next, that type of thing.

Q. Do you still think in fatalistic terms? Or is that a way of thinking you strategically took on just during the war?

I guess I still am fatalistic. That is to say, I don't believe I have a pre-destined direction or that somebody has got a plan for me, that I am fulfilling this plan. My reaction is that you live in a world where all sorts of things are happening. Events occur, and it's how you react to them. But you don't control events. You don't control the world around you.

Q. When you say you're not living out some plan, does that mean something like a god is out of the picture, or is not that important?

Religion provides a lot of strength for a lot of people. Religious belief keeps a lot of people going. I am not religious. I was raised religious. My mother was very devout in her religion. In about my teenage years – maybe when I went to college – I basically broke with organized religion because I couldn't accept the premises.

As I began to lean toward the scientific side of my schoolwork, I began to find things that contradicted the assumptions of the Bible. That caused me to lose faith in what you might call the truths of the Bible. There's a lot in the Bible that's very worthwhile. The ethical teachings, rules on how to live: all are very important. But in terms of their being a creator who made the world in his image and likeness and who's overlooking it, I couldn't believe it. I ceased to believe in a One who had a plan for the world and a plan for me or anything of that sort. You then substitute something else for it.

Q. And so what did you substitute for it?

Fatalism. In the beginning, you are born. You don't choose your parents. You don't choose the date. The same way when you finally leave the world.

Q. You told me once you took an online course on religion and discovered you were Navajo.

When I looked at other religions and their beliefs, I found myself more in tune with some than with others. I discovered that if I were a religious person, I would be more likely to be a polytheist. I would believe in multiple gods. That this one central, all-purpose god who looks over everything and everyone is like the federal government. About as competent, too! The Navajos believed in individual spirits: the sun god, the rain god. I can relate to that. They can provide sacrifices to him. Or give gifts, if you will. It was a polytheistic view. The gods they worshipped were essentially various elements of nature. If I were to be anything, I might have been a Navajo. The Hopis and the Zunis have similar concepts. You have to have something. We humans, we come up and say, "Who am I? Why am I here?" These are the questions you ask. It's a puzzle to any human.

Q. Have you found answers for yourself to those questions?

I think I'm here by pure fate. Or, the urges of my father and my mother, if you get down to it. The fact that they were married and decided to have children, that's why I'm here. And what am I here for? I don't think there's any purpose that they had in mind for me. Maybe they had in mind that I would support them in their old age, which I did.

Q. So let's go back to the war's end. What did you do after the war?

After the war? I went back to school. They had a G.I. bill and I wanted to get more engineering education. So I went back and did two years of graduate study in electrical engineering at Stanford. It was at the end of my second year that my father had the stroke. I went to work to be able to provide support.

* * *

Q. How do you want to be remembered?

I don't expect to be remembered. I really don't care. I have no legacy I want to leave. I have no memorial. I don't need an obelisk someplace. Rest in peace. That's it. Somebody has passed through. I've enjoyed my life. I'm glad I had it.

Frank died on November 21, 2010, shortly after this interview.

NOTES

1. Emilio Aguinaldo y Famy, born March 22, 1869, was a Filipino freedom fighter, general, and politician. Aguinaldo played an instrumental role in both the Philippines' fight for independence against Spain and the subsequent Philippine-American War (also called the War of Philippine Independence) that Frank described. The youngest Philippine president, Aguinaldo took office when he was only 29, and died on February 6, 1964, at age 94.
2. U.S. Navy Fleet Admiral Chester William Nimitz (February 24, 1885–February 20, 1966) was a five-star admiral with dual command of Commander-in-Chief, United States Pacific Fleet (the "CinCPac" that Frank refers to) for U.S. naval forces and also the Commander-in-Chief of the Pacific Ocean Areas (CinCPOA) for both the U.S. and the Allied air, land, and sea forces. Nimitz was the leading Navy expert on submarines during WWII.
3. John Choon Yoo (born July 10, 1967) is the UC Berkeley Law School professor and former official in the U.S. Department of Justice during the George W. Bush administration who wrote what has become known as the Torture Memos, detailing the use of so-called enhanced interrogation techniques, techniques critics say far exceed the traditional concepts of interrogation under the Geneva Conventions.

3 PREJUDICE, BIGOTRY, AND HATRED. LOVE AND LUCK

Laura, Holocaust Survivor on Schindler's List

By surviving the Holocaust I was given the gift of life a second time; that's how I look at it. I was incarcerated from May eighth, 1942, till May eighth, 1945, which happened to be my mother's birthday. At that point I didn't know she had been killed. I was still searching for her. And why were they killed: my mother, my father, my brothers? All in all sixty-three members of my family were killed. Why? Because of prejudice and bigotry, and hatred. So how do I live with that? How do I forgive them? What do I do? I always wanted to be the best person I could so that no finger could be pointed at me and say, "She's a Jew. She's not righteous." I always wanted to do the best I could because of what happened to me, to prove I was worthy of having stayed alive.

Many times when I speak at schools, students ask me, "How come you stayed alive when your family and the six million did not?" I could never give an answer to that. I didn't know myself. Only by sitting down and writing my book did I learn how I survived. It was a set of circumstances. It was luck. It was where I stood at a given time, and of course what time of year it was. In my little prison dress, it was no stockings, just wooden shoes. Standing at the place where they counted us it was freezing cold or else it was so hot. It took me nearly twenty years to write this story and finally I figured out by writing. I could never find the voice I wanted to give it. I started writing in the third person. But when one does that, then we move one's self from what really one wants to convey. So I started all over again in the first person. That gave it the right voice – the voice of my voice when I was your age or younger. I'm now eighty-six years old and I was sixteen when it happened.

Before all this happened, we lived in this small town in Northern Germany, not far from the North Sea. I was one of five children. We had many non-Jewish neighbors. We celebrated each other's holidays.

I went there on Christmas. I loved sitting under the tree and hearing them sing carols. Easter also was fun. They came to our house on Hanukkah. I don't know if you know what Hanukkah is. The Jewish people celebrate when the Temple was theirs again, before it was destroyed. We Jewish people celebrate it.[1] My neighbors would always come on Passover, too. They liked the unleavened bread the Jewish people eat, called matza. It was a wonderful life. We were in and out of each other's homes. We played together.

Then comes 1933 and everything changed. Hitler made these powerful speeches saying Jews were not worthy to live and everybody was entitled to take away their possessions. Jews could not attend public schools anymore. It wasn't allowed, and why? Because they were born of the Jewish faith. No other reason. Hitler became bolder and bolder. He took away our jewelry. Anything of value was taken away, including our house. We then lived in a small apartment, in a ghetto setting. You know what a ghetto is? A place where people are confined. They can't get out. That's where they stay. That's where they live.

Then came a night I will never forget. November ninth, 1938. *Kristallnacht*: the night of broken glass. They not only broke the glasses in all the businesses and looted them; they also started fires in synagogues all over Germany, not only in the synagogue I went to. That night the Nazis banged on our door and said all Jews have to come out, get out. My father told us we should wear warm clothing. It was November and we didn't know where we were going. The Nazis paraded us in front of our synagogue. They wanted us to see how the prayer books and Torah scrolls were going up in flames. They humiliated Jews as much as they could. Afterwards, when everything had burned down, they took us to a hall and made the men do calisthenics and sing. They humiliated them in every way they could while they stood laughing. Then women and children were allowed to go home. My mother, two brothers and I went back into the ghetto. We took out a prayer book, huddled together, and prayed my father would come back home. It wasn't until dusk that my father returned. He looked pale and very, very tired. This is what he told us, "All men are going to go to a concentration camp tomorrow. They are all incarcerated now in a German prison but tomorrow they will all go to camp." Why then did my father come home? My father fought in World War I. He was severely wounded. One leg was shorter than the other so he wore special shoes and socks. We couldn't figure out why they sent him home. Perhaps someone recognized him, maybe even served with him in the same regiment. We'll never know. But this gave my father the false belief he would be safe, that nothing would happen to him. "Nobody will hurt me. I can stay." But of course that wasn't so.

My parents had to find schools for us since we were not allowed to attend public school. My brothers were thirteen and fourteen at the time and they went first, to Jewish school in Cologne, where they had to live in an orphanage. They were not orphans but that's where they had to live. I was sent to Berlin to a Jewish girls' school. I was often very homesick for my parents. Some of my schoolmates had gotten letters that their parents had been deported. From that moment on, they never heard from their parents again. It was as if they never existed and why? I can't repeat it often enough: only because they were born of the Jewish faith. While at the school, I received a letter from my mother one day. The letter said this: "Your father is no longer with us. He's in prison. I believe he's already in the Buchenwald concentration camp." They lived in a city called Weimar, only an hour from Buchenwald concentration camp. My father was assigned to slave labor. Since he had one leg shorter than the other, it was hard for him to walk far. But Jews were not allowed to go on public transportation so he had an old bicycle he rode. The Gestapo, the secret police, stopped him and said, "You're not allowed to own a bicycle. Jews are not allowed to have them." For that, they took him to prison. My mother was beside herself but she couldn't look for him because it was curfew. Jews had curfew. She waited until the next morning and went to prison with the special shoes and socks he wore. She begged them to let my father have these things. They only laughed at her! "He doesn't need anything where he's going, lady. Go home and take that with you." Six weeks later the postman brought a letter. My father's name was Martin and it said the following: "Martin Wolf, age forty-seven, died of unknown causes." Then they sent a little urn, where you put ashes when someone dies. My father had died! My mother wrote to me, "Our father is no longer with us. What am I going to do? How am I going to exist?"

But that wasn't all. A few weeks later another letter arrived from the secret police telling me my mother would be deported to the east, whatever that meant. They didn't explain it. They just said she was going to the east. But we knew from other people, from my classmates who had gone through the same thing with their parents, that going to the east meant going to labor camps and concentration camps, and with not much food and lots of beatings.

I was heartbroken. It was raining hard, I remember. I seldom left the school but then I did. When I came back into my room, one shared with two other girls, I knew what I had to do. I wrote a letter to the secret police and asked them to allow me to be deported with my mother and brothers. The Gestapo sent an answer just a few days later that I could. I could take the train from Berlin to Weimar; they had assigned me a seat. I left most of my belongings behind and I went to Weimar to be with my mother and brothers. If I had to do it all over again, I would do the very same because we were together for another few months.

One night they took us to a ghetto and then a labor camp. They took my brother Wolfgang away. They said they'd bring him back in the morning but we never saw him again. After the war I learned he was taken that night to the infamous concentration camp Auschwitz, and there he died. Fifteen years old, born of the Jewish faith.

My mother and brother and I were again separated when the camps were emptied out. We were sent here and there. One day I went to the one street that ran from one end of one camp to the other. I always looked to see if I couldn't find my mother or brother. I always hoped they would be there. Someone tapped me on the shoulder, saying, "Hannelore" – that's my German name. I changed it here to Laura – and he repeated that a few times. I didn't know who that was. He looked like an old man but he could've been a boy. His clothes were in tatters and when he coughed you could hear the rattle in his lungs. "Have I changed that much? I'm your brother. I'm your brother, silly."

He was near death. He'd been beaten and didn't have enough to eat and he was growing so fast. They took him to the infirmary and wouldn't let me in. Two days later they buried him in a mass grave with thousands of others. Again, I was sent to another camp and another camp and eventually I met the man I was to marry after the war there. He worked in the kitchen and was able to give me a piece of bread or maybe a boiled potato or some hot so-called coffee. It wasn't real coffee. Those things helped me stay strong. But it also was loving someone. My friends said, "This is no place to love. What do you think is going to happen to us?" But I couldn't be persuaded and we found ways to see each other, if only a few minutes. Again we were separated. Different camps.

Then I was assigned to be a maid to a Nazi camp commandant, and the woman who lived with him. They wanted me to be their maid because I spoke German. I got a clean dress and was taken by a policeman to this couple's house. It wasn't their house; it belonged to Jewish people. I could tell because a mezuzah was on the wall. They made me take hot water up from the basement so the woman could take a hot bath; the hot water didn't reach the third floor. She complained to the commandant that I was lazy and didn't do my job. So one day he took the two pails of water from me, doused me with water and kicked me down three flights of stairs. If I had broken my legs or arms he would've shot me right away. I would've been of no use. But I didn't break anything. So with my wet clothes, I had to go to the salt mines. That's where we shoveled the salt from the sides of this cave into layers so it could be brought up. Things went on like that until we were led into Auschwitz, the hell hole of society – if you can call it society! Everybody suffered in Auschwitz. Very few people came out. But Oskar Schindler put me on his list. Oskar Schindler wanted me to be on that list. He had drawn up a list of people who worked for him. I had never met him before but he put my name on the list and that's how I was able to leave Auschwitz. Oskar Schindler paid with gold bars to have three hundred women released and I was one of them.

Q. Do you know why he put your name on the list?

Yes. The Nazi who had thrown me down the flight of stairs was to be the new commandant of that camp that Schindler opened far away in Czechoslovakia. He said it was for ammunition making. This Nazi insisted that my name go on that list.[2] Once he had tried to kill me and now he put my name down on the list. There was no rhyme or reason for anything. But they had so much power that if you walked down the camp, he could take his pistol out and shoot. And he did! Those of you who have seen *Schindler's List* and read the book know what it was like. It was all over like that! A Nazi saved my life by getting me on Oskar Schindler's list. So ironic. We got out of Auschwitz because of Oskar Schindler. We were liberated four or five months later. My late husband was also on this list because he had been a German prisoner of war at that time.

That's how I stayed alive. Now, I hope you have lots of questions for me.

Q. Why did Hitler have such hate for Jews?

They say his grandmother or great-grandmother was Jewish. I don't know if that's true so I shouldn't even repeat it.

Q. Can I ask you – I don't know if this is possible – but can you make sense of all this? Was there anything you took out of it to help you understand things?

You have to know what happened in prewar Germany. One day bread was five marks and the next day it could be fifteen marks. The government printed money but people were out of work so no one produced any goods so there was massive inflation. It was very, very bad for people in Germany at that time. They needed a scapegoat and Hitler said he could get them out of their difficulties. Hitler had such charisma! While he was in prison he wrote this book, *Mein Kampf, My Struggle*. So who's to know? In every century, there's a bad person who wants to kill. Hitler was one of them. The pharaohs of Egypt at another time were ones also. Somebody else now.

Q. Prior to Hitler coming to power, what was the status of Jews in Germany? Were they equal to everyone else or were they slightly lower status and looked down on by some people?

I grew up in a small town but in the big towns there were painters and musicians and scientists, and many of them were Jewish. In Vienna, too. They concerted a lot. But in the small town where I lived, I wasn't exposed to that at all. We were as cozy with our non-Jewish neighbors as they were to us. First names with our parents and helping each other out. When a child was sick, my mother would not ask are you Jewish or not. You would help.

Q. What did the neighbors do after Hitler came in? Was there any effort to help you?

No. They immediately put on the uniform, my neighbors. Brownshirt, brown pants, and the black boots. They put the swastika on their arm bands. They were so delighted with this because it was a poor town really. No one had money in this town. They wanted some of what Hitler promised them: Jewish houses, jobs, and everything. Because everybody was dismissed from their jobs, they had a hard time, I know.

Q. So you find a materialistic explanation for the Holocaust?

Yes.

Q. Then why do you think someone like Oskar Schindler did what he did? All the evidence I've seen suggests he was not a laudable human being before, or even after, the war. But for some reason he did something very good during the war. How do you make sense of this, you, who knew him?

You've seen the movie, *Schindler's List*? He approached these Jewish people and said, "They're taking your factory away anyway. Sell it to me; give it to me and I will employ you." The Jews made so much money for Schindler. In the meantime, Schindler saw what was happening. He saw Jews being killed for nothing. He saw what was done in the ghetto, too. Remember that scene when the little girl in red runs? Schindler finally saw he was a Nazi and that it was all wrong. That the Jewish people who made him rich, who had worked so hard for him, were just like everyone else. That's when he decided he wanted to save some lives. He could open an ammunitions factory and the Jewish people who worked already for him – though not in ammunitions – they could be of great help to the Third Reich. Of course the Nazis never knew we never made anything that worked. Nothing worked. We sabotaged it. All the weapons we made, none of them worked. We did that so our weapons would not help the war effort. Schindler would go buy real weapons so when the inspectors came our goods would pass inspection. He had a real conversion, so to speak.

Q. Were the movie and the book accurate depictions of what he was like?

They were much, much too mild. Nobody would go and see the movie had they shown the reality of it. But Schindler was like the character depicted in the movie, yeah. He was a womanizer and he drank a lot. But to me he is a hero. He was a hero.

Q. I heard his wife was unhappy with the book, that she thought it made him look too good and that the depiction of her as accepting and forgiving him was not accurate.

He always had a new girlfriend. This movie depiction of his giving up other women for his wife, this was not accurate. She hated him, of course, for humiliating her all the time.

Q. And your life after you were liberated? Where did you go? As "Schindler's List" ends, you see prisoners not knowing where to go. The guy who liberates them says, "They don't want you in the east; they don't want you in the west either." What was it like for you when you were suddenly liberated?

That's a good question. Both the Russians and Schindler told us not to take the law in our own hands. We had two warehouses that belonged to the Germans. One was filled with vodka and the other with material, mostly blue serge for Navy uniforms. Schindler gave us the key and said somebody has to distribute it. My boyfriend did. I want to show you a picture of my wedding dress. That's blue serge I'm wearing.

My husband was quite courageous. He got us something to eat from the village and said we're going to hop on trains. My girlfriend Eva was with us. Trains didn't run on schedule. Everything was out of whack. We sat not on seats but on the floor, and changed trains often. My husband's cousin lived in Prague. She was an internist. We thought she'd still be there because she had married someone who wasn't Jewish. We went as far as Prague. My husband went from police station to police station, looking for his cousin. Nobody knew where she was. Only after the war did we learn she had five patients in the hotel where we stayed. We were then in Prague, but Czechoslovakia was occupied by the Russians, the English, and the Americans. One needed a three-zone pass to get out of Prague. We didn't have that; we didn't have anything. Just that bottle of vodka. So my husband went to the Russians, gave them the vodka and got the three-zone pass. We again hopped trains and headed for the American zone.

Q. Were you conscious you wanted to be with the Americans? Were you afraid of the Russians?

Very much afraid. They did all kinds of horrific things. But then I got arrested by an American soldier. He said, "You are German. You are not from the concentration camps." They put me in prison. The next day I said, "Can you bring me a Jewish prayer book? I'll show you I can read every word out of it." Then he finally, finally realized I came from the camps. If I can read the Jewish prayer book then I can't be the kind of German you want to arrest. So they apologized. They gave us cigarettes to trade. My boyfriend and my girlfriend waited for me in that town until I was free. Then we went on until we came to the English zone and a displaced person's camp where the English fed us. The women were separate from men and it wasn't great but we were out of danger. It wasn't far from my hometown so I took a bus to our old house. The woman opened the door. I saw all our furniture there but I didn't care. I didn't need it. She said to me, "You're still alive. You shouldn't be here. Are there any others of you?" I just ran, ran, ran away. I ran to the displaced person's camp. We waited two years to get a visa. My husband's uncle vouched for us and we came to New York. We lived in a boarding house where the bathroom is shared with ten other roomers. I got very ill at that time. It was rough, very rough. But eventually, we crawled out of this all.

Q. Did you know the woman who was living in your home?

Yes. My mother had been very good to her.

Q. How do you deal with something that's basically neighbors turning on neighbors? That must be extremely difficult to deal with.

The bigger issue was where is my mother? Where is my brother Wolf-gang? Never mind that woman. Where is my family? That was the bigger issue. That was the second punishment. Not only being in camps but no family. When I finally married in Germany I cried so hard the chaplain said, "Why are you crying?"

"Because I have no family. My family isn't with me on this day." We got married October 1945 in a small town near Munich. The American army, they made the wedding party for us. They were very nice to us. But I had no family there. I had one sister who went to England in 1939 and became a registered nurse. The other sister went on those little boats Leon Uris describes in *Exodus*. She arrived in Palestine and was sent to prison for coming illegally into the country. My father's uncle lived there. He finally arranged that she got out of prison. She worked in a house as a housekeeper and married the son of this family. Unfortunately, that sister died at fifty-four of leukemia. The other sister lives now in Dublin, Ireland. Her husband died when she was forty-nine and she remarried this lawyer in Dublin.

Q. So you have one member of your family left?

I have my sister. She's very ill now and can't walk much but before that, after my husband died, she and I went to Switzerland together. My son went to school in Switzerland for two and a half years. Here and there, we'd go on vacation. I visited her a lot more than she visited me because it was easier for me. I had only one child and she had two daughters; her second husband had four children so that made six.

Q. How was your sister able to escape Germany?

She had friends who got her an affidavit so she could come. It was hard to get out. Prior to the war Jewish people tried to flee the Third Reich. The United States said no. We won't take you in. Every country said no. Roosevelt didn't want them. There was a boat, the St. Louis, that sailed to Cuba with Jews. It sailed all around trying to get someone to let them land. A friend of mine was on that boat. He was safe but not everyone stayed alive on that boat.[3] Most of them went back to Hamburg and were killed in the concentration camps.

Q. You started your conversation with us by saying, "How do I live with this? How do I forgive them?"

That's a very difficult question. Elie Wiesel once addressed that question. "How can I forgive them when my parents aren't alive to give me permission to forgive them? How can I do that?" I go a little further than that. I've been to Germany a few times; when I see people my age, I start to tremble because I don't know if they killed my mother, my brother. Maybe they were the ones. Can I forgive them? I don't know. I don't think so. I have been a guide in the Long Beach Museum of Art. When they have German students come, they always ask me to conduct the tour because I can speak German with them. I have no animosity against these people. They weren't even born yet. It's not their fault. But to forgive someone my age is very, very difficult. I don't live with hate at all. Not hate. But forgiveness is very, very difficult.

Q. You said you don't live with hate but how do you not live with hate? What made you able to do this, to give up living with hate? Did it happen naturally? Was it something consciously you made a decision to do?

I found that once I stayed alive. That was very difficult and it took time. The guilt for staying alive, most of us had guilt feelings. Why didn't my parents live? Why did I live? Guilt feelings were there but then as time went on, I said to myself, "Yes I survived and now I have to make a life for myself." Especially if I wanted a child. If I wanted a child – and I wanted that very much! It only took me 10 years to have a child – I knew I had to have a different environment from always being together with people who were there. Always the talking about the war, and the talking about what you can't change. You have to do it privately. When I get really in despair sometimes – and who doesn't – I leave my house, get in the car, and go to the beach. I live near Seal Beach and I go on the pier and walk. The breeze is wonderful and people are in the water and it cures me. That helps me. Writing this book helped me a lot. It was my catharsis. It really was.

Q. How has your faith changed throughout everything you experienced? Have you maintained it or is it something you just can't let go of?

I maintained it. I am a practicing Jew. I maintain the holidays. I'm not so strict but I always said in the camps, "Oh, God, what have you done? Why do we have to be in this situation?" I never said there is no God. When my husband said, "There is no God," I would always say to him. "I can't prove it to you but I feel it in my heart." My son has become religious recently and so has my grandson.

Q. So even throughout the whole experience and throughout your horror, your faith remained?

Yes.

Q. Is there in Judaism, as there is in Christianity, an emphasis on the concept of forgiveness?

Yes, I'll tell you why. Did you hear about the holiday called Yom Kippur? That's the holiest day. That day we say a lot of prayers. First we have to forgive everyone we might have hurt, everyone we might have injured. Only then will God forgive us. We do want forgiveness from God. I certainly do. For having said something I shouldn't have said, for having hurt someone with a certain remark, for having invited one person and not the other and they were hurt by it. Those prayers are about just what you said: forgiveness. They encourage forgiveness. That was written before the Holocaust.

Q. I think the point you are making is that the Day of Atonement is before Yom Kippur. You have to forgive other people before you can ask for forgiveness for yourself.

God will not forgive you unless you forgive others.

Q. Does that mean you feel under pressure to try to find forgiveness for others?

Not at all. It's a relief. It's a relief you know. One of the things in Judaism is to avoid a bad tongue, to not bad-mouth people. You can hurt them very much if you make a remark about someone, whether that remark is true or false. That comes up, too, on Yom Kippur.

Q. Does that holiday take on new meaning since the Holocaust?

Let me think about that a minute. I don't think so. There's nothing special written about this in the prayer books. We have prayer books for the Sabbath, for Rosh Hashanah, the New Year which is coming up very soon, and Yom Kippur – they're all the same prayer books.[4] Only in the Haggadah when we have Passover, do we read about the exodus of the Jews from Egypt. There is a certain prayer in there that I am made to read every year, about the 6 million who perished in the Holocaust. I think not every Haggadah has that passage. My son collects Haggadahs; he has about thirty of them. Some of them say that prayer. We always say it and I'm the one who says it.

Q. Why do you think people who were running the camps continued to do what they did? Do you think they did it out of fear of what other people would do to them if they refused? Or was it more because of the power they had?

I can't tell you. I can't give you an answer to that because I really don't know. I don't know why they did it, not having talked to them. I've never talked to them. I tried to avoid them. Even with Schindler and why he did it, I can't tell you. I can only tell you about my own experiences and what I saw in the camps. But I can't go into their minds obviously and I too was restricted.

Q. You were a young girl, too, when all this happened to you.

Yes.

Q. You talked about Schindler. He liked women. He liked wine. You also talked about some of the camp guards who didn't do anything. From the sound of this, can anyone be a camp guard? Can anyone be Oskar Schindler? Is there anything special about them that they happened to be who they were? Or was it just because of chance?

That's a difficult question. A very difficult question. I can't answer that.

Q. Let me formulate the question a little differently. I don't know if you know of the social psychological experiments that came out, partly came out as a result of the Holocaust. The Milgram experiments on willingness to obey authority grew out of concerns that the Holocaust occurred because Germans were authoritarian. In fact, what Milgram and his associates found was that – if put in certain situations – most people will do what they're told to do. Then there are the Stanford prison experiments. Since your son went to school there, you know about those, too. Zimbardo set up a lab in the Stanford psychology department basement and had some students take on the role of guards and some take on the role of prisoners. The underlying assumption on which all these experiments are predicated is the idea that there is an environmental influence on our behavior. These experiments contradict the view that some people have a personality that simply will not allow them to do certain things. But it turns out that personality sets a moral agenda for roughly a third of those people. Only one-third of people didn't obey, didn't follow orders in Milgram's experiments. So here's my question. As someone who lived through this period, do you think it's situational or do you think there are certain personalities that would withstand the kind of pressure to do evil things?

First of all, if they didn't comply, the person next to them could say that so-and-so didn't raise his arm and say Heil Hitler and you should question them.

Q. But you, at the age of seventeen, told them you wanted to be with your mother and your brothers, an act that you would've known was going to put you in a difficult situation, at best.

I know. But my father wasn't alive anymore and my brothers were too young to help my mother and I thought I could help her. My going meant we did get to spend four months together, those four months where we had to work very hard. If you read my book it tells you every little detail and I don't want to go into it again here. Had I not gone, I may have lived and I may not have lived, who knows? I feel good that I did it. It must have given my mother some kind of comfort although she kept saying, "Save yourself."

Q. Do you know what made you do that?

Love. Love for my family. We were very close. We were orthodox Jews and Friday and Saturday nights were so much fun in our house. All my uncles and cousins came and we ate and we sang. My parents were very good parents. I always say that. I wrote several poems about that. Because they gave me the love, I was able to love others. It's so important in the early years and the middle years because of that.

Q. Have you been able to reconnect with Holocaust survivors other than your sister?

Yes. One lived in London and she's no longer alive. One lived in New York and I lost touch with her. My friend Eva lives in Israel and we phone each other every other week.

Q. What is it like to reconnect with people who have gone through the same experiences as you?

Like part of my family. When Eva and I call, we call each other sister because we are sisters. We went through a lot in our lives.

Q. Do you feel that even after so long you still need to have that connection and need to talk to people about it?

No. We don't. Most of my friends are not survivors.

Q. A lot of people with whom I talked said that after the war, they came here and they put a big "Do not disturb!" sign on their memory. They

didn't want to deal with the war and the Holocaust. I was wondering if you ever did anything like that.

I didn't but my sister hasn't read my book. She hasn't read anything. She can't. She said, "I can't. I feel so guilty for having left you." (She left in '39.) I told her my parents were happy she left, knowing at least one child was safe. But I can't convince her. She doesn't want to hear anything about the Holocaust. Nothing.

Q. I can understand that. Forgiveness is difficult, especially forgiving yourself. Coming back to forgiveness, what do you feel when you meet Germans of your own age and older, as opposed to younger Germans, like the ones you mentioned meeting at the museum. But Germans born before the war, what is the internal feeling you experience toward them? You say you don't forgive them but you don't hate them. There's a very interesting distinction in that statement. It's a beautiful statement in many respects and I wonder if you can give me and others here some clue about the difference internally for you. You said you trembled – and you still tremble – when you meet people your own age and older from Germany but not the younger generation. You bear them no fear, no ill will. What is the difference internally for you?

People my age could well have been the executioners of my parents. So it's difficult for me. Very difficult. But hate is such a negative feeling. It would take over my life. I enjoy life. I like to go to plays and concerts. My friends take me out and I have a lot of friends; most of them are non-Jewish. It doesn't make a difference. They wish me Happy Hanukkah and I wish them Merry Christmas. We come together for parties. In fact recently I had to have physical therapy and the girl who did it was a German girl, maybe thirty. She is from a city which makes very good cookies. When my son goes to Germany for work I ask him to bring me some of those cookies. He always does. This girl knew I liked them so she gave me some, too. She told me her parents were coming to this country. It was Christmas time and I said to her, "I would like to invite your parents to have coffee and baked cookies." They came to my house. It was a wonderful visit. I felt I had overcome another step. I had grown.

Q. I had a question about memory. It seems one reason you wrote the book, the reason why you're here today, talking with us, and the reason why memories are important is that you don't want to forget what happened. How important is it to remember what went on, and do you worry about not being able to remember? Do you worry that the rest of us will forget?

I worry that the rest of you will forget. I'm eighty-six. How much longer can I live? So many of the survivors, they are that age or older. After we go, who would talk about it? It isn't easy for me to go to all these schools, to attend plays like the Anne Frank Opera where I met your professor and her daughter. It's very difficult. Most of the time I don't want to talk about it. But it's my duty. It's my duty to speak until I no longer can, so that we will be remembered. That's how the book started out. But then I always ask: Why did I survive? I survived and the book will tell you why.

Q. So talking gave you a purpose in some way?

I do a lot of volunteer work. I work with HIV infected teenagers at Willows hospital and now cancer children. I do art work with them and poetry. I was a guide at the Long Beach Museum, for seventeen years, until my back gave out. I do a lot of things.

Q. What did your husband do?

He was in the liquor business. When you come here without education, you have to make a living. It was a lot more than being incarcerated. It was losing your youth, your parents, your education, your social skills. All these things are part of the punishment.

Q. What does the number 287 mean to you?

That was my number on the list, on Schindler's list.[5] That's not the number I was given in the camp. I have this camp tattoo, too, if you're interested. The people of my town raised a thing with the names of the people that perished. My parents' names are on there. So are my brothers'. I took my grandson, who was sixteen at the time, and we went to the area to visit. He said the Jewish prayer, the Kaddish, there. I showed him all the places my relatives have lived. We were there four days.

Q. That must've been really important for him. Did you and your husband follow the trials that went on in Nuremberg directly after the war?

I vaguely remember them. I do remember the one in Israel. I followed that closely.

Q. Let me ask you a question about why the Holocaust happened in Germany, which remains a great puzzle to many scholars. Germany before World War I was the apogee of civilization, in learning, music, art, science, and so on. Germany had a cultured people. How could the Holocaust happen there? You seem to suggest the Holocaust happened – at least in

part – because of the shock of losing World War I and then the punitive actions of the Versailles Treaty, which were very unfair to Germany. That's a widely held view. Recently, a different explanation was offered, suggesting anti-Semitism was particularly virulent in Germany.[6] A lot of scholars disagree, pointing out the many Germans who spoke up against anti-Semitism at earlier points. Do you have thoughts on this, since you are German yourself? Do you have any thoughts about why the Holocaust happened in Germany? Is it just an economic explanation? Just the shock of losing the war, and the unfair reparations?

Don't forget I lived in a small town; it was a really small town.

Q. But the people all turned on you.

They all turned on me. On us. Every one of them. A friend of my father's came one night and said, "Martin, you have to get out!" My father said, "I don't have to get out. I fought in World War I." He did! I have this picture of him, with his uniform on.

Q. A lot of Jewish people thought that having fought in the war would protect them. A lot of people were very shocked when it didn't protect them. But as you say, here's a man who sounds as if he was trying to protect your father by saying you needed to leave. But your father didn't believe him.

Yes. My father said no.

Q. That's another interesting question. Why did some people quickly assimilate the fact that Hitler was something different and not just another politician? A German- Jewish rescuer named Margot told me she remembers being in coffee klatches with people saying, "Oh well, we'll try this Hitler for a while. What harm can he do? Someone has to get us out of the economic hardships." This echoes a joke in American politics, saying no matter who you elect, you end up with someone in the center. But in fact, there are politicians that are not in the center and who definitely turn the country in a different direction. Do you have any thoughts about why some people were able to realize Hitler was something qualitatively different than other politicians when other people were slower to grasp this?

You don't want to believe something that bad. I imagine the people your friend Margot mentions had a nice house and they all got together for coffee, things like that. They were so comfortable, and you don't want to believe anything bad can happen when you're like this. But there is another reason why my father didn't leave: he had no money. He couldn't pay for five children and two adults to emigrate because he had nothing left.

Q. So part of it was comfort; part of it was opportunities. It was during the depression after all. It was hard to get someone to sponsor you. Do you have any ill feelings for your neighbors for basically betraying you?

No. I completely shut them out of my life. I have to help myself. I never wanted to speak with a psychologist though people often recommend it. It's not for me because I would uncover things that better stay hidden. There's so much I have to repress, that I don't want to let come to surface because I can't handle it.

Q. So your ability to move on and to not hate people is complex. Part of it comes from your policy of not forgiving them but not hating them. Some of it emanates from a conscious desire and knowledge that if you don't do this, it'll cripple you psychologically. Part of it is coming from a deep emotion which is your desire to have a child. You wanted to raise this child in an atmosphere where he could be whole and not suffer from hate and the old prejudices and wounds. Finally, part of it is an act of will on your part to simply suppress certain things. That's incredible that you can do all that.

My friends always say I might be a slight person but I have a steel blade in my back. But it's important to me. When things aren't important, I let them go.

Q. What did you tell your son? You said something while we had lunch that I thought was a lovely thing to say about a child. That you're very proud of his accomplishments but you're most proud that he's such a wonderful human being. What was it that you did to help him become this way and what did you tell him of your own experience? Did you talk to him about the Holocaust? Did you talk to him about your experience?

Interesting, when my son was in graduate school at MIT, he called me one day and said, "I've just seen a film about the Holocaust, about a couple in the army. It wasn't that bad. It was made with a very light touch. Did you go through that? Is that what you went through?" We said to him, "When you come home next time we'll tell you the whole story, now that you're old enough to know." We didn't want to cripple him at an early age. He knew we had been in a camp and that we were different certainly because we had accents. We were not the ordinary couple. That's what we did. He handled it very well. Just before my husband died my son did a video of him in which my husband opened up a lot more. He never wanted to talk about it. My husband never opened my book, just like my sister. They can't handle it.

Q. You said you met your husband in one of the camps and that this was a positive part of the experience. Are there any other positive things you took from the Holocaust, maybe found meaning out of the suffering?

Perhaps the fact that little things don't upset me so much. Black or white, or green. Who cares? Somebody says something they shouldn't have said. Little things, I can forget. I don't analyze them. I don't want to think about those things. They're not important. When my daughter-in-law says, "I was so busy I couldn't call you for ten days," I just said, "It's okay. I think about you and that's good." Another mother-in-law might say, "Oh, she didn't call me."

Q. How have you been able to be so positive about this and not let it make you bitter?

I think it's all the love I received when I was a child. That's what it is.

Q. I remember my mother telling me once after her mother had died – she was very close to her mother – and she said waking up in the mornings was hard for her. She finally decided she would take all the love her mother had given her and give it to me. I'm hearing something a little similar in what you're saying; that you had this love that was given to you that kept you whole and helped keep you whole throughout this whole experience. In some ways are you passing this on to your children?

Yes. I wrote a poem about it. Many years ago I think it was published in some little magazine. The poem is written to my mother and says I'm able to give the love she's given to me to others. Maybe I could fish it out and e-mail it to you.

Q. Is part of what you're doing here today, going out and talking to young people – as you have done here today – is that a part of that process? Is it part of the healing process for you, as a witness? And a duty to remember your mom?

Remembering my parents and brothers.

Q. You said you had a duty. Who was that duty to? Is it to us? To your parents? To God?

To my parents who have no voice, who were silenced. My mother was forty-four and my father was forty-seven. Too young to be killed and leaving five children.

Q. You said you were able to forgive because you were able to give the love your parents gave to you. But why do you think, assuming your sister had the same love for your parents, that she's not able to talk about it and open up too?

I don't know. I can't go into her mind. I think it's guilt on her part for having left but she doesn't need to feel guilty. How do I tell her that?

Q. Do you feel because you lived you have a purpose? Or is it more that you have a second life to do something that you have a purpose for?

Just being a good person and giving back to this country what it has given me, that's my purpose. That's why I always like to volunteer. Not for something easy but something that is a little more difficult. So I like to give back by volunteering, by helping people, by doing a good deed. That's what I like to do. Whether that's my purpose I don't know. I also love my grandchildren very much. I was part of their lives and that incredible closeness means so much to me, and my daughter-in-law and my son. They're very nice to me.

Q. So in terms of finding your own moral compass it was the love your parents gave to you. What would you tell young people here as they go into their own world and as they go into finding their own purpose in life?

Never give up for one thing. If you have an idea in your mind, what you want to do in your life and where you want to go, there's always hope even if there's a fork in the road. Pursue what you want to do and above all be true to yourself.

NOTES

1. Hanukkah (also Romanized as Chanukah or Chanuka) is an eight-day Jewish holiday commemorating the rededication of the Second Temple in Jerusalem during the second century BCE Maccabean Revolt. It is observed for eight nights and days, beginning on the 25th day of Kislev according to the Hebrew calendar, a day that occurs sometime between late November and late December, according to the Gregorian calendar.

2. The historical facts concerning many of Schindler's activities, including the construction of the famous list, are murky and in dispute. It seems relatively uncontroversial that Schindler purchased a factory in Krakow shortly after Germany conquered Poland in 1939. Schindler employed many Jews from the Krakow ghetto until it was closed, at which date most of the Jews were sent to the Plaszow labor camp, located a short distance from Krakow. At this point, Schindler seems to have obtained permission to house Jews in his factory. During most of this time, Schindler made a fortune by paying the Jews in his factory lower wages than the non-Jewish Poles would have demanded. Schindler later opened a factory in the now Czech Republic, near his hometown, Brunnlitz.

   The contention comes over who actually drew up the list, with the best evidence suggesting it was not Schindler but that Schindler instead gave explicit guidelines concerning the kind of workers he wanted to SS-Hauptscharführer Franz Josef Müller. Was Amon Göth the person Laura describes as having put her name on the list? This character, played by Ralph Fiennes in the movie, figures prominently in the movie/book's depiction of the list's construction and adds his own mistreated maid to the list. Göth does seem to have been the psychopathic Commandant of the Plaszow camp, the one who shot prisoners from his balcony, as Laura's narrative mentions and as is depicted in the movie. He well may be the Nazi Laura describes who kicked her down the stairs. But Göth already had been arrested by the SS on September 13, 1944, and hence was in prison in Breslau at the time Schindler's list was constructed. Further, according to David Crowe, Marcel Goldberg was the person who actually prepared Schindler's list. Goldberg was a Jewish prisoner of questionable morals and a member of the Ordnungdienst, the Jewish police force in the camp. Regardless of Goldberg's personal character, the historical evidence does seem to confirm that he was the assistant of SS-Hauptscharführer Franz Josef Müller, who was the SS official responsible for transport lists. The best evidence also suggests that only about one in three of the Jews on Schindler's list had been workers in his Krakow factory. Had Schindler simply closed his munitions factory in Krakow, instead of bribing the officials so he could move it to Brunnlitz, most of the men in the factory probably would have been sent to the Gross Rosen concentration camp (a camp with no gas chambers) and the women and children probably would have gone to Auschwitz. Most probably would have perished.

3. The St. Louis sailed with 937 Jewish refugees from Hamburg. Each passenger had a valid visa for temporary entry into Cuba. Sailing on May 13, 1939, the S.S. St. Louis was one of the last ships to leave Nazi Germany before Europe was engulfed in war. When the boat arrived in Havana, the Cuban government declared the visas invalid. The boat waited for 12 days, off the coast of Cuba and Florida, while negotiations with the United States and with Cuba failed to produce a change in refugee policy, and eventually the boat had to return to Hamburg. Four weeks after the St. Louis first left Hamburg, Belgium agreed to take its refugees. Three days later, the French, British, and Dutch governments also agreed to provide temporary asylum until a permanent home could be found for the refugees. The ship docked at Antwerp and the passengers dispersed to their temporary destinations. Once the Nazis occupied their countries of destination, most of the refugees not placed in Britain perished.

4. Rosh Hashanah means "head of the year" and is the celebration of the Jewish New Year. It is the first of what are known as the High Holy Days and occurs ten days before Yom Kippur.
5. Hannelore Wolf is listed on Schindler's list as number 287 and a *schreibkraft* (typist) with camp #76490.
6. Goldhagen 1996.

4 EVERYTHING WENT DOWNHILL AFTER THAT

Gunther, Refugee and Displaced Person with an SS Father

My name is Gunther. Usually when somebody asks me where I was born I always say I'm not from around here. My earliest recollection is of the fancy sort of a castle near Vienna that was a refugee station for the war. My actual birthplace as far as I know, well some people say the Northern part of Yugoslavia. But that's not what I understand. I understand Novi Sad.[1] This was initially Serbia. It didn't become Yugoslavia until 1918. That would be on the border of Croatia, close to the border of southern Austria. I have no recollection of that since we had to get out because of the war. It was not popular to be German in what was considered Russian territory. We had to get out of there. We got half of a train because my people were part of the military and we went to Vienna through various steps. How we got to Novi Sad in the first place is beyond me. It could have been for religious reasons. We initially came from the Black Forest region, sometime around the First World War. All the way from there to Czechoslovakia. So we come from there. That's a long way from Germany.

Q. How old were you and when were you born?

I was born in 1942; it was the middle of the war. January sixth, 1942. I lived through the war and I've actually made it until sixty-nine.

Q. You said some of your first recollections were of Vienna?

We lived outside Vienna. We went there occasionally. We weren't very well off but the situation was ideal if you were a child because the area where we lived touched on a forested area. The hillsides were covered in grapes, a lot like Napa. It's pretty ideal for a child. It might have been bad circumstances. But as a playpen it was excellent. Me and my cousin Helmut, we had a pretty good time there. We would have been four years old. We occasionally went into Vienna and even though it was bombed a little bit, it remained a pretty fancy city. So we had some pretty good stuff.

Q. So you were living under Nazi occupation then?

Yeah. My people, we had to choose sides so they all joined the German army; actually they joined a faction of the SS, an armored division, like a Panzer division. I think one of my relatives, Uncle Fritz got grabbed by the partisans and was butchered. The rest of them never came back from the war. This was the beginning of being sort of an alien. First you can't go back to where you came from. The property was gone. Anything you had was gone. So we had a fresh start. We were still with the same people. It was just being a displaced person. Not only that but with all the men gone, it was just the women running things, so that probably screwed me up a bit too, you know? It's very one sided, plus they were slightly hysterical because we were occasionally bombed. I'm not sure by whom. We could have been bombed by the Russians, the Americans, or even the Krauts. I'm not exactly sure how to retrace that to determine what territory we were in but I remember the women in the family telling how they ran from bombs and sought shelter so they must have passed a lot of fear to us subliminally. If they're scared it rubs off on the kids. That's probably why I'm kind of paranoid. Anyway, nobody was destroyed by the bombing but it was still a terror. I have no recollection of any of that but I'm sure some of it rubbed off somehow, psycho-logically.

Q. What were the names of your parents? Obviously Oma – my Grandma – was your mother but who was your father?

My father, his name was Franz ___. His background, I'm not sure about that because ___ is actually an Irish name according to what I know. He could go off in another direction totally and have some Irish because the Germans did a lot of mercenary work at the time. They fought for anyone who'd pay them. Ireland was one of the places they fought. My parents must have met somewhere near the Black Forest area, or in Germany or the Serbia area. When the war broke out, the Second World War, they had to get out. Get out or be butchered.

Q. You said before that your family and the neighbors around you had to choose sides when the war broke out. Can you explain how that choice was made, and if it was even really a choice?

There wasn't much to choose from because there was a community of all Germans; they didn't intermarry with anybody else. I'm not sure about their religion, probably Roman Catholic. They kind of stuck to themselves. As far as I know, my father had some kind of textile company. They probably did business with everybody but stuck mostly to themselves, staying in their little enclave. When the post-war sides were drawn there were certainly Russians in the area and there's no way my people could be there so they had to get out. Germany was definitely the enemy and the aggressor so we had to get the hell out. Especially my people with the SS tattoos. Those tattoos were completely out there. They didn't like them even in Germany. In fact, when my father came home once on leave he had to wear civilian clothes because the SS uniform was not considered cool at all. Anyways, all those people were killed. That was the worst situation you could be in: being SS and losing the war. Nobody came back and we don't know exactly what happened. Who knows? Maybe they're in South America. All I know is that they didn't come back.

Q. So you are positive your father was SS?

Oh yeah. I have pictures. A lot of that stuff had to be destroyed because otherwise we probably would have been dead, too, since we were intercepted by Russians when we were fleeing, going from place to place. We could not be German. My aunt and everybody else, we passed ourselves off as somebody else. All birth certificates, anything connected with Germany had to be destroyed. We couldn't have any evidence. All that stuff had to be destroyed. Any kind of pictures or documentation, it all had to go. The women also faked having tuberculosis so that they looked less attractive, to fend against rape and whatever else since they were pretty young. They passed themselves off as not German; I don't know exactly what though. Maybe Hungarian. That whole area was part of the Hungarian empire for quite a while. In fact, my grandfather was in the Austro-Hungarian Calvary. It was all intermixed there. That whole area was covered by the Austro-Hungarian Empire and the Hapsburgs. Then it started breaking up, even before they put Germany together, you know, when Germany was united finally as a country. So somehow we ended up down there and then we had to get the hell out and we have been moving ever since. Maybe that's why I'm such a gypsy.

Q. Do you remember at all when the war broke out? Did your family then move into Germany?

We moved out of Germany across Austria into the Northern Czechoslovakia area, wherever concentrations of Germans were. They were like pioneers, like somebody going from New York to California in the old days of the United States. Eventually we wound up down south. We always stuck to a bunch of Krauts. The war, I have no recollection of that. I have recollection of the rubble after the war. I saw stuff like that when I was little. I never saw a bomb explode, and I don't recall that I ever heard a bomb explode so I missed that. I remember rubble and I remember people being not too well off. I remember getting care packages from the Americans. Those were the occupying troops. There were occupying troops in Vienna. They used to drive around in jeeps and stuff. Four people I remember, an English man, a Russian, French, and American. Most likely they were all officers. They used to drive around; I don't know what they were up to. But they used to drive around and we would shoot at them with slingshots. The enemies, you know; they were considered the enemies.

Q. Even though they were providing help and care packages to you?

Yeah. They didn't belong there. They were the occupying force. We got little presents and stuff like chocolate bars or whatever, but this went beyond that. We thought they had no business there. They were outsiders. We used to play war games. We found a tank in the woods, and that was our clubhouse. We played war games and slingshots were our weapons. There was still stuff lying around – the occasional grenade or whatever, weapons to be found – but we were just little kids. We had slingshots. Our little fort was the tank. It was a cute little childhood right in the wine country, which is not too bad.

Q. How old were you when you left Europe? How did that work out?

When you're in one of those refugee camps, you are not going anywhere. There are a lot of people in refugee camps all over the world right now going through border disputes, wars, and whatnot. It's not a perfect situation. It's totally unstable and you never know what's going to happen so most people never get anywhere. I guess what my people did is put our name on a possible immigration list. We knew a few people in the United States; if they sponsored you, you could put yourself on an immigration list and immigrate. My people had nothing going on. Nobody was coming back. Everything was destroyed. They said, "The hell with this. Let's start over." So they tried to get to the United States.

They put their name on the list and we were golden. That started more gypsy stuff.

Q. What do you remember about the refugee camp? Do you remember the name?

I don't remember the name. We called it the refugee camp. It had no special name. You weren't hated by the people but you weren't liked because you were a drain on society. A lot of the churches would give you stuff. We weren't that popular here either, especially after the war. People just aren't so generous. There's not so much to go around. You're not considered an enemy, more an irritation – a drag. You're not producing anything; you're not working. You're this and that. In the refugee camp there was no future so they put in the paper work to immigrate. Eventually they worked out that if you were healthy enough you could immigrate. You still had to be examined. They didn't take your word for it.

Q. How many people were in your family?

My immediate family was my mother, my sister Elga, and me. Then we had Mom's sister, my Aunt Alice. She had three kids, Bruno, Bertha, and Frieda. There was another sister, my Aunt Mary. They were all together. I don't believe Mary had any kids. So it was all sisters. My Aunt Alice, she was the strongest one. She took charge of everything. That's principally what it was. That was the family unit: three women constantly pushing everyone around, and I guess to this day it still bothers me. I ran mostly with my cousin Bruno. We were little troublemakers.

Q. All the men were SS and they were killed in the war?

Yeah, I'm sure they were. My Uncle Otto was killed by partisans, vigilante groups who made up a faction against Germany or Germans. They operated as part of the communist party. It was like a secret little death clique. You didn't want to get caught by these guys. My Uncle Otto was blinded, castrated, and bayoneted in a public square. That wasn't too pleasant for him! So you did not want to get caught by the partisans. You did not want to get caught by the Russians with an SS tattoo, that's for sure.

Q. How old were you when you immigrated to the United States?

When we got the clearance to go, I might have been close to twelve. I think we might have taken a train to the northern part of Germany, maybe Hamburg, which is a port. Then we took a battleship. Actually, a fancy little Caribbean cruise line but originally it was a battleship. We took that to New York to Ellis Island.

Q. So you lived in Europe until you were twelve after the war ended? How old were you when the war ended?

I must have been three years old.

Q. So did you live under communist rule?

Where we were at, it was temporarily under four influences: British, French, American, and Russian. 'Cause we were in this refugee camp, located just outside of Vienna, and Vienna was administered as a divided city, that's where we spent most of the time. But we were in a couple other little camps, maybe not as attractive. They weren't in the wine country, which was sort of elegant. I would say if you went there right now, it would probably be first class. You could compare it to Napa or something; everything was built back up again.

Q. Were you born in the refugee camp?

I would have been born en route, probably coming out of Serbia. I used to make up little stuff because I never heard the complete story. An accurate story is hard to get because everything needed to be destroyed; everything was hush hush. Theoretically I could have been born en route, getting out of there. My earliest memory would have been right outside Vienna. Not bad huh? It was a pretty fancy little city; that's an image you want to remember, not like being in a trailer camp.

Q. So before the war your mother, and your father, they lived in Serbia?

The area became known as Yugoslavia after the war. After World War II ended, all those countries were united. Now all that stuff is broken up again. They went back to the old ways. But each one of those countries then had German influence. Croatia sided with the Germans so it was popular to be in Croatia. It was safe to be in Croatia if you were German. We had to get out of Serbia because they sided with the Russians and that was bad news for us. We didn't have very far to go. We could have just hopped right over the border. But because my people had some military influence, they got half of a train to put their stuff in and get the hell out of there. That's why they went to Vienna.

Q. Each family got half of a train car, is that what you're saying?

Something like that. At least that's what I heard. Each family got half of a train car. You put your stuff in there and your kids and you're gone. This was all an overland train. You stop here and there. It was no luxury thing. It wasn't like an express train to Vienna. It took a long time. It's like hitchhiking; eventually you get to where you are going. When we got there, we were just put in a camp because we had no place else to go.

Q. When you were in these refugee camps, was there any schooling for you and your sister?

I went to a public school in Vienna. There was no school in the camp though there could have been a kindergarten or something. I do remember going to a Catholic school somewhere in Vienna, close to the Danube River. Vienna was walking distance from the camp, I remember that. I don't know how many grades I went there; could have been a couple of years. I must have gone for four years and finished grammar school.

Q. Do you remember anything specific they taught you?

Some history; mostly Austrian history. I don't remember any mathematics or anything; lots of gymnastics. Gymnastics was a big deal. I don't remember a lot of specifics, but we must've had mathematics because their schools are pretty good. I don't remember any sort of real schooling until I got over here to the United States.

Q. So you and your family immigrated when you were around twelve years old and you went on a battleship to Ellis Island?

Yeah, that was my first sight. The Atlantic Ocean and then you're standing in front of the Statue of Liberty!

Q. How long was the ride on the battleship?

A week. It was not a luxury thing because everyone was as sick as a dog, except me. I didn't get sick from that sea stuff. It was quite an experience coming to America. Then you're actually in front of the Statue of Liberty. You go through immigration and do tests to make sure you're not bringing in anything, no germs or disease. When you get passed you get your five bucks or whatever and you're on your own.

Q. Were there any major problems in the camps? On the ship? Lack of food, or anything like that?

No, I don't remember any of that.

Q. So you didn't have luxuries but you were definitely taken care of?

Yes, we were fine. Occasionally we got some stuff from the Americans. I remember Mrs. Grass's noodle soup with an egg and noodles. I remember a lot of cod liver in a can, which I happened to like though most people hated it. Cod liver was really good for you; maybe that's why I'm still alive. So yeah, I got basic food. I was young so I didn't care because we'd raid fruit trees and so on. We were pretty wild, me and Bruno. We ran loose all the time. Not that my mother and the women didn't care; but we weren't controlled that tight. We didn't get into trouble so it was, "whatever."

Q. Was the refugee camp fenced in or could you leave?

You could leave, sure. We weren't fenced in but you had no business going anywhere else. We went to the woods every day to pick strawberries and flowers. We ran all over the place. Occasionally we even went into the city. I remember going down into the city once by myself, too, which was pretty far out. But yeah, we could go anywhere. I remember fooling around in town, right in the heart of Vienna. There's a huge cathedral there called Stephansdom,[2] other museums, and palaces, of course. There was a big amusement park with a Ferris wheel so it was pretty nice.

Q. Do you remember ever having to make any tough decisions or moral decisions?

At that time, no. It wasn't up to me. No one asked me should we go or shouldn't we go. If it was up to me, I don't know if wanted to stay or go. I think I wanted to stay and not even come to the United States. Everything was such a thrill. When you're twelve and you're coming into a new country, everything is such a kick. It didn't start to go sour until a little bit later.

Q. How was it moving to a completely new country?

It was pretty shocking. Vienna was a thousand-year-old city with a lot of architecture and class. New York was just the opposite. Like a canyon of skyscrapers. It was pretty powerful, very dramatic. Overwhelming, really. But we were only in New York for two or three days. We didn't speak any English so we couldn't say too much. The only word I knew was "ice cream," and I did manage to get an ice cream bar some way. After that we took a train from New York to Chicago, which was pretty cool. One of our sponsors lived in Chicago. Chicago was also a big city. Different than Vienna and quite a bit different than New York, too. This was 1951, around then.

Q. Do you know who your sponsor was?

Aunt Elizabeth or Aunt Mary. You had to have a sponsor to come. Someone had to say they were responsible and would look after you, try to get you on your feet. They didn't want any liabilities. No people getting on welfare right away, like it is now. Yeah, it probably would have been Aunt Mary who sponsored us. Then she took off and went out to California. My mother wanted to learn English so she joined an English class, where she met my stepfather. Once they got hooked up everything went downhill from there as far as I'm concerned.

Q. What do you mean everything went downhill?

He was also a Kraut, from the middle part of Germany, near Hanover. He was in the *Wehrmacht*[3] on the eastern front, so he was probably damaged goods himself. We never got along. We could not get along at all. He didn't like the idea that we were not his children. You know how it is. They got married and there's children from another marriage, he can't handle them. Like we were scumbags. We never got along so I got the hell out of there as soon as I could. I may have been out of the house by the time I was fourteen years old. I moved into the basement in the same building, and was completely out of the house by the time I was sixteen. I mean gone! Then it was just the occasional visit. I learned English pretty quick. When you're fooling around on the streets all the time you learn pretty quickly.

Q. What did you do? You moved into the basement, but then after that, where did you go?

We were like street people.

Q. Who's we?

I always found alliances; I always had friends and people in similar situations. They were not Europeans, except for one guy who was also a DP [displaced person] from France. Then we met Bernardo. We met some other guy with similar circumstances, an American Indian.

Q. So your friends were an American Indian and a Frenchman?

When I first got on the streets I was alone. But at night when you got no place to go [Gunther shrugged]. You make alliances for survival with people in similar circumstances. Somehow I met somebody else who was also alone and I said, "Where are you going?" That person didn't have any place to go, so we were kinda sticking together. Once you're not alone it's not so scary because now you got someone watching your back. Whatever misery and joy you're going through, you got someone to share it with. That part's not so bad. But it's still rough and tough. If you're on the street in the winter time in an abandoned building with no heat, in Chicago, it's tough! You're a vagrant and the police don't like vagrants.

Q. Did you ever have to do anything you regret because of your situation?

We never did any major crimes but I remember stealing a lot of bicycles! I never had a chain. So I'd steal one bike. I'd leave it; someone else would steal that bike and I'd steal another one. I stole a lot of bicycles to bop around. I never chained them up. They would just get passed around like Europe is doing now. But we never did any burglaries. We didn't rape anybody. Kill anybody. It was rough and tough but we did okay. We stayed in abandoned buildings. I've slept a lot out in the park, practically in the snow too, but you can't do that for long. You've got to get out of the weather. We'd usually find an abandoned building or break into a basement or something. Find an open window, which was pretty scary, because someone could wake up and shoot you. We gambled a lot of the time. We broke into lots of hallways and slept in between floors, on the landing or whatever. Sometimes we'd put up notes saying, "Don't call the police; we're just sleeping." It was a constant hassle because vagrancy was not a serious crime but it could still get you in the lock-up, you know? Of course we were always armed with an ice pick or a razor knife, even sometimes a pistol. So we were armed. We were vagrants and we had a concealed weapon. Whenever we did get grabbed it was always for disorderly conduct, nothing criminal. They'd hold us overnight and tell us to get out. That was in the sixties. They don't do that anymore. Now you'd serve some time.

Q. When you made the decision to leave home, what was going through your head? What triggered you to leave?

My stepfather and I got into a few scuffles. I could never kick his ass but I was not welcome. Eventually I got the drift and I just moved out of the house. I would sneak back to the house when he was not there cause of my mother. I'd take a shower, grab something to eat. There was not a lot of bread so every now and then I'd grab a couple dollars. Usually I'd go there once in a while, take a shower and then get out. We all had to be on the sneak. After a while even that got to be too intense. The years went by, lots of years. They didn't even know if I was dead or alive.

Q. What did your sister Elga do?

She stayed at home; she probably felt the same way. I know for a fact that she refused even to attend my stepfather's funeral out of principle because he was an asshole. So she has pretty strong opinions. But she didn't leave. She stayed at home and went to school. She eventually went to college and got married. She didn't play the street game. That's mostly a guy thing. She would never make it out there.

Q. So you're out on the street, just surviving. Other than occasional money from your mother, how did you get food?

Odd jobs. For a while I delivered pizzas. Between the three of us, someone ran into something. We always had girlfriends. One of us always had a girlfriend we could hustle for food or a couple dollars. But that situation would never last long. It was a game. If you had a girlfriend for a month, you were lucky. One way or another you ran into people. You hustled. You did odd jobs. This and that. Got me how I survived that long. At the time I never thought I'd make it to twenty-one years old! Never any way I was going to make it to twenty-one. No fucking way. You know what I mean? But it turns out I did, not only to twenty-one but another forty years more than that. It's amazing to me. For a while there, it got to be pretty weird because we got involved with the drug Benzedrine, which was a big drug at the time. Back in the Jack Kerouac days, there was this whole beatnik thing happening. I ended up cutting all ties with everybody and joining the military because I knew I was going to have a problem. I needed to get out of the scene I was in.

Q. Wait. You wanted to join the military because you didn't like the people you were around anymore? You didn't like the situation you were in?

Yeah. It was dangerous because you could wind up in prison or wind up dead. I figured I'd change it completely. I could've changed states. I could have moved to Missouri. But I wanted to make a completely different change. That didn't work out because I didn't get what I wanted. I wasn't a citizen. I wanted to do counterintelligence, you know, espionage. But they wouldn't give it to me because I was not born here. Well, it got me off the streets.

Q. What did you end up doing in the military?

I went through basic training. They gave me some crazy duty but I balked because that's not what I signed up for. Nothing could be done because I couldn't get the security clearance since I wasn't a citizen. Eventually I went AWOL. I eventually turned myself in and got placed in the stockade. I got out of the stockade pretty quick. Previous to the stockade, I used to find the military hilarious and I'd laugh a lot, which caused some of the officers to think there was something wrong with me. I had psychiatric testing, which I volunteered for because it was interesting.

Q. Why did you think that would be interesting?

Military life was so boring. There was nothing going on. I thought it was ridiculous. I mean, after living off the streets of Chicago all that military stuff seemed ridiculous. It was a game. A joke. When I didn't get the assignment I wanted, I went AWOL. Because I had this little psychiatric episode, they did some tests on me since I'd made some outrageous threats when I was in the stockade. They took it seriously and took me out to what they called Ward 57. Kinda like *One Flew over the Cuckoo's Nest*. I needed mental evaluation but they could never make up their mind about anything so I kept getting shipped around, eventually flown shackled into Phoenix and moved around some more. Eventually they offered me a discharge. That's not what I wanted. But I didn't care as long as it was under honorable conditions. I still wanted to be a spy but that was out so they gave me an honorable discharge, which I took because it was a huge threat to be put in a nut house, you know, a mental institution. It was total blackmail to get me out of the military. I had no real choice. I had to get out of there.

Q. What did you do after that?

I wound up going back to Chicago and I looked up the trinity. We called ourselves the trinity, and we started all over again. This time we had more connections. We used to hang out at this pizzeria and they knew I was getting out. So when I go to the pizzeria, there was a note there and a train ticket to go to Dayton, Ohio. John had stolen a bunch of money from the mafia. So they were all hiding out in Ohio.

Q. These were your friends?

Yeah. John and Bernard.

Q. They stole money from the mafia? The Italian mafia?

The Chicago mob. Some bookie or whatever and they were all gunning for us. So we had to get out of town even though only John took the money. They knew all three of us. So we all met down there on the run in Ohio.

Q. How much money did they take?

A lot of money at the time. It was about twenty-five thousand dollars. That was a lot of bread in the fifties, or rather sixties.

Q. Were you ever caught?

Not by the mob. We'd be dead! [Laughs.] No. We bought a car. We rented a house, got art material. It was a great time. We hung around in Ohio until all the money ran out then we came back to Chicago when the heat had died down. They were no longer gunning for us.

Q. Did you ever work? How did you get money before the so-called twenty-five thousand dollar bonus?

Yeah, I worked, I did odd jobs. This and that. Eventually I did get a couple of jobs. I worked at a fancy bookstore, Kroch's and Brentano's. I had a bunch of little jobs. I used to rent these rooms, like little sleeping rooms, whenever we had money. We'd rent something and when I got a little money I got a room, which you'd pay for a week at a time. As long as you paid, you had a home. A place you could take a hot shower. One of the places I rented, the owner was in the electrical contracting business. He asked me if I knew anything about electricity and of course I said yeah. I didn't know a dicky bird. But I got into that and I started doing electrical work. Now that's a whole different ballgame. Once you had a trade, especially electricity – everyone likes electricians – it got a little easier. I could earn a bit of money. It's a higher paying trade. When everyone was making a dollar fifty, I was making five dollars. That helped a lot. I never did any investing or anything but the story goes on and on. I had a couple girlfriends. Even ended up getting married for about a year, but that didn't work out.

Q. After moving out of the house and living on the streets, how did you deal with education?

I was in school, in high school, but that got to be impossible because when the school day ended, there was no place to go. It became a question of survival. We got tossed out of school for making trouble; we weren't able to function. We would make up for it by hanging around the University of Chicago and schools like that because they tolerated people that were "beatniks," or off-color, and otherwise burdens to society. But along with all that stuff they had at the university, there's a lot of stuff that's free. We could attend lectures. Film festivals, plays and musical events, and whatnot. You can go to all kinds of stuff. We got a lot of free stuff. Most of it was free. Some of it we snuck in because we knew the system and we knew the schools. We had two years of that stuff. While I lived in Chicago, I mean it was a big city anyways. We practically lived at the Art Institute. You get an education by hanging around museums and being in the right place. It was our scene. Plus it was warm. Well, one time, we did one thing. For about a year, we started a party and kept it going at my friend's house for about a year. That was almost like a sociological study because we had everybody there. We had hookers, burglars, cops, college professors. You name it. We had all kinds of IQs: dumb, smart, whatever. That went on twenty-four hours a day for a year. Eventually the year went by. Later on down the road I got more drug research. It was the right type of climate. These were not dumb people. These were pretty smart people we're talking about, not burglars. A lot of these people were up there in the high 180 IQs. These are not fools. Some of that intelligence rubbed off on us and kept us from becoming criminals.

Q. After you and your family emigrated to Chicago, were you enrolled in any formal school?

Yeah. I had to start over and I went to grammar school. It was quite a shock actually. It was an all-black neighborhood. I had never actually seen anybody black until I came over here. I went to an all-black school, which was pretty crazy. I actually went to two of them, one by my stepfather's house, which happened to be by Forty-seventh Street in Chicago, which was sorta a ghetto.

Q. You mentioned it was very extreme. Was that because it was a new environment? Can you remember any particular crazy things that happened?

There was a lot of violence at the school. I remember I was always armed with an ice pick or a bayonet. This was a grammar school, which was pretty unbelievable. The police used to come in and line up all the boys and search them. That doesn't even happen in high schools today. It maybe happens in some of them. It was pretty unusual. It was a racial thing. I was pretty outnumbered. I was the only white boy in there. I was never a threat but I drew some good attention.

Q. Did you yourself ever feel personally threatened?

Oh yeah. I got into a lot of stuff: knife fights, fistfights, stuff like that, after school. It got dangerous but you form alliances. I hung around certain similar tougher black street members. You can get killed. [Laughs.] No problem.

Q. You mentioned earlier that you and your friends would get into trouble in school. What did you do to get in trouble?

We were probably disrupting class because some of the stuff just didn't gel. Like I've said, we were sleeping in buildings so some of the stuff that came up didn't click with the reality we were living. We made a lot of trouble. We cut a lot of classes. We hung out at a lot of coffee shops. We were all in accelerated classes. We just did a lot of arguing with teachers. It was part of the times. We're talking about the sixties. We're talking beatnik days. Not everybody followed. Eventually we started getting fairly decent grades. There was a lot of cutting class and not turning in work and this and that. We felt we were above it anyway. It just didn't click. I eventually transferred from the school in Chicago to one in St. Louis temporarily but that didn't work out either because it was the same shit. At that time I lived with my aunt, which was a real family but that didn't work either probably because I was too acclimated to the streets. I couldn't really obey any rules. So I got kicked out of there and then I decided to leave. I just wasn't material for high school anymore. So that was the end of that. I came very close. I probably had enough credits to graduate high school but I never did. We always thought we were way above that anyway. Turns out we weren't. That's just a casualty. That kind of lifestyle, a lot of people end up dead. A lot of people end up in prison. A lot of people end up damaged. None of those things happened to us. Except whatever damage happened to us was probably psychological and physical.

Q. When you were in school you mentioned you and your friends had to arm yourselves? Did you feel that was absolutely necessary? Did you not feel any protection from the school or police?

Oh yeah. In the neighborhood. But in the black schools, when I went to high school – which was a mix – I was probably armed there, too. It was kind of a routine of life, going to those schools. Some of those neighborhoods we went to, I was armed with something. I didn't stab somebody everyday but when you did get jumped or something – and you were easily jumped, because you were white – you either had to get the hell out of there or get some kind of weapon to at least be a threat. I wasn't really intimidated by that. I always felt I was kind of immortal, that nothing could happen to me no matter how many people jumped me. That attitude worked for quite a while. You got the occasional boo-boo or something, but most of the time I walked away with nothing serious.

Q. You were targeted because you were white. Did this cause you to develop racist tendencies?

Of course I was targeted because I was white. I was an automatic mark. When you're in a black neighborhood, even to this day, there's some tension. But that didn't turn us against the blacks. That was just the way it was. I'm sure I have some racist tendencies but I used to sing with black guys on the street corners. Like the doo wop stuff in the old days. I ran around with black street gangs. In fact, I probably had my back covered more by black people than by white people. It was just you were the wrong color and not too many people knew you. Sometimes because you were white, you were ignored. It was a problem.

While I was still at home my stepfather had some buildings he managed in the ghetto and I did a lot of work there. So I had to go into those neighborhoods and of course you were always the wrong color. This was not an affluent area; it was rough and tough. You were always a mark.

Q. Do you remember how your family acclimated to a new country? What did your mother and stepfather do for work?

Mother had some little jobs, odd jobs, occasionally. She stayed home though after they got married. My stepfather ran some buildings. He belonged to some janitor's union. He'd collect the rent and fix the boilers. Stuff like that. Actually I did a lot of that stuff, too. But yeah, they liked it just fine. Compared to Europe it was better. Not architecturally speaking. Architecturally it was inferior to Europe in those neighborhoods. It wasn't as clean as Europe but as far as survival and having a lot more freedom and say so, it worked out pretty good. Buildings had phones and other amenities. Any money you saved, you could bank. It was a lot easier. In the refugee camps there wasn't anything at all. It was charity. Here you could hustle and make a buck. I was running around, working on boilers, but I was only twelve years old. I always had a helper I could tell what to do so that worked out okay. That was earning my keep. So I wasn't exactly mooching off the family.

Q. You didn't really know your real father; you just knew of him?

I was too young. I have no recollection. I saw pictures but I have no recollection of this person.

Q. Knowing your father was part of the SS, did that make you feel ashamed of him or proud of him?

No. I didn't have any problems with it. It wasn't like he was running extermination camps like Auschwitz. These were strictly elite military units. They would be something equivalent to the Rangers or the SEALs in the U.S. Army. Of course he was going to join the German army because he was German. At that time a lot of people, a lot of younger people, came through and switched to the American side. I was in the American army myself. At the time it was the thing to do, and if you were a Kraut, you swung with the Krauts. It was patriotism. I had no problems with what he did. What do I know about attacking a situation with tanks? I could imagine it but at least he wasn't shoving people into the ovens.

Q. Your stepfather, you didn't get along with him?

Nah. I guess we rubbed each other the wrong way. He knew when he married my mother she had two kids. That was on the table but I guess he couldn't handle it. Like I say, he was in the German army. Sent to the Russian front so he was probably damaged goods, too. He couldn't handle it. Far as I know he couldn't handle his own kids either. He just treated everybody like shit. That was the best he could do. We didn't get along so I got out of his way. There was no point in being there.

Q. Did you know if he had problems entering the United States because of his affiliation with the German army?

As far as I know, no. He was in the German army and they didn't have anything against him. Unless he didn't admit that. I don't know his immigration status but he didn't sneak across the border. I know he came in legitimately. He got papers. He did okay. Mostly he just ran buildings. He was part of those janitor unions and they ran buildings. It's not like he owned the building. You weren't *exactly* a pawn but you were a pawn. If you get the help and got all the work done, you got pretty good pay. Most of those people, they were frugal from the war. So they would save money. They would get a house in the country and get a boat. Even a lot of times they were able to buy the buildings they lived in because they were frugal and pooled their money. So yeah it worked out okay for some of them. Most of them did okay because they knew better than to be spoiled. They couldn't be spoiled. They were war babies.

Q. In your younger days, after you were honorably discharged from the Army and you took the money from the Chicago mafia with your friends, did you ever feel ashamed about it?

No, not really. That was John's play. I just got hooked into it. John was one of our boys. He looked a lot like Elvis Presley. All the girls would swoon over him. There were plenty of chicks silly enough to fall for him. But he was a total mercenary. If these chicks happened to have any money, he would get it. Right? He had no interest in these girls except to hustle them. One of those chicks was the daughter of a bookie. When he was able to get at her bread, that account was empty! That money was gone. Sayonara. Because we were so tight, and everyone in that neighborhood knew we were so tight, we all got sucked into this thing. They were gunning for all of us. When I came out of the army I found out about all of this. I didn't know anything before that. They said to meet in Ohio. There were tickets for me to take the train down to Ohio; it wasn't until I got there I found out the real story.

Q. Were you mad that John had done that?

Not really. It's like Robin Hood. He didn't kill anybody. It wasn't armed robbery. He wasn't stealing from unfortunate people. It was stealing from predators. I didn't think anything of it. I didn't like the idea that we had to be out of Chicago while people were gunning for us. That was pretty serious. Morality wise, I didn't think much of it. It worked for us because it gave us a house. We had money to burn. We were all artists so we had plenty of money to buy art supplies, which the town found amazing. John was a sculptor and he wouldn't just buy a pound of clay, he would buy a truckload. [Laughs.] You know what I mean? We got paints because we were all painters. We always had lots of materials. We were considered the big spenders in that town. Because we were so weird, people would drive by our place just to look at us. On the weekends it was something to do, like a curiosity. We used to hang around Yellow Springs, Ohio. It was a college town.[4] Very progressive. That was one of our hangouts. It's probably still there; it's a no-grades kind of college. Pretty heavy people went to this college. We had a purple VW. We used to hang out there and never cut the grass, which would piss people off. We had it four, eight feet high. People would come by on the weekends, bring their kids, and look at the weirdos. But we were the weirdos because we had the bread.

Q. How did you get into the art scene? Was it natural for you?

Yeah, I always considered it the number one game to play. One of the high games. You could be a plumber, you could be anything. But I considered an artist one of the higher games. Unfortunately it never did click for us; we could have been somebody but we never had a place to paint. You can't be on the street lugging canvases around. You know what I mean? There's no place to do it. So whatever got done got done and left behind. All that art, it's probably still around somewhere. With a proper studio and support, we could have been something like de Kooning or the New York Art School.[5] We did pretty crazy stuff. But survival took precedence over everything. We weren't stable enough to stretch a canvas or build anything. Sometimes we would have a place for a few days and knock something out, but it would get left behind. Hitchhiking around the country we couldn't schlep anything around. It's an impossible trade without space or somebody who looks after you, somebody with a house, or somebody to sponsor you. Without those things you can't get away with it. We did that whenever we could. I still do it to this day. I'm still struggling, to this day, to get a proper studio. It's a luxurious game. Who has time to paint? Plus paints are expensive. People have real bills to pay, real problems to deal with. Painting's a luxury I managed to squeeze in a little here and there but not as much as I like to. There's not enough money, not enough space, not enough time, you know? A lot of the artists in the old days had similar problems. Some of them overcame it; some didn't. The ones that had the space managed to get the stuff done and would even be recognized. But anything that was done in the abstract, we were doing stuff like that, we had no problem.

Q. If someone were to ask you how you identify yourself – ask how you view yourself and what group you identify yourself with – what would you say?

I would be a total outsider. I don't like gangs; I don't belong to any gangs. I don't like political parties. I'm pretty much like a freethinker. I would call myself an existentialist. I invent myself as I go. I'm not counting on anyone telling me who I am or what I am. I just make it up, and if that doesn't work, I just change it. You reap what you sow. Depends on what you do. If you're doing a bunch of bullshit you get a bunch of bullshit back. If you're doing a bunch of good stuff, you get good stuff back. I would pretty much say I'm an existentialist and underground artist, no particular training. I do what I want to do. If it works, it works. If it doesn't, I change it.

NOTES

1. The second largest city of then Yugoslavia, Novi Sad, suffered extensive NATO bombing in 1999.
2. Located in the heart of Vienna, St. Stephen's Cathedral is the seat of the Archbishop of Vienna. Standing on the ruins of two earlier churches, the first one a small parish church consecrated in 1147, it is one of Vienna's most recognizable symbols.

3. The simplest definition of the *Wehrmacht* is the armed forces of Nazi Germany, including the army, air force, navy, and SS. A fuller explanation is more complicated. After World War I, the German armed forces were disbanded into a *Friedensheer* (peace army) in January 1919. The Treaty of Versailles imposed severe constraints on the number of German armed forces and general conscription was abolished. Germany soon began covertly circumventing these conditions. After Hitler assumed the office of *Reichspräsident* and became commander-in-chief, all German officers and soldiers were required to swear a personal oath of loyalty to the *Führer.* Conscription was reintroduced on March 16, 1935, and the conscription law introduced the name *Wehrmacht.* Thus both the name and organizational structure of the *Wehrmacht* are Nazi creations. The insignia resembled the Iron Cross used as tank and aircraft markings in World War I. The creation of the *Wehrmacht* was announced officially on October 15, 1935, and was abolished by the Allies in 1945. Gunther's father and stepfather thus both were in the *Wehrmacht* but, presumably, by referring to his stepfather as *Wehrmacht*, Gunther suggests the stepfather was not SS. In practice, the SS functioned autonomously and existed in parallel to the *Wehrmacht.*
4. Antioch College.
5. Born in Rotterdam in 1904, the Dutch American artist Willem de Kooning (died March 19, 1997) became famous after World War II for his style of abstract expressionism or action painting. De Kooning was part of the New York School, a group of artists that included other well-known painters such as Jackson Pollock and Mark Rothko.

5 IN THE MIDDLE OF A HAILSTORM, ONE DOESN'T FEAR FOR ONE'S OWN LIFE

The Red Princess and the July 20th Plot to Kill Hitler

Born January 31, 1912, the Infanta Dona Maria Adelaide of Braganza was the last surviving granddaughter of a Portuguese monarch. Known as the "Red Princess" because of her socialist beliefs, the woman code-named Mafalda by the resistance studied in Vienna during World War II, traveling at night to help war victims, including Jews in hiding. She worked with the von Stauffenberg group and was arrested and tortured after the group failed to assassinate Hitler in July 1944. The Nazis condemned Mafalda to death but Salazar – fascist ruler of Portugal – is believed to have intervened with the Germans, possibly because of her royal status. This intervention resulted in her release and immediate deportation. In 1945, Mafalda married Nicolaas van Uden, a Dutch physician, with whom she worked as a nurse and social assistant caring for children in Vienna, Africa, and Portugal.

For more than 50 years, Mafalda never spoke of her wartime actions. Her grandson learned of them when he was assigned The Hand of Compassion in a class in Vienna. In one chapter, Otto Springer describes his resistance work and mentions Mafalda, whom Otto suspected carried secret messages from Churchill to von Stauffenberg agreeing to conditions for German surrender if Hitler were assassinated. Otto described trying to track down Mafalda but noted that he had failed. When Mafalda's grandson read the chapter on Otto he called his father, saying, "I think this is Grandma." His father used the internet to contact me, received what information I had, and quizzed his mother, who finally owned up to her role in the resistance movement. Eventually, my son Nicholas interviewed Mafalda in Lisbon in October of 2010, with her family in attendance, learning for the first time about some of their mother's activities. Questioners are Nicholas (N), Mafalda's son, and Mafalda's daughter. Mafalda died not long after this interview, on

February 24, 2012. After her death, I learned she had a sister named Dona Mafalda, who died in 1918. I do not know if the code name was chosen by Maria Adelaide to honor her sister or whether the similarity was chance.

It is true. I was in prison because I was working against the Nazis. But I heard the news about the Stauffenberg plot [which failed to kill Hitler] from the other side. The general public wasn't supposed to know about plots to hurt Hitler. It was Thurn-und-Taxis who helped me afterwards, after the plot failed. He was a prince of [the] Thurn-und-Taxis family and was put in prison the same time as me.[1] The difference between what the book [*The Hand of Compassion*] says and what I told you is that I didn't have any contact with the man [von Stauffenberg] who made the attempt [on Hitler's life] before he did it. I knew about von Stauffenberg and I heard he wanted to do something. But he was in Germany and I was in Austria. He was only in Austria as a prisoner the day after the bomb, after the attempt at killing Hitler. That was the only moment. So I am not as interesting as they think I am. I worked in the resistance, of course.

When it came to dropping bombs, the English went during the day somewhere in Austria. We had to tell them where bombs should be thrown. I told the British about papers with names of the Austrian underground people whom the German wanted to eliminate. The Nazis had lists of those people. I had the telephone number of the man who threw the arms for us. We needed the bombs thrown.

N: How did you originally get involved with the resistance?

The Nazis did things which none of us could approve. All of us were against it. I don't remember when I initially contacted the underground people. We were all underground and against the occupation of Austria. It was terrible for the Germans to enter Austria and do what they wanted. Of course we were underground! The Americans [had] the planes during the night. The British were better during the day. The Americans were alright during the night and knew where to shoot their bombs. We wanted them to destroy the fewest number of people working on our side. We tried to tell the Americans how not to drop bombs on the hiding places of our people, especially where our imprisoned people were taken by the Germans. We knew where the Nazis had their lists of the underground people they wanted to catch. So we asked the man who threw the bomb, to throw it exactly on that place, to destroy the lists of underground members. I didn't want the Nazis to know those lists. I tried to alert the Allies where to drop their bombs.

Even when I was in prison, I wasn't afraid of being killed. It doesn't matter somehow when it's one person against others. It's the idea that counts. So even while in prison I tried to get them word, "You throw it exactly in that place," [Mafalda made a swooping gesture to imitate a bomb falling]. I knew the other side of the corridor where I was imprisoned in that ancient hotel was where the Nazis had the list of resistance workers. That list needed to be destroyed, even if I died too. Of course, normally the people wouldn't find that decision very natural because it meant killing one or two [of us] probably. But well, that's what a person does. I told the man in the underground exactly where the list was kept and he threw the grenade there. It didn't open my door, my door was closed and somehow the bomb couldn't open that. It could break part of the door but not all. Then there was the corridor, then the washing room, and down there was the list. The resistance threw it exactly there. So it all went down and the list was destroyed.

N: But you were not destroyed.

No. The door, it was all broken. Then when the attack was all finished, then came the guards and took us abruptly to another prison. But I remember the moment they threw the bomb there. I was so insistent that the bombing site had to be targeted just right, to destroy the paper with the Nazi files. These files needed to be destroyed and I thought I would be killed, too. [Mafalda shrugged.] It was very interesting. Anyway, the Nazis couldn't catch the people that were on the list. I made sure of that.

N: How were you able to tell the man with the bomb, while you were in prison, where the list was?

With a telephone. That was the only telephone number I had. It's astonishing that I had this chance. It was really a sensation. That you knew that the plane would come and to say [to] him where [and] how he should throw it. It was hard work really to make him do it, but it was alright, the man from the plane. He was English, of course, or American. Probably American. Those [who] worked with us were British or American.

N: So after the bomb they took you to a different prison?

I couldn't open the door. The guards came along and took me away to another prison. I hoped that it would be possible to get out, but it was not. About the telephone. When we were in prison, of course I had no telephone. Thurn-und-Taxis [had] told the bomber where I was. Thurn-und-Taxis is my brother-in-law. He married my sister. He was put in prison at the time, before me. He went to prison before me. He stayed there until the end of the war, and then he was let out. Thurn-und-Taxis was put in prison because he got caught listening to the news from the British radio. That's why he went to prison. Another sister of mine went into prison and [only] came out when the war finished. Afterwards I nearly was put to prison by the Russians, but they found out I had protected one of the communists. When the communists found out that, they didn't send me to Russia. Otherwise I wouldn't be alive. I think you know everything that you wanted to know. Is that everything your mother wanted to know?

N: She gave me some questions. So let me ask you, how were they treating you in prison?

They weren't very cruel. Nothing interesting. They were harsh. I knew of people they tortured. But I thought they wouldn't do that to me because I was a princess of a neutral land. Of course, when it came to it, they did do the same to me. I didn't have water to drink for two days. That's the worst. To eat, to not eat, it's all the same. But to not to be able to drink water is bad. Some more things happened while I was imprisoned but I always found little things to tell them so the torture would stop.

N: What sort of things did they want you to tell them? What sort of information?

What they were interested in, naturally, was who had told us about the location of the list of resistance people they were looking for. They wanted to know other things about our people in the resistance, or if I knew who it was who was the big boss, the head of the organization. They wanted to know who headed the political group against the Nazis in my land. They wanted to know, for instance, which of their people told us things. They didn't know that.

N: What was your life like after the war?

[Laughing.] I began to study medicine, I wanted to go to America to specialize in one field of medicine but after the war it wasn't possible. I hadn't finished completely my study of medicine during the war because the Nazis politicized the universities. During the Nazi occupation, how you speak about politics affected whether or not you'd get to go on. I was told I was too outspoken and it would be better if I would leave. So I went away. But I had nearly finished. I lacked only two exams to finish medicine. Well, actually it was a nursing degree.

Mafalda's son: In the meantime, you got married, you started to have children. You went to Switzerland. You made plans to go to Kenya.

Oh yes. But that didn't work, going to Africa.

N: Why were you going to Africa?

To help the black people. I got married and my husband was a professor of the university but he went to Africa for quite a long time, nearly a year, from one place to another, always to help the blacks. I couldn't go. I wanted to go but I was having another child. Then there were four and my husband said, "No. You can't go with four of them. It's too much for now. Later on." So later on I went with the children. This one is number two. [Mafalda pointed to her son, who smiled and said, "I always have been number two."]

N: What was your life like before the war?

I wasn't in Portugal at the time. We went to Portugal afterwards. I think at the time our family wasn't allowed into Portugal. But then the big man in Portugal [Salaazar] said, "Of course you can go to Portugal." So we all went. It's always politics. Religion and politics.

We had a large farm and at that time I was the head of our farm. I brought the animals in stalls and studied. Two things I wanted to be. I wanted to be a doctor, but we hadn't the money because a sister of mine was studying already. So I wasn't able to go. I studied only for health, for nursing. There was a possibility of three years in America but then between the Portuguese civil war and World War II, there was not any more possibility for it. What I really was interested in was medicine. Because I couldn't do medicine, I had to do nursing. Afterwards I continued with my work. During the war everybody was hungry so of course farming was necessary. So I went on with my farming.

Then I was asked to go to Africa as a nurse. That's when I finished nursing and my husband finished medicine. In Africa where there were no people, there were only animals. We had the possibility to work there but then my brother wanted us to return to Portugal. He said, "Come on, come back to Portugal." So then we went to Portugal. We continued to get children. We continued to work with children and politics and then I made social assistance here. The places where the most people were hungry were where we worked together with the social assistance officials. They accepted me as if I were one of them. I worked with them. That was my occupation afterwards. I was a social assistant. They had a home for children whom I cared for. The house was meant for thirty-five children and they had nearly eighty children so it was very difficult. The communist party thought people wouldn't like me, but they did like me because I worked in these camps. The communists gave food for the children. Every day we would have one meal for the children, food we got from the communists. Everybody was astonished that the children were so brave, but they understood the scene.

So that's what I did after the war, if your mother wants to know. I worked in the social assistance. First I worked in Africa, then I worked in the social assistance in Portugal. For years I had a children's home. I took care of the home. I fed the children. I got together all their papers and sent them all to rich people so they would help me feed the children. It worked very well. Then when the communists came back, they didn't like the children's home outside of the town. They wanted them inside with the working class. They said, "No. No. You must have them inside the city." I told them, "Okay, you take care of them all." I was already quite aged by then.

The elder children came back to me when they were grownups and they said, "It's terrible, terrible that they took our house away and the other children have to be in town. Not like us who are here with the animals and garden and space to play. The communists don't want us here. They want us to be inside town because they can contact us."

I said, "Well, I haven't anything to say now." But it was nice for the young man and he brought me money to help. He came from war. He was a soldier at the time. He gave me money for the children, children in both the city and the town.

What else does one do after a war? What did your mother do?

N: My mother was born after the war. My mother's parents, like you, came back from the war. Her father came back from the war and they had children and that was my mother. During the war were you involved in housing or rescuing Jews, political targets, or people you knew the Nazis were chasing?

During the war it was for the countries. When the Germans took over, of course, I worked one hundred percent against them. I was not initially in the resistance. But the moment the Germans took over, I worked, of course. After the Germans came in, then yes we helped Jews and so on. It was something naturally anybody from our family, any of our people would do that. It was necessary. But not before because then there was no persecution. There was no need to do anything. Before the war I worked for our people. Afterwards, when the Nazis took over, yes, of course.

N: Did you help people hide or help people get out of the country?

My brother had a quite good organization to help people get out and get to America. Of course we worked in those organizations. Naturally. You couldn't have helped doing such work! To see what was going on! That's why I went to prison. I went to prison because of these things and because I had listened to the news from the other countries, which we weren't allowed to hear.

N: Is there anything else you can think of you'd like to say?

No. I told you about my moment in prison when the man came to throw the bomb. Afterwards I thought it quite funny that I had no fear whatsoever at that moment. I felt so strong that I could observe them throwing that bomb exactly in the place I lived. That is strange but it happens. In the middle of a hailstorm one doesn't feel afraid for one's own life. It doesn't happen at the moment. Then there were the interrogations, which I did not think they would do with me. But they did. I invented stories to tell them why this and that happened. I just made up things. Now it seems strange that somehow during the interrogations they didn't catch my lies.

I suppose in retrospect it's interesting. First I worked in politics all the time. Then afterwards I was busy taking care of the children and of other people. Afterwards, taking care of dogs. Afterwards it was breeding dogs. Boxers.

Mafalda's son: There was a time where we had eighteen dogs in the house. My elder brother and I went to my mother and said, "That's too many dogs in the house. We can't live together. You have to decide whether you want dogs or children." She took a very deep thought on it and decided in one second. "I've had you for nineteen years; now I want the dogs." So we went to live in the apartment next to the house. I will always remember that. [He laughed.]

At the time I had four dogs and social assistants.

Mafalda's son: And children. [Laughter.]

NOTE

1. One of Mafalda's sisters was Princess consort of Thurn-und-Taxis (1894–1970). Mafalda thus may be referring to Franz Joseph, ninth Prince of Thurn-und-Taxis. I have no evidence of his arrest by the Nazis. He died in 1970, making it possible but not clear that it was he with whom Otto corresponded.

6 BELONGING TO SOMETHING

Herb, Austrian Jewish Refugee from the Third Reich

I was born in 1927 in Vienna. My parents came from Eastern Galicia, which during World War I was part of the Austro-Hungarian Empire. My father was actually a soldier in the Austrian Army. My mother came separately. They both came from the same area, now part of Western Ukraine. My wife and I just visited there in '97. This was the first time I was there. But I was born in Vienna and I was eleven years old when *Anschluss* came. I was there for a year after the *Anschluss* experience. We managed to get visas. They were semi-legal visas to go to Belgium in the spring of 1939. After about a year under Nazi rule we went to Belgium where we were refugees waiting for our American visas to come through. It took a year, but fortunately by the spring of 1940, we got our visas and left for the States. We made it out by just a few weeks. The war had started in the meantime; the French were already in the middle of the war. Our boat was sunk by a U-boat on its next voyage. Not on our voyage fortunately. We arrived in New York April eighth, 1940.

Q. What was it like to arrive? How was the feeling?

Good.

Q. Do you remember anything about the day of the *Anschluss*?

The specific day, no. I don't have any specific memories relating to that date in itself. I remember a great deal about the experience and about the year. You have to remember, I was eleven and a half years old, so I was still very much into it. I have a sister who is a couple of years older than I am, and I was very well informed. We knew very well what was happening. We insisted on being kept up-to-date. Our parents respected that. By November of 1938 we had been evicted from our apartment. We had lived before that in a, well – what do we call it – public housing, in Vienna during the period of socialist rule of Vienna. They had very big housing projects, quite desirable housing. Our father was able to get an apartment there because of the status of the family. Maybe also because he had been a member of the Social Democratic Party. I don't know if that was a factor as well. My father was a small businessman. He owned a small store with my uncle. They sold laces, silks, and textiles by the yard. It was a very small store downtown. The store was closed in November 1938. All stores owned by Jews were closed. We had been evicted from our apartment because they evicted Jews from the East from public housing apartments. I saw a book published in Vienna, just a couple of years ago, about that old program of evicting the Jews from the public housing projects. The book told the stories about paraplegic veterans. There were Austrian veterans who also were evicted; they had asked for special treatment because they were veterans and paraplegic as a result, but they were not granted special treatment. This was after *Anschluss*. The Nazis were very efficient. They worked very quickly. A lot of things were put in place. I assume some Austrians probably marveled at what already had happened in Germany since the Nazis held power. Of course there was a big Nazi underground in Austria so everything, the whole hierarchy, was in place. Overnight we learned, for example, that our neighbors in the apartment below us – the high school principal; the wife was a teacher – were Nazis. The only relationship we had with them was that periodically they would complain that we made so much noise. We didn't have rugs on the floor and we had two children who moved around. After the *Anschluss* was over, he then became some kind of official. The interesting thing is that my father went to him when we were evicted and he helped us find an apartment to move into. You know how Vienna is organized. It was in the traditional Jewish district. In Vienna, we got an apartment that another family of three was living in. They were getting their visas for the United States so they were about to leave. But they had not left yet. So we all lived together at that apartment. We were all there at the time of *Kristallnacht*, of the night of the broken glass. We were all in that apartment together.

I knew very early in the morning that something was afoot because it was in a Jewish neighborhood. I looked out the window and I saw a small Jewish-owned grocery store. I saw people pulling a man out of the store. They were marking out the windows and locking the store. I don't think they broke the windows but they took him away. It was pretty clear something important was going on. My father was supposed to open the store that morning and he decided it wasn't safe to go. I suppose we should have known this could happen. What actually happened is that they would pick up Jewish men on the streets and drag them away to the police, some to concentration camps. Some were beaten; it was arbitrary. We knew what was happening. My father didn't go into the store. We knew my uncle would come in later to the store and wonder what happened, why the store hadn't been opened because it was my father's day to open the store. We hadn't a phone at home, but we had a phone at the store so I went down to the phone booth to try to tell him why my father couldn't come to the store. But to do so without revealing too much. I was worried about saying things on the phone. A short time later my uncle walks into our apartment. We open the door and he sees my father alive and well. Not so well perhaps, but alive anyway. My uncle got angry! He was an impetuous man. He walked out in anger, saying "All this time I thought he was sick!" We tried to stop the argument, but he just marched out and then – I don't know whether I was asked or I offered – I was chosen to be the one to follow my uncle and clue him in on what was happening, tell him there was a pogrom underway. I was Orthodox at the time, more Orthodox than my family. I took off my cap and my glasses so I would look less Jewish, and I walked through the streets to the store. I was not disabled by leaving my glasses. Even now I can get along without any glasses, but reading is very hard for me without them. So I could see. Walking in the street is not a problem. I walked and I came to the store and the store was locked. We learned later the building's janitress came to my aunt and uncle and said, "There are rumors there will be some accidents here. It's probably wise for you to go home." So they locked up the store and went home, and were safe. The store was closed. We never got back to it; that was the end of it. My aunt did go back at night on a couple of occasions to take some laces and the most valuable things.

Also on that day we heard the boots on the stairs and the knock on the door. The frightening knock on the door. They were a couple of storm troopers. They were checking who was in and searching for weapons. They looked around and messed things around. This was the second time we'd been visited. On this occasion they took away some books but they didn't do anything else. Nothing significant anyway. These same men broke furniture in other apartments and beat up people. Maybe they put some people away. The thing that is most dominant in my memory of this event is its total arbitrariness. I knew we were being subject to totally arbitrary treatment. They could do anything they felt like. If there was anything they didn't like about you – something you said or some way you looked or whatever – they could beat you. They could break your furniture. They could take things away. Fortunately, they left and we stayed on. But I do remember that date and I remember all of us just huddled together. It was four of us and three of our apartment mates. I had another aunt and uncle, not the ones from the store but my father's sister and her husband, who was an old man already at the time. They came to be with us during that day. We were all huddled together at this apartment, spending that very frightening day. That's probably the most traumatic memory but life is full of things of this sort during that period.

Q. Did it help having your parents with you? Did you feel comforted and safe with them?

The fact was that not only during this period, but throughout the entire war we were together. Obviously, not the whole family. I lost uncles and aunts and cousins. It's so hard through the Holocaust! But our nuclear family remained intact. That was probably the major factor in making this whole experience not a classically traumatic one. Obviously, it was traumatic but only in the looser sense of the term, and my parents tried very hard to keep it that way. As with all Jewish families, they were entertaining other options that might become necessary, including splitting up of the family. There were various ways children were being saved, essentially by being sent to Palestine without their parents. So at least the children could be saved. I think my parents looked into these options and kept them as possibilities. But my parents were very determined to use this option only under the greatest duress. Only if nothing else was available. They could see keeping the family together was of primary importance. The big problem in those days was not getting out of Germany or Austria but finding a place to go. Here again, we were lucky. We had cousins to whom we were very close. Interestingly enough, this cousin got out early and got into Italy. Then he got caught in the war and in the end he survived the Holocaust by hiding out in a monastery in France. But he was in Italy and although I don't know the details, as I understand it there was a Belgium Consul in Italy who made visas available for a fee. They were semi-illegal in that they were legal Belgium visas issued by a Belgium Consul. But *not* the consul who was entitled to issue visas to people living in Vienna. So, in other words, they looked like Belgium visas but if you looked at the passport carefully you could see it was not the appropriate consul who had signed them. I don't exactly know how or what but our cousin got these visas for us. So we have these visas and our passports and we initially planned to leave with my aunt and uncle, as the partners. This is my mother's sister and her husband, who had no children and whom we were very close to. They also got visas through my cousin. Initially we were going to take the train into Belgium. But then word spread in this Jewish community that a Jewish family with similar visas was turned back at the border of the train, which means presumably somebody saw that these were illegal visas. It was recommended to not go by train but to go by plane. We left fairly soon, by plane, after we got the visas; you didn't want to wait around. There was nothing to wait around for. You have to remember, we had no income. My sister and I had been expelled from school at the end of the school year, in 1937–38. We were assigned to a Jewish school. As I recall, not everybody got a placement to school. We did get placements at the school but after November tenth it seemed not safe to go there, so we stopped going to school. We were just waiting to get out. That was very clear.

Most important, we didn't know what was going to happen at any time. My father could be picked up, et cetera. So we made the arrangements. We took a train to the crossing point. I remember the crossing point. I remember the German customs. But our papers were okay as far as the Germans were concerned so that wasn't a problem. They searched us very carefully because you weren't supposed to take out any property. My father and I were strip-searched. Remember, I was twelve years old at the time. My mother and my sister apparently got a woman agent who told them, "Wait a few minutes. I'm supposed to search you but that's alright. Just wait a few minutes." She let them through. We were searched very carefully at least on the male side. We got in and went on the plane and when we landed in Brussels, nobody challenged our papers. Then we took a small plane and reported to the Jewish aid organization helping refugees, partly supported by America, if I remember correctly. We got support from them for the year. The reason Belgium was the preferred place to go to was that they had a policy that if the Jewish refugees from Germany got in, by whatever way – I mean some came in the way we did, others walked across the border at night, there was a whole business of helping people cross the border, of course for money and so on – but by whatever means you got in, the moment you were there you could register with the police and they would not send you back. Except you were not supposed to work. You were not supposed to take jobs away from Belgians and so on. Of course we had no money; you couldn't take anything except pocket money from Germany. So we were penniless but as wards of the Jewish community. They gave us enough money to pay for a room, maybe in somebody's house.

My father persuaded them to give us the money it would cost for housing and let him make his own housing arrangements instead of putting us up in that room. He managed to find a tiny little house. It was a cold water house. Every morning I had to wash my face and hands with cold water. Tiny house, but enough space for our family and my aunt and uncle. It was tiny quarters but it was our own; we didn't have to live in a room in somebody else's apartment. We made a decent life there. My mother spent most of her time finding bargains to eat. We had meat only once a week on the Sabbath and even then it was a special cut of meat, which actually I liked. We made do with the aid we got. After the first couple of months, my schooling experience was very good. I was in a Jewish day school and was doing very well and learning a lot. So from that point of view, I was doing well in school. This was important because it was a very central part of my experience. After the *Kristallnacht*, my sister and I joined the Zionist youth group and that became the center of our lives. We continued in the sister organization in Belgium and that was the center of our lives there. From all sorts of points of view, that Zionist group made this actually a good experience, despite the fact that we were poor, our future was uncertain and all of these things. But this Zionist group was very important for all sorts of reasons. Perhaps most relevant to what we are talking about now, it buffered my self-esteem in such a way that the whole part of the experience – not the Holocaust at that time, not my whole Nazi experience – none of this threatened my self-esteem in any way. It threatened me, but not my self-esteem.

Q. Things like being strip-searched, though. I'm thinking about my young son at twelve. That's a hard thing to go through for a young impressionable boy.

It just affected me by making me aware of the danger. Remember, during this time when you walked on the street – a Jewish kid, adult, women too, maybe men more often, and most often men with visible Jewish signs, either the classical facial features or a beard, that kind of thing – these people could be stopped and forced to wash the sidewalk with a brush and so on. That was a classic humiliation tactic. Fortunately, that never happened to me; but it could have happened to me. It happened to kids I knew. So being strip-searched by a customs agent was, at least in that context, I don't remember it as being humiliating. I do remember thinking it was a real good thing we weren't carrying any hidden things. You know what else they did? We had some rolls. They broke up the rolls to make sure there wasn't anything baked into them. They were very serious. Of course, you're right; all of these things are terribly humiliating. But I don't remember them as such.

Q. As you go through these memories, are you conscious that this is something that happens to everybody in this category? And if so, does it thus become less threatening in a personal way? Does this knowledge then defuse the personal aspect of the humiliation or the attempt of humiliation, as it was in this case? Do you think joining the Zionists helped you as a psychological protection?

That's very definitely true. I've been thinking through this period, particularly why I don't feel trauma, and I never felt the experience was a major traumatic experience. I'm trying to distinguish between being subjected to the experience and having the experience feel frightening and being dislocating. It was not a good experience, I assure you! But it didn't really attack my sense of self. To begin with, my sense of Jewish identity was strong. The youth group movement helped keep it very much in the foreground. The youth movement did that. I assume that if I were more assimilated into Austrian society, or came from a family that was highly assimilated, in the sense in which we use it in Central Europe, in Europe in general, and if I saw myself as really an Austrian of the Mosaic faith, that kind of thing, that would have been much more devastating for me because I would have had to ask myself, "What's wrong with me?" That's a question I don't think I'll ever have to ask myself. I knew the reason this was happening to me had nothing to do with me. It has to do with the fact that I am a Jew, and being a Jew is a good thing. It's not a bad thing. It's not something to be ashamed of; it's something you should be proud of. It's not something to be desperate about; it's something to be hopeful about. So I think it gave meaning to my experience but it also gave me a sense of worth, which I think made me less vulnerable. Not that I wasn't afraid of being hurt and of course even more afraid of my father being hurt or dragged away. Not that I didn't feel humiliation. I think it's a little different. You can feel humiliation without feeling it reflects something rotten about yourself. That's the part I was protected against.

Q. Is there also an element of prediction and therefore control? You talked earlier about the arbitrariness of it all. It's a terrifying thing for people to feel that the universe is random and unpredictable.

Exactly.

Q. I'm wondering if this kind of factor determined why some groups did well in surviving in a concentration camp, when others did not.

People like Jehovah's Witnesses, for example, who understood there was a reason they were being persecuted and that therefore, even though they didn't feel they should be persecuted because of this reason, there would have been an element of choice for them. They had decided to be Jehovah's Witnesses. This was an important part of their identity. Therefore, because there was some kind of rough relationship here to control in a sense that presumably you can say, "I don't want to be a Jehovah's Witness anymore. I can stop and therefore stop the persecution." Perhaps that's not control in the classic sense but it provided a sense of understanding the causation that was there for them. Whereas Jews, especially assimilated Jews with a strong German identity, couldn't find any logic or reason for their persecution. I'm expressing this very poorly, I apologize.

Not at all. And yes, I see. You're saying control is related to not feeling a victim, to having a choice. That's the whole thing about being a Jew. Being a racial Jew in a Nazi system, you had no control. You can see all around you people who tried to exercise control. But they could not be allowed to exercise it; even if you were a converted Catholic, you were still a Jew. So control, no . . . causation. I mean, I do think it's an important factor. It's hard for me since I've been teaching about this for some decades and I use the same points you are making both about the concentration camps and about the Chinese and Korean brainwashing experiences. People who had ideological commitments were able to withstand the situation better because in a sense they knew why they were there and it made sense at some level. It was partly, "Okay I'm witnessing for my beliefs and for my identity and so on." That's exactly the kind of thing we are talking about here. The persecution would not really undermine your identity. If anything, it confirms your identity. So, I think that . . . I don't know whether I'm saying this about my personal experience or as a scholar because I have been rehearsing this over so many years. But I certainly agree with the theoretical assumption of what you are saying. I do think my Jewish identity played a role, an important role, in fact. How much was I conscious of it at the time? I don't know. For example, my sister was the leader – she was two years older than I – and I was a good follower. Shortly after the Nazis came, we went to our parents, with whom we negotiated, particularly during that period, and from then on, we negotiated about a lot of things. At that point, I don't know whether we – or she, too – had expressed an interest in joining the Zionist youth group. I know my parents weren't too eager for us to do it. They didn't want us to be out of the house, beside whatever other reasons they had. After the *Anschluss*, we came to our parents. I say "we," but I think my sister did most of the talking. But I don't know. I can't remember the details here. We said, "Now really things are so hard for us. We should be allowed to fall in a group." My parents agreed. I never asked them the question, but I wonder whether they understood. Partly it could have just been a matter of indulging the children. I mean, "Life was going to be so hard. Let them have this pleasure." But I wonder if they understood it signified more than that. That it was going to give us an opportunity to belong to something. After all, we were basically expelled from belonging to society. I wonder to what extent my sister intuitively felt that, too. Whether or not this was in anyone's consciousness, I don't know. But it certainly had that pattern of effect.

Q. It wouldn't have to be conscious to be important.

Right. Right.

Q. Does that have anything to do with what we might call "ontological security"? Something that strikes at the security of your being, of your sense of who you are? I'm wondering if this is what you're talking about by joining the Zionist youth group and staying with your parents. You didn't feel particularly secure in the world. You knew the world was a random place and had a lot of ugliness in it. But those two factors were important in protecting your sense of ontological security, the very essence of who you were.

Yeah, I think that's a good way to put it, though I'm not necessarily buying into that term.

Q. Okay. Let me ask you two last questions. You're talking about leaving Austria. You never went back to the store. It's difficult emotionally to walk away from everything, from your whole world. What was it that enabled you and your parents to do this? The second, closely related, question is this. In real life, as things unfold, nobody expects the Nazis or the Spanish Inquisition. They're events so far out of the normal political life that it's just hard to wrap your mind around them. I think there has to be something that happens, maybe cognitively, to let someone grasp what's occurring. I don't buy the distinction between emotion and cognition. I think emotion does feed into cognition. I think they are much related to each other in subtle ways that we don't even understand yet. So assume there's an emotional component to the comprehension, a sinking into one's consciousness that things have changed dramatically. How was it when you were confronted with such a situation? Something has to

get shattered about the traditional way of looking at things, doesn't it? The mind has to stretch, has to realize that the traditional parameters of political discourse, behavior, especially ethical behavior, everything is changing before you. How is it that this cognitive process occurred in your case, in your parents' case, when the political world changed? You said you and your sister went and negotiated with your parents. Another question is, you're one of the few people I've spoken with who alerted your parents to what was going on. Was it a mutual thing? Did all four of you realize it at the same time? I'm just asking about the process by which that happened.

No, I think my parents probably realized sooner or later. I give them a lot of credit. The most dramatic part of it was the decision, within a few weeks of the *Anschluss*, maybe five weeks or something like that, to register for American visas. That saved our lives. I just found a letter in my father's papers from the American Consul in Vienna, which was a sort of form letter. It said, "To Those Who Registered for Immigration Visas, if you register after such and such date, don't call us. It will take a year." It took two years for the visas to be processed. Had my father waited two or three weeks, it would have taken another year. Even if everything had gone the same way, we would have been caught in Belgium. The war would have happened in the interim and trapped us in Europe. So he was aware. He took action.

Q. Why did he move so quickly?

In part, I must give him credit for having foresight and planning; he was that kind of person. But I think in part it was the fact that we were not that well integrated into Austrian life. We had an advantage from that point of view, compared to some people who came from families that were natives and better off financially. We were struggling financially, barely eating meat. I mean not poor in a sense of doing menial jobs but in that we lived in a public housing apartment. We had a nice apartment, although it was an apartment without a bath. That was quite common in the low-middle-class housing. But it was a decent apartment in a pleasant neighborhood. There never was any problem with food and so on. My parents arranged ice skating lessons for the children, but not skiing lessons because we couldn't afford to go to the mountains for skiing. We didn't have places to spend summers. We didn't have some of the things neighboring kids had. So it was a struggle, really, a financial struggle, and also being of East European origin. East Europe was part of the Austrian Empire, but still we were East European Jews, and in a sense immigrants. Interestingly enough, as I have increasingly reconnected with Austria in the last few years, I've discovered how integrated my family was. I always knew my father loved the German language, which he taught himself as a late teenager. We spoke Yiddish at home, and Polish probably was the more formal language we used. German also, because it was the language of the Empire. The peasants spoke Ukrainian. I don't think my parents ever learned Ukrainian. But my father actually became a writer, a frustrated writer. He tried to be a writer. He finished a play that might even have had a chance had the war not intervened. So culturally he wanted to belong. But I also discovered to what extent my mother, in her own quiet way, had become integrated. She did this through little things. Eating out in general as I do, I find I get the kinds of foods that my mother made at home. She adapted to the Austrian cuisine, which of course is a conglomerate of other cuisines. She did crossword puzzles, which both my sister and I inherited from her. You have to know the language and the culture to do crossword puzzles. We spoke German, Yiddish, and Polish. We attended Yiddish theatre on a regular basis and life became embedded in Yiddish language and culture. At home we were and we tried to be an Austrian-Jewish family. But still I think they didn't come from there and I knew we didn't come from there. I knew there was a difference between me and even some of the other Jewish kids. My sister knew it even better than I. I think she was – maybe as a girl, I don't know – more sensitive. She saw the differences between herself and the others. But I also have some sensitivity to the differences and to the fact that financially we were not doing well. So the idea of leaving and trying to make your new life in America was something my father could entertain more readily than somebody who would have been more deeply embedded in the society.

Q. Let me see if I understand this. There are two aspects that you're highlighting. One is that life wasn't so great financially so you weren't leaving so much behind. This meant a traditional cost benefit analysis made it easier for you to leave. But the other part of it – and it sounds as if this may have been even more important; please correct me if I'm wrong here – was that you didn't have the sense that "This is my land. This is my culture. I'm a part of this. Of course they wouldn't do anything to me." So the lack of a sense of belonging may, ironically, have made you more comfortable leaving. Your parents were still trying to belong but in some ways the fact that they were more marginal meant they could recognize the threat. "Yes, they can do it to me. This can happen to me." Whereas

people who were Jews who had lived a long time in Vienna, who were
more assimilated, less Jewish in their identity and their religion, I think
you used the term "Mosaic religion." . . .

That's fairly used there. That's the term that was used on the papers of
Jews. Mosaic was the choice. Mosaic. Moses. It's parallel to Christian
from Christ to Mohammad and Islam.

**Q. I've talked to different people who said they didn't think of themselves
as Jewish. It wasn't a part of their identity. But those people who felt they
were German, Austrian. . . .**

Shock. It was more of a shock to them. It was harder for them to recognize
what was going on. It was all of these things put together. Even the first
part, I wouldn't put it in just conscious terms. But I would put it more in
terms of emotions. It's hard for you to imagine a life outside this life that
you have. You are so embedded in that life that it's very hard for you to
imagine a life outside, and so you don't. That then leads you to maybe
deny the signs that that life is gone. So it's not just an adjustment and a
shock. Of course part of it is. But it's, "If I go I'm leaving my house. I'm
leaving my business."

Q. But that was more minor.

I wouldn't say it was minor. But it was not in cost/benefit terms because
if they really understood the cost and benefits, they would have known
what is more important. Life couldn't exist anymore, and their life was
in danger. You have to imagine both the horrors that are going to come,
which I think was far easier to imagine for somebody who was embedded
in their Jewish identity and who had experience with pogroms and
discrimination in Eastern Europe. You therefore are not all that convinced
that it can't happen here. You aren't convinced that it can't happen to
you. So you have to imagine there is another life that you may try to
create for yourself as good as or even better than what you have.

For my father that wasn't too hard to do because the life wasn't that
good. But another thing that happened in his case was the one that I
mentioned: because being Jewish was your identification you took the
Nazis extremely personally. I mean, Father lost German culture, German
literature. He embedded himself as a young man, as a late teenager, in
this language and he admired it and he was very knowledgeable. The
house was full of German classics. The idea that out of that strong culture
Nazism could emerge was a tremendous disappointment to him. Also,
he was coming out of that little tiny village. You can't imagine; he came

out of a two-block building. The only Jewish family kind of thing and coming out of that and identifying with this German culture and then finding what this German culture has done, I think it broke the spell. A kind of cynicism set in and that freed him. "Okay. To hell with it." He probably also exited because a cousin and two of his sisters were in the United States and they helped to arrange affidavits for us and all that sort of stuff. Initially he wasn't going to emigrate perhaps because he was culturally making himself at home there. But now that was gone. This is partly what made it able for him to realize what was happening.

Q. It's very interesting. I started out the interview telling you I'm interested in how identity can change choices and now you're helping me fill in how that works. I think you're saying we're all embedded in an identity and thus we don't imagine a different one. We have to imagine something different before we can see certain options. Is that correct?

I think the other question we should address before we stop is what I've heard lots of people say: "How could the culture that gave us Goethe give us the Nazis?" This was a great shock, that question. It broke the cocoon or the sense of place and embeddedness that your father had protected.

Yes, yes.

Q. Some of the conversations I've had with people about the war are the first times they've talked about it. They just put a "do not disturb" sign and didn't even talk about things with their families.

I certainly didn't talk about it as much when I was much younger as now. But part of it is that nobody asked me. At least ten or so years ago, a friend was going to do a film on the Holocaust. She never did it. But she interviewed me as part of that project and I remember I spent six hours with her. I'm really sorry she didn't do anything with it. But I was quite open. This is what I mean when I say that it was not traumatic in the classical sense. Talking about this doesn't open up new wounds. It doesn't today and it didn't when Hilga interviewed me ten years ago.

7 HARD TO ADJUST AFTER ALL THAT

Grace, Interned Japanese-American Teenager

America entered World War II after the Japanese bombed Pearl Harbor in Hawaii – not yet a state – on December 7, 1941.[1] Concerned about invasion and terrorism on the part of Japanese living in the United States, President Roosevelt signed Executive Order 9066 on February 19, 1942, empowering local military commanders to set aside "military areas" from which "any or all persons may be excluded." In effect, Executive Order 9006 declared the entire Pacific coast off limits to people of Japanese ancestry. The only exemptions were internment camps. Approximately 110,000 Japanese-Americans living along the Pacific coast and over 150,000 living in Hawaii (over one-third of Hawaii's population) thus were relocated and interned by the U.S. government in 1942. These Japanese-Americans – over 62% being U.S. citizens – were settled in what were called War Relocation Camps. The Supreme Court upheld the constitutional legitimacy of the exclusion orders in 1944.[2] Although it denied it for years, in 2007 the U.S. Census Bureau was found to have helped in this internment by giving confidential information on Japanese-Americans. It was not until 1988 that Congress passed legislation, signed by President Reagan, acknowledging and apologizing for the internment, admitting the internments were based on "race prejudice, war hysteria, and a failure of political leadership." More than $1.6 billion of reparations were eventually disbursed to the internees and their heirs.[3]

There were four children in my family in addition to my father and mother. We lived in Watsonville, near Santa Cruz, California. My father was a World War I veteran. He had a strawberry farm and we raised strawberries when we were young. One night we were struck by a drunk driver so my father got his leg injured. My mother, brother, and I were also injured. My two other sisters were not. My father went to a veterans' hospital in Palo Alto. He was there for a long time and then they operated on his leg. It didn't take the way they wanted it to so they operated again. In those days they had ether, kind of a gas that knocks you out. They gave him ether and he didn't come out of it. He just went to sleep. So my father was thirty-seven years old when he passed away. This was 1935. After that my mother couldn't – we couldn't – run the farm or raise strawberries anymore because we had to have somebody plow the field, things like that. So we came to Watsonville. We stayed there and went to school. We had a bus that picked us up and took us to school. That's all minor, daily life stuff.

It was a real nice day in 1941. December the seventh, 1941. The day my sister got married. We went to Stockton and that's where she got married. We were all there. They started on their honeymoon; then they came back. We didn't know why. You know what day that was, don't you? December seventh, 1941? Pearl Harbor day. So we went to the wedding and then we came home and my sister and my brother-in-law also came home. We came back to Watsonville. We started to school but they wouldn't let us go to school anymore. It was barely half term.

Q. This happened the following school day, immediately after Pearl Harbor?

Yeah. The next school day we weren't allowed to go back to school. We were at Watsonville High School. They wouldn't let us go back to school.

Q. Was this school-wide or just because you were Japanese?

No. Because we were Japanese. All the Japanese couldn't go to school anymore.

Q. Okay, so just the Japanese students. All the other students were still attending school?

Yes. All the other students were still in school. Just the Japanese couldn't go to school anymore. So we did all kinds of things. We went out to work, stuff like that. Till we had to go to Salinas Assembly Center. There was a line; we lived on one side of the street and my mother, she couldn't stay with us anymore because she was on the wrong side of the line. So she went to go live with her friends. So me and my sister and brother had to stay by ourselves. You know how scared I was? I kept a hammer under my bed. This was a long time ago so it wasn't as bad as it is now. My mother was over there and we lived over here, and we had to clear out our house. There was a neighbor's house down the street where we put all our things. Out of all of our belongings, we could only take to camp whatever we could carry. We couldn't take anything else. We got a bag and put our things in that 'cause we could only take so many things. Only take what you could carry. That was all. We then went on a bus to the Salinas Assembly Center. There was a rodeo, a horse racing thing there. We stayed there for a while then we were transported to a camp in Poston. You know Poston is in Arizona? Poston had three camps: one, two, three camps. The first camp had all of the medical hospitals, things like that. The second camp had just a clinic and the third camp also just had a clinic. If you had something wrong with you, you had to get on a bus and go to the first camp. So we had three camps.

Q. Were people living in each camp?

Yes. Oh, yes. You can look at the map. We had long barracks, a mess hall, a clinic, a place to wash clothes, a fire station. Things like that. We had all the necessities there.

Q. Before you were sent to the camp, how were you notified you would be sent to these camps? Were you even notified at all?

Oh, yes, they notified us. Go get on a bus and go to Salinas Assembly Center. That's not far away. We were all there for a couple of years. Salinas was a horse racetrack. They built barracks there, inside the racetrack.

Q. Do you have an accurate memory of how many people were living in this camp?

I don't know exactly but that's where all of the Japanese from Watsonville, Salinas, and Monterey went. We were all there. It was a very large place. We had barracks.

Q. How old were you when you were imprisoned?

I was seventeen when I went into the camp. The principal from Watsonville High School came to give us our diplomas. We missed a whole half a year. We only went to school until December but we all graduated. We got our diplomas and we graduated at the Salinas Assembly Center.

Q. So you were still being educated while at the Salinas Assembly center camp?

No, we were not. We were done. They didn't have school in the camp in those days. They did when we went to Poston. They had schools but not at the Assembly Center, no.

Q. So you were taken out of school midway through your senior year of high school and relocated to the Salinas Assembly Center and then you received a diploma?

Yes. We all received our diplomas.

Q. How aware were you of what was going on at the time? Did you know what had gone on at Pearl Harbor? I'm sure they told you why you were being imprisoned.

We heard. We didn't know. They had people up on things, with guns, you know, watching us. So it wasn't a place where you had fun or anything. We were young, though, so we never thought about things like that that much. All we knew was that we were in camp and then on a train and on our way to Poston, Arizona, to another camp.

Q. Did you have family in Japan at the time?

Yes, my grandmother and grandpa. There was no contact with them. After the war my mother did contact them. But not during the war, no.

Q. How long had your parents been [in the United States] before World War II?

Let me think. My mother was born in 1900. In those days they had picture brides. She came to Hawaii first, where she married my father. My mother and father then came over here. So my father was in Hawaii but my mother came to Hawaii from Japan. She was going to school at the same school as my father's sister. His sister brought my mother back to Hawaii and that's when my mother and father got married. They stayed there for a while and then they came to California.

Q. So your parents' siblings were in Hawaii at the time of Pearl Harbor? Did you have family there?

My grandmother and grandfather were in Hawaii. My father had eight brothers and sisters. Most of them are gone now except some of my cousins. My father was born in Hawaii.[4] So he was born in the United States and my mother was born in Japan. My father was a U.S. citizen. That's why he was in World War I. He fought for the U.S.

Q. Do you think that if your father still had been alive during the attack on Pearl Harbor and the subsequent interning of Japanese that you still would have been imprisoned even though he was a war veteran?

Oh, yeah. We still would have been imprisoned. That didn't make a difference. Anybody who was Japanese went. *Everyone* was sent to camps. Everyone: my mother, my sister, and my brother; it was the four of us.

Q. Can you explain what a day was like in the internment camp?

First thing when we went to camp in Poston, we walked into our barrack. The barrack floor had holes in it between the large planks. There was a pile of hay there. That was for our mattress. We had to stuff our mattress to put out our beds to go to sleep. The first meal was cabbage. I still remember that. Then the days just went. We were young and we had never seen so many Japanese in our life! Everybody, everywhere we looked there were Japanese! It wasn't like in Watsonville. So we were there and then we did what we wanted. I first started working in the kitchen. You would clean the floor or wipe dishes or whatever. We had these terrible dust storms. We would wipe the tables and then a dust storm would come and we would have to clean it again because it was all full of dust. Arizona had a lot of dust storms. After that I went to work at the clinic. Then after that I went to church.

Q. So you were able to express your religious beliefs there? That wasn't restricted at all?

Oh, yeah. You could go to whatever church you wanted to go to. But inside the camp.

Q. You said you worked in the clinic?

Yes. I was a receptionist at the clinic. Everybody did their own thing. They did whatever they wanted to do. You didn't have to work but you could work if you wanted to. There were all these different things you could do. Piano lessons, things like that. For us at our young age it was more getting to know a lot of people, I guess because we were young.

Q. Was a lot of time spent with people your age? What was the predominant language spoken?

We all spoke English. If you were older, you spoke Japanese. A lot of cultures want their children to learn their own language but Japanese people, we just didn't do that. For us it was all one language, English.

Q. On a day-to-day basis, how would you eat? Was it provided for you?

We had breakfast, lunch, and dinner there. In our room, there were four of us. There are pictures of barracks in the book. [Points to a book on the camps.] Maybe not of the inside but it has pictures of how the barracks looked.

Q. So were you in a room with your siblings?

Yes, four of us were in one room. It was done by family. You had a small family, you had a smaller room; a larger family, a larger place. One barrack had about five families living there.

Q. Was there privacy?

Oh, yes, because we were blocked off. They didn't know what we were doing and we didn't know what they were doing.

Q. And the same way for the restrooms and showers?

They were in the center and we all had to go there. They weren't in our barrack. We had a place to go and wash clothes.

Q. Your mother, was she in this room with you?

Yes, she was there. She worked in the kitchen. She was a cook. I don't know what kind but she was a cook.

Q. How were people assigned positions?

You would just go up and ask. Nobody had to work if they didn't want to. I think we were paid eight dollars an hour; no, eight dollars a month. If you were a doctor I think it was about sixteen dollars a month.

Q. So the camp itself was basically run by the Japanese interns?

Yes. It was run by us. Every block had somebody who was in charge of it. These people were Japanese, the people who ran everything.

Q. So no non-Japanese Americans were inside the camp?

No. There were just the guards on the outside of the camp. But a lot of things happened there. There was a man who hung himself. You'd have to talk to somebody who was older to find out more about that. But they're gone now.

Q. Well, it's just as important that we get insight from you as well because your perspective is just as important.

We were young. What would you do if you were seventeen and eighteen? Go out and have fun!

Q. What would you do for fun?

What would we do for fun? We had movies there. If you wanted you could visit another camp. I went to visit my sister. She was in another camp. I forgot what camp she was in but I took a bus to go visit her. My nephew was born so I went over there. So there were things you could do if you wanted to.

Q. So probing a little bit deeper...

Yes, you can ask me whatever you like. Then it's easier for me.

Q. It doesn't sound like you were particularly angry about what was going on, about being put into these camps. A lot of people look at it as something that was a step backwards for America; yet in a lot of ways you're describing the experience as fun and enjoyable, one you kind of made the most out of it.

A lot of people had farms and businesses; these were all taken away. We didn't have any of that because when we came to Watsonville to work my father was in the hospital so we did something called a half share. We had a family that let us stay there and they would do all of the heavy work and things like that. That's what's called a half share. We did that so when we went to camp we didn't lose anything. We didn't lose a house. So many people lost their homes. They sold things cheaply because they had to get rid of all of those things. They couldn't take them with them.

Q. I'm noticing a picture here showing an evacuation sale where they're selling things.

They had to sell their stuff because what else would they do?

Q. So you didn't have a lot before you went to the Salinas camp?

No. We cleaned out our house and we put it all in a spare house that our friends let us use. They told us that an airplane fell on the house. But you could see that they raided it. We had a lot of things that my grandmother had sent to us from Japan, pictures and personal things. They were all gone. We didn't have anything when we got back.

Q. That didn't make you angry? It didn't frustrate you when you got back?

But what could we do? There wasn't anything we could do. I'm sure a lot of the older folks had a hard time because they had to leave their farms. Some people had people take care of their things and when they got back to California, they still had them. A lot of people sold their place and when they got back they had to start all over again. This happened to my husband's parents. My husband and I had a poultry farm right down the street. But then when everything turned into commercial space, we sold it and then we bought the house here. But we not lose anything because we didn't have anything.

Q. Going back a bit, what was your mother's experience? Did you get a sense from her of being worried for her children?

She was worried about us. My father was already gone; he had been gone. My sister was married and in Stockton so it was just the three of us. My younger siblings went to school in the camp.

Q. How old were your siblings?

I'm eighty-six and my sister was three years younger and my brother three years younger than my sister.

Q. Did you feel any concern for them? Did you feel you had to take care of them and watch out for them?

No. They ran off and did their own thing, too. They went to school and then they were there for lunch or whatever. It was like a regular day at home.

Q. While you were in the camps, you were never concerned about your own well-being or that of your family?

No, because we were able to eat. I was going to go to college when I was in Watsonville because the bus stopped right by my house. I was going to some kind of college in Salinas. But then after that I didn't go.

Q. Did you miss your old way of life after you were put in the camp? It sounds like it was a similar routine.

It was the same; the only thing is that we didn't have to work. Living at home before, we went to school and we went out to help my mother with her strawberries. After we got back from school, we would go out and help her. When we were in the camp we didn't have any chores to do after or before school.

Q. Do you think that what the United States did to its Japanese residents was justifiable?

No. I don't think so. They said it was for our safety but what did they mean by safety? We weren't that close to where the war was going on.

Q. While in the camp did you feel like you didn't belong there as an American?

I don't think it was fair. A lot of my friends went to war from camp and they didn't come back. The 442nd infantry, a lot of my friends were in that infantry; a lot of them didn't come back. They went overseas to fight and saved a lot of people.[5]

Q. Do you still have contact with the people who got out?

I have pictures but I don't have any contact with them.

Q. You were saying earlier that you slept with a hammer under your bed after the war began?

Yeah. Just after the war started. My mother wasn't with us. Just my brother and my sister. I was so scared.

Q. What was it specifically that scared you?

I don't know why. I was afraid someone would come and do something I guess. I was seventeen, my sister was fourteen, and brother was eleven. He wasn't any help and we went to camp not very long after that. We had to pack up everything and go.

Q. Did you have any interaction with non–Japanese Americans after the Japanese bombed Pearl Harbor? Did you feel discriminated by them?

No, I didn't. No. We were in the country when it happened. But a lot of [Japanese] people *did* feel discriminated against. I didn't feel it though.

Q. But you did have interaction with Americans before going to the camp?

No, I don't think so. No. I didn't.

Q. But from your friends, did any of them experience some sort of racial discrimination after the events?

Oh, yes, some people did but not me personally.

Q. And your mother, how did she take all of this?

My mother didn't talk about it too much. She didn't say much. She was a very strong person and she didn't say much about anything. She would say, "What could I do?" There wasn't much she could do.

Q. What would have happened had she voiced her opinion to somebody? I'm sure there were complaints within the camps.

In our camp? Well, yes. They did have people who really voiced their opinion. They didn't receive any punishment. They just voiced their opinion. There was someone who was very vocal but I don't remember his name.

Q. You didn't participate in any of this?

No. I didn't want to. There wasn't much we could do; we just did our daily thing and that was it.

Q. How long were you in a camp?

I was in the camp for about three years. My sister was in Chicago so I went up to Chicago after that. She was in Arizona too but she moved to Chicago after. There were a lot of camps, in Arkansas and a whole bunch of others.

Q. How did you find out that you were free?

After so long they said we could leave. They opened the gates and said we could leave. They had to check to see if you were okay to leave. My mother, my sister, and my brother stayed behind and I went to Chicago with my older sister. My sister and brother-in-law were in Chicago so I went out and before I knew it they said they were going to move to Michigan and raise strawberries. So they left me behind. I didn't know what to do so I took care of a little girl, a lawyer's daughter in Chicago. I was about twenty at this time. Afterwards I went to work for a company called Perfection Electric. They made speakers. I went to make speakers. In the meantime, before that I got married; I met my husband there. My mother was working there so I got a job there.

Q. So your mother went to Chicago with you after?

No, my mother went to Chicago for a while and then my sister wanted her to go to Michigan and help out at the farm.

Q. So when you were released you saw that everything was looted from your home, and everything was taken? So you figured why not start a new life and make the best out of it?

My mother stayed there and worked.

Q. Was that a challenge for you?

I didn't find it challenging. She did.

Q. It seems like your life had already been a struggle so being interned was something that made you stronger and helped you adapt to new environments. Was it a big struggle for you to readjust?

I think it was for everybody. It would have been for anybody. It's hard for someone to adjust after all of that. I guess we had to just make the best of it. A lot of people worked for *Life* magazine. They had to work to survive.

Q. Did the U.S. government help you at all once you were released?

When we left camp they gave us twenty-five dollars. Something like that when we left. They turned us loose and just expected us to get by with that.

Q. That doesn't make you angry or frustrated at all? After taking three years of your life, here are twenty-five dollars?

After the war the government sent us a letter saying that all of us that were in camp and survived got twenty thousand dollars.

Q. How long after you were released was this done?

It was before my husband passed away. It wasn't very soon. They decided that we would get paid twenty thousand dollars for all of the misery and whatever we all went through I guess.

Q. You wouldn't say you went through much misery while you were in the camp?

Well, I didn't. I was young and kids have fun. So I didn't really.

Q. So upon leaving and after everything that went on did you feel any discrimination after being released? Did people treat you differently because you were Japanese?

No, I didn't feel anything different. A lot of people did but I didn't feel anything. I didn't have anybody tell me anything.

Q. And your siblings and mother, did they ever talk about feeling discriminated against after the fact?

No, no. I don't think so. If my mother did, she didn't say anything. She went back to Watsonville. Afterwards she stayed with her sister so I don't know but I didn't have anybody say anything to me.

Q. The experience overall, do you feel like you lost any part of yourself? Any part of your dignity or your humanity?

I think so. I don't think it was necessary that we had to be put in these camps. We didn't do anything wrong. We weren't the ones involved in Pearl Harbor. But it happened, and we were all hauled off to camps. It wasn't fair but we had to go.

Q. How did your mother explain it to you and your siblings that you had to go to these camps?

My mom never said anything. She never mentioned anything. I had to pack up and get everything ready, our clothes and stuff. Because you could only take what you could carry on the bus so that's what we did. We got our stuff and left. I don't know how I did it now. We were scared; we didn't know what to expect. When we first went to camp we landed in Camp One. None of our friends were there but my mother got us to move to Camp Two, where a lot of our friends were. In Camp One we didn't know anybody.

Q. How did they designate what camp you went to?

People in Watsonville, Salinas, and Monterey, we all went to Poston and into Camp Two. I don't know why we were placed in Camp One but my mother got us to move into Camp Two.

Q. Today in retrospect, after everything that you have experienced and having grandchildren, do you talk about this often? Is this something that you tell people about?

You know, I don't even want to think about it.

Q. You just try to push it back out of your mind?

Yeah. Besides, I don't have to be worrying about it at my age now. Not with everything else going on in the world today. It was something nobody should have to go through.

Q. Did you feel like they weren't treating you like a human being?

Yes. How would you feel with guns over your head when you hadn't done anything wrong?

Q. Did you feel you were being treated like a criminal even though you had done absolutely nothing?

Nothing. We had done absolutely nothing!

Q. And your siblings . . . are they still around?

My brother is; my sister passed away.

Q. You and your siblings never talked about what went on in the camps?

No, we didn't. Plus my brother was in Vietnam. I think that's where he went. He never talks about it. He never says anything about that war. He pushes it out of his mind, too. He doesn't mention anything. A lot of people don't talk about it. They never say anything.

Q. Are there any lessons you pulled from the experience? Did your experience in the camp shape you into who you are today? Anything you can derive from that experience? Because you seem to have pulled a lot out of it already, like how you've been saying that you made the best out of a very bad situation.

There wasn't much anybody could do. You just had to do what you had to do. What could we have done? There's nothing. We had to stay where we were.

Q. Did anyone ever try to escape from the camp?

That I don't know. All I know is that a man hung himself from a tree. I don't know about anyone trying to escape.

Q. When you were in the camp, how often did you long to leave? Did the thought ever cross your mind that you wished you were somewhere else and not in the desert?

No. I knew there wasn't anything I could do. It was simply one of those things that just happened. It wasn't anything we did. I think the world is in a worse shape right now than it was back then.

Q. In what respect?

There are wars everywhere. The government can't seem to be able to settle anything. Going into Afghanistan was bad. Health issues are bad.

California is in debt. Everything is just a mess. I don't know who is going to settle all this but anyways [shrugged].

Q. Do you think Roosevelt was a good leader during World War II even though he allowed you to be placed in these camps?

He thought he was doing the right thing. He thought he was doing the right thing for the country to get us out of the way.

Q. So you don't feel like the government's excuse of having you there for your protection was justifiable?

No, it wasn't. We didn't need the government's protection.

Q. I'm trying to put myself in your position as a twenty-two-year-old. Had I been in your situation I don't think I would have been able to live imprisoned like you did for so much time.

There were U.S.-born guys who didn't even want to go to war. They refused to leave. They wanted to just get out of the camp. What they would do is send them to another camp where all of the defectors were sent and then they would send them to Japan. After the war most of them came back to the United States. Most had no family in Japan. They knew nothing about the country, not even how to speak Japanese. But yeah, there were young people who refused to listen. They were the ones who were punished.

NOTES

1. On December 7, 1941 – a date Franklin Roosevelt famously declared "will live in infamy" – the Imperial Japanese Navy attacked Pearl Harbor, presumably hoping such a preventive attack would cripple the U.S. Pacific fleet's ability to engage effectively later to aid or protect Dutch and British territories in the Pacific. The attack killed 2,402 Americans and wounded 1,282. Although only 65 Japanese servicemen were killed or wounded, and one Japanese sailor captured, the attack proved counterproductive since the outrage it created immediately ended American isolationism, and America issued a formal declaration of war against Japan on December 8, 1941. Japan's allies – Italy and Germany – declared war on the United States on December 11 and the United States reciprocated that same day.
2. *Korematsu v. United States*. The majority opinion was written by Justice Hugo Black.
3. 100th Congress, S. 1009, reproduced at internmentarchives.com. and "WWII Reparations: Japanese-American Internees," Democracy Now! http://www .democracynow.org/1999/2/18/wwii_reparations_japanese_american_internees.
4. Hawaii was annexed to the United States by the Newlands Resolution in 1898, at which point it became the Territory of Hawaii and was granted self-governance

in 1900. Hawaii tried to become a state for 60 years, achieving statehood only in 1959. Because he was born in a U.S. territory, Grace's father would have been a legal citizen.

5. An all Japanese-American unit, the 442nd Regimental Combat Team fought valiantly in Europe beginning in 1944. Its combat experience in Italy, southern France, and eventually Germany made it the most highly decorated regiment in U.S. history, with 21 Medal of Honor recipients.

PART THREE

OTHER VOICES, OTHER WARS: FROM INDOCHINA TO IRAQ

Part Cold War military conflict, part decolonization, the Vietnam War raged through Vietnam, Laos, and Cambodia, involving France, the United States, plus some other anticommunist countries, from November 1955 to the fall of Saigon on April 30, 1975. The Viet Cong were a dedicated if lightly armed South Vietnamese communist-controlled insurgent group and the official U.S. government justification for participation was to prevent a communist takeover of South Vietnam and, eventually, all of South Asia, as part of a wider strategy of containment of communism. (The so-called "domino theory" argued that if Vietnam fell, so would the rest of Asia.) The North Vietnamese government considered the war a fight against colonialism, fought initially against France, backed by the United States, and later against South Vietnam, widely regarded as a corrupt puppet state.

Although U.S. military advisors began arriving in 1950, the war did not escalate until the early 1960s. After 1965, U.S. combat units were widely deployed. The Vietnam People's Army (also called the North Vietnamese Army) fought both a guerrilla and a conventional war. U.S. and South Vietnamese forces initially relied on air superiority and overwhelming firepower, engaging in search and destroy operations using ground forces, artillery, and air strikes. Just prior to the period described by Tuan (Chapter 8), the conflict spilled over into Laos and Cambodia. Events climaxed in 1968 with the North Vietnamese Tet Offensive. Facing increasing and divisive public opposition at home, the United States began withdrawing ground forces as part of its Vietnamization policy. The Paris Peace Accords were signed in January 1973 and the Case-Church Amendment passed by the U.S. Congress (1973) prohibited further U.S. military action in Laos, Cambodia, and Vietnam. In April 1975, the North Vietnamese captured Saigon, and North and South Vietnam were reunified formally in 1976.

Varying estimates suggest the war killed from 1 to 3 million Vietnamese soldiers and civilians, 200 thousand to 300 thousand Cambodians, 20 thousand to 200 thousand Laotians, and more than 58 thousand U.S. servicemen. The war cost Lyndon Johnson his second full presidential term and Hubert Humphrey the presidency. It caused massive political chaos in Southeast Asia, and indirectly led to the regime of the Khmer Rouge in Cambodia, discussed by Kimberly and Sara (Chapters 9 and 10).

8 FOR MY FAMILY

Tuan, South Vietnamese Soldier

My name is Tuan. I am about fifty-eight. My childhood was spent in Vietnam in the small village where I was born. I go to high school, then one year of college. After that I have to go to the army. My family has three brothers, then two sisters. I was drafted at twenty. I was studying law and was disappointed. I tried to study more but I had no choice. I had to join the army.

Q. What did your parents say?

They were disappointed but no choice because of the war.

Q. Were you married already?

After the communists took over my country in 1975, I met my wife. We got married in June 1975. After the communists took over my country they put me in a re-education camp for a year. Like a jail. You have to work the fields. Like Cambodia, like prison. They took me because I joined the army in South Vietnam. We lost the war so they took me to go to the re-education camp. So, stop there?

Q. You can tell us as much as you like. Perhaps tell us about fighting in the war. Did you go to training?

Yes. Training for the war took about a year. Then fighting for two years. I never killed anyone. Well, we didn't know. When we were in battle we didn't know. You don't know who was from the south or who was from the north.

Q. Did you get paid while you were in the war?

Yeah, like soldiers get paid. Like a soldier over here, with benefits.

Q. Did you get injured?

Just one time. I got shot in my leg, right here. [Tuan gestured to his left foot.] I wasn't afraid because when you fight together you don't know what happens. If it happens, it happens. You know it happens every day. Many die any day. We hear bomb every day. Boom boom, every day. We know someday it's your turn to die so we don't scare. I don't scare.

Q. Did you have friends who died?

Yeah. A lot of them. We see them today but tomorrow they were gone.

Q. You say that every day, every night you knew it could be your last. What went through your mind at the end of a day?

We are alive today but maybe tomorrow we don't know. Day by day.

Q. Were you thankful every night? Did you pray?

Yeah.

Q. Are you religious?

I am Buddhist.

Q. Were you more religious during the war?

No, I don't think so.

Q. How did you feel about the United States coming into Vietnam?

Better, much better. It was a lot different. When the communists took over my country, the communist police can stop you anywhere they catch you. You can't speak. No freedom of speech. No. No way you can go anywhere you want. If you go somewhere, you have to ask them for permission. They can do anything they want. They can catch you anytime they want. They can come to your door in the night and take you, with no reason. So we were scared, really scared.

Q. Did anyone ever come to your house at night?

Yeah.

Q. What did your parents do? What did they feel?

Scared too.

Q. What did the communists do when they came?

There is nothing you can do. They knock on your door and if they don't like you, they don't like you. They had you, you know? My parents had a business where they sell parts for the motorcycle. The communists didn't like that. They want to take over. They came to my house. They knock on the door at night and made you scared. They searched the house. Some days they didn't want anyone to come in or out so they would close the shop and would take our stuff. The motorcycle parts we sold, they took them all. Just like that. They stole them.

Q. Did any of your brothers join the army?

My brother, my big brother was in the navy. When the communists took over in 1975, he escaped to the United States. He didn't come back to the country. He came to the United States. He sponsored us here. He brought the family here. Yeah, he was smart. If he came back maybe he would get killed because he was a Navy officer.

Q. You stayed?

Yeah.

Q. Did you stay only to wait so you could come here? Or did you choose to stay?

We missed a message from him. I waited for five years, and then we talk together again. We did the paperwork, the sponsorship, the visa to come here.

Q. Did he bring over all your brothers and sisters?

Yeah, all the family. In-laws too. Oh, I forgot. When he sponsored me, it was from Indonesia because I escaped from Vietnam to Indonesia by boat in 1981.

Q. With your wife?

No, I was alone.

Q. How did you escape?

We go together one time, but they caught us. So the next time, I went alone because it was better.

Q. Please tell us the story. When you were trying to escape with Mom, were my sister and brother already born?

No, only your sister was born.

Q. Why did you escape and how did you get captured?

The first time I tried to escape, it was with my wife and daughter. She was young, only four or five years old. There were two or three families gathered together in order to purchase a small boat. The plan was to get a small boat and go behind a bigger boat. But the communists found out about the boat so they shoot it. All the families spilt up and we had to run away.

Q. Were you trying to escape to Indonesia?

No. We didn't know where the boat was going.

Q. Did you split up from your wife and child?

No. We ran away together.

Q. Tell us about the decision to escape. What went through your mind?

There were people outside in the sea. We thought maybe if we were out at sea we can get lucky and somebody would find us and rescue us. Save us and help us. So the boats did not have any particular destination. We were just trying to get to the ocean, so someone would come back in a big boat and rescue us.

Q. What led to the decision to leave for an unknown destination with your wife and child? What was it like with them? Were you scared for their lives? You do not need to answer if you do not want to.

Life was very difficult. There was not enough money to live. There was a lot of depression. We had to get out of the country.

Q. What about the second time you tried to escape? Why did you go without your wife?

About three years later my friend asked me to go with them to escape again so I went with him. Like the first time except my wife didn't come with me. She was home. She knew I was going. She let me go. She was with my parents. My friend bought the boat. I didn't have to pay so we go. We escaped. About one or two days and not enough oil, not enough food, no water. No nothing. We stayed in the water. We were hungry and thirsty. There were about thirteen people in the boat, including a lot of children. I was one of the oldest. They asked me to drive the boat. I didn't know how but they kept on asking so I did. After two days it stopped running because it was out of oil. Then we saw a bigger boat. I lit a fire to come rescue us but they did the opposite. They came so close we thought we are saved. But they left. I don't know why. Then our boat broke down because there was no oil. We were on the sea for about seven days.

Q. Seven days! Without food or water?

Yeah, yeah. Four adults and nine children. They were fourteen, maybe fifteen and under.

Q. How did the children cope with having no food and no water?

One die. One died after that. They asked me, "I want water! I want water!" They tell the parents, "Give him money. Buy water for me!" They said like that all the time. We finally gave one kid the ocean water. He drank it, spit it out the ocean water, and he died. He died. I think he was about four, three or four.

He died in the boat. That family, they had two kids. They had two children and one already died and then the other one was about to die. The other one was a girl. Her parents told her just to lie there next to her brother, waiting for her to die so that they can throw both children into the sea together. So she just lay there. The boy died first. The girl almost died but didn't. After seven days, then the rain came. Yea! Yea! Water! So the girl was alive. Every night we prayed. We prayed then and when we woke up in the morning, I saw the boat come over. We think that is the communist boat come to catch us. We don't care. If they catch us we go to jail but we are still alive. But that boat escaped from Vietnam like us. They helped. They didn't want to go too close so they asked me what happened. I then said that the boy died. The captain of that boat jumps into our boat. That boat towed us to an island with a rope. We didn't know what island it was. Later we find out it was Indonesia. We saw the island. A small island. We are so close! But it took twelve hours to get there. They helped. They help everything. We got to the water first. We go to find water. The people who live on the island, they took us to water. So the people helped give us water. Whatever we had, like gold, jewelry, anything like that, we gave it to the people on the island in exchange for water and bananas. After that morning, maybe the day after, they got the food and the bananas and everything. Then I went out and buried the kid, the son that died. His parents, they were too exhausted to bury him, so I had to do it. I picked a place on top of a mountain or a hill. I was so dizzy. I was so tired. We stay there one day and then they came back on a boat, a big boat, and take us to refugee camp in Indonesia. I stay there about one year.

Q. Without your wife and daughter?

My wife . . . she think I die. [Laughs.] I couldn't communicate with her.

Q. Was mom pregnant with Khoo [brother] at the time you left?

Your brother and sister were already born. First time we tried to escape only my daughter born. The second time my son was already born.

Q. So for one year you didn't speak to your wife or family?

Yes. I had contact with them about six month later in a letter so she know I alive.

Q. Then what happened?

I stay there one year, and then my brother sponsor me to go to here.

Q. During that one year what did you do?

Just stay. In the morning you go to the school and learn English. That's it. The re-education camp that I was in, back in Vietnam, I almost died there because every day I only wear shorts and a T-shirt. Every day we would have to work in rice fields. We had to work in the rice patties – stuff like that – to make a canal. We would have to dig up the dirt and move the dirt. They only gave you a small portion of rice. That's all they gave you for food. I almost died during that time. I was so weak. So hungry. I didn't have any energy. I didn't have enough energy or strength to go on because I was hungry and really weak.

Q. Was there a certain amount of time that you had to be in the re-education camp? When did you get out of the re-education camp?

One year.

Q. Was that mandatory?

It doesn't matter. One year. Ten year. You really lucky if you know. They caught a bunch of people, and whoever worked well, people they like very good they would let them go, but if they were really bad at it they would just keep us, making us work. They caught so many people they needed to let some of them go. One of my friends, he died. He just works too hard. No food. No food. When you sleep, they crawl, the bed bugs, they biting all over. And the mosquito. Oh, and leeches! These bite while you work because it's in the water. It would be itchy and you'd yell "Oooh!" You look down and go whack! Then all the blood come out.

Q. Did that happen to you?

Yeah. So while I was digging the dirt I got injured. Oh, blood come out! [Tuan gestured to his left foot, the same one he had previously pointed to when he said that he got shot. He gestured as if it was a shovel that took off part of his toe.] Same foot I got shot in is the one injured after the war because of the communists. This was right before I escape.

Q. You said you weren't scared of dying. What was your greatest fear at the time?

I was the most scared when I was in the re-education camp. I was more scared in the re-education camp than in the war. Every day, when I was in the war, I knew that each day could have been the last. The war, I knew what to expect. But in the camp I didn't. You sick, no medicine. There's nothing. You don't know when you get out. That's the re-education camp. I die there. If I stay there longer, I will die.

Q. How did you get released? They just let you go?

Yeah. They let me go because there was too many people. Then I come back home. Stay with my family.

Q. What about your family? Did you have any contact with them when you were in the camp?

My wife comes to see me a few times, but when I see her, I cry and cry. But you can't cry. If they catch you crying, they keep you longer. So you keep it in, like that. You hold your breath. Terrible. Terrible.

Q. Was it all men there, no women?

No women.

Q. How long could your wife visit you?

Sometime once a month. Sometime two or three months.

Q. How did you meet your wife?

Before I go to war. My friend's sister's friend and my wife go to school together. I met her when I come to my friend's house. I saw her; after that we talk and then after that we married. I know her long time, four or five years, before we marry. Six months after the communists took over the country, we get married.

Q. What was your wedding like?

Ah, it was good. When the communists come, she is afraid. She don't like the communists. She fears maybe the communists will take her because she was very pretty. So we married.

Q. Were there any restrictions when it came to marriage?

Yeah. When the communists first come in, they act like stupid people. They really stupid. They don't know nothing! They don't know how to ride a car. They don't know how to use the toilet. They were so stupid they took toilet water and cooked like it was clean water. All the communists came from the field. They don't know anything except the country ways. In Northern Vietnam they were more guerrillas. They were always in the fields and the jungle. They didn't know what toilets are.

Q. During the war, those years you were fighting, what was your assignment? What did you do?

When I was soldier? We had a barricade – like in movies – where they have people stand outside and take turns in rotations. If anyone comes through, we shoot them. We protect the capital. We're something like a capital guard. They switched out every time.

Q. So you were standing guard for long periods of time?

Yeah, about two hours we stand up.

Q. But you never had to shoot anyone?

No.

Q. Would you have?

When they attack me, yes. Somewhere else, not on my place.

Q. Would you have been able to shoot a man?

Yes. You have to. You have to. You don't shoot them, they shoot you! So we had to do that. The war, even that friend. They attack, I had to do it. I heard in 1954 when the Vietnamese cut the country in half, some brother and sister go the north and other go south. They choose. Brother and sister go to north and other go south. They go to army, communist army and when they meet together, we had to shoot. You understand what I'm talking about? Families are divided. No choice. My mom and aunt got separated into North and Southern Vietnam. My aunt's husband, he was the captain in the north. So if I see him, he attack me. I shoot him. No choice. He shoot me. I shoot him. After the war we get together and we shake hands and hug.

Q. At this time, so many bad things happened. Did you even think things were going to be okay? Internally, what did you tell yourself? What was your source of hope? What drove you to say, "I'm going to be okay"?

If I didn't think that way, if I didn't think, "I gotta do what I gotta do in order to survive," I would be like any other person, any ordinary person. Like any other person out there. My thought was I had to do, like I just had to do it. There was no questions.

Q. You had to act like you acted then so you could survive?

Yeah.

Q. What about your family, were they a big motivation to survive?

Of course. I had to stay alive and I come back to see them. I stay alive for my family.

Q. So we know [your story] up to when you went to Indonesia and the refugee camp.

I went training, went to war cause the war broke out. I went for three year. I trained for a year and two years in the war, and then I got married six months after the war. I went into the re-education camp but I don't remember when I went to the re-education camp. I was there for a year. Me and my wife tried to escape once with my daughter and then I tried to escape a second time.

Q. How much time passed between the two escape attempts?

I lost my memory, you know? I'm old now. Not good memory. When I go to the army, my boss and everything I don't remember. Bad memory. I forgot. All my paperwork I don't take with me, 'cause if I get caught maybe they kill me so I destroy everything. That letter I only sent it to my wife, my family over in Vietnam. I sent a letter to Vietnam, that's how I got into contact with them. The letters, like the visa and the sponsorship, I threw away all those papers because if I get caught then I will be punished in Vietnam. If I was ever to get caught with them, like perhaps in the boat [trying to leave], say the communists caught me and saw those papers, I would get punished. When my brother sponsors me, the papers and everything match up.

Q. When did you come to America?

After a year in Indonesia. 1981, or 1982. I come alone. I go to Riverside. My brother lived in Minnesota and he move over to Riverside. I live with him. Then me and him did the paperwork together to sponsor for my family. I was here three years without my family. I go to work. Earn money. I work in Riverside. I sell furniture. I make furniture. Eventually I sponsor everyone: my mother, my father, brothers and sisters and their husbands and wives and their children. We have a large group, a large family. But at that time, they open the door to you. It was easy to bring people to America. Not now. I am a citizen now. My whole family is. After 1985, we had about twenty people living in one house. A small house. Small rooms, like really small. Five bedrooms. Original was only three bedroom but we built two more. We add two more room because it not enough. Too many people. We live together to save money. My family still live in Riverside. We still own that house, too.

Q. Have you gone back to Vietnam?

Twice. My sister-in-law died.

Q. Would you have gone back if that unfortunate event hadn't occurred?

My wife does. Her family is still there. I don't want to go.

Q. You wouldn't want to go back there to live?

No. Because my family is all here. But my wife's family is still there. She's more attached.
    I think that's enough. That's enough right?

Q. One last question. Do you have any regrets? If you could go back and change something, what would you change?

Yes. I hope the communist time is over. No more in my country. I want that they be a free country. Free speech. Everything I want to come back if no more communists.

9 BAD MEMORY, BAD FEELING

Sara, on the Khmer Rouge

Ruling Cambodia from 1975 to 1979, the Khmer Rouge were the Communist Party of Kampuchea led by Pol Pot and his followers in the state known as Democratic Kampuchea. The regime was notorious for social engineering resulting in mass murder, famine, diseases, arbitrary executions, and even purges and torture of its own members for violations such as engaging in free market activity. Once the Khmer Rouge regime fell, the remaining guerrilla forces became known as the National Army of Democratic Kampuchea. The party itself was dissolved in 1981, to be substituted by the Party of Democratic Kampuchea, itself in turn succeeded (1993–94) by the Cambodian National Unity Party. Both Sara – also called Navy Cheap – and Kimberly (Chapter 10) lived through the Khmer Rouge period. Each has a quite different response to that time.

Q. Hi, Auntie. How are you?

Good, good. Still hungry [after Thanksgiving]. So what you want to know?

Q. How old are you, Auntie?

Me? Old; next question.

Q. Aren't you just around forty, though? About mid-forties?

Yeah, forty [is a] good number. [Sara laughed.]

Q. Okay then. How old were you when Pol Pot's regime occurred?

I just a little girl, younger than you. I came to this country and went to junior high and then high school.

Q. Okay. The Khmer Rouge forces entered in 1975? Where were you when it happened? What were you doing?

I think I was at home. I don't remember. It [was] so long ago.

Q. Do you remember what happened to our family?

They closed my school. I was happy because I thought to myself, "No more school!" But then I realized it was bad. The people who destroyed my school, they were bad.

Q. What about our family?

You know you're supposed to have two more uncles? The Khmer Rouge, they killed them.

Q. What about you? What happened to you?

One time Khmer Rouge asked me questions. They asked me about family. They asked me what I was eating. They asked those things to find out if we were rich. If you said you were eating candy, then they knew you were rich. I was a little girl and I liked to eat candy a lot. Your grandma told me not to tell them that. And your mom? You know she hates rice. She still doesn't eat rice. She only eats bread. That is a sign you have money. Poor people, they cannot afford bread. They can only eat rice. And your mom . . . in the [labor] camp . . . she kept stealing bread. So it was bad. . . . [Long pause.] I lied a lot, you know?

Q. How did that make you feel?

Good. If you didn't lie, then you would die.

Q. Lying saved your life?

Yes, of course. Everybody lied. We were people, so we lied all the time.

Q. Was it the situation you were in that forced you to lie?

I didn't want to die. You lied so you were able to survive.

Q. What about life before the Khmer Rouge? Could you describe how it was before?

Before we lived in big house, big stone house with three stories. We had TV and radio. It was . . . [Sara sighed] it was so nice. So nice. We had peace, and big, big house. My dad – your grandpa – he owned a business, a factory. Many people worked for him. The family was well off. We had everything. Your mom, she was so spoiled. She was the first born daughter so your grandpa, he give her everything. Your grandpa's factory, the Khmer Rouge destroyed it. It's gone now. They destroyed everything. We lived a good life.

Q. Are you angry about it? Whom do you blame?

The communists. They're so bad. They destroyed everything . . . my home, my life, my family, my friends . . . they destroyed everything. Pol Pot and [the] communists . . . they're evil. Terrible. So many bad people. I don't understand. I don't understand why they killed so many. If you kill, then you are bad.

Q. Are you more sad or angry over this?

Angry! The communists. All they do is kill . . . and . . . and. . . . [Long pause.] You know your mom's story, right? About her in the truck in Cambodia? When they almost . . . almost took her? They grabbed her when we didn't know, when no one was looking. They grabbed her and put her on the truck with other people. I was with your grandma. I was next to her. She ran after your mom. They were so busy and everything was so loud. So chaotic. Nobody was looking, so your grandma ran after your mom and grabbed your mom from the truck. Your grandma just grabbed your mom from the truck and ran back to me. No one saw what happened.

Q. Do you know where the truck was headed?

No. I don't know. I think special camps. But they took her – I didn't know why they wanted her. I think maybe they took her to work or maybe to kill. I don't know.

Q. Were you scared? Were you afraid they were going to take my mom? That maybe both Mom and Grandma would be taken?

Yes. I was young. I didn't know what was happening. I didn't understand. My heart . . . it was going so fast. It made my stomach sick. I was so scared. You know your mom got into trouble a lot? I told you. She kept eating bread. She would hide the bread. Your grandma got so mad at her. She was not supposed to eat the bread or they would find out. They would know she was rich. [Long pause.] Did Grandma tell you about going back to Cambodia the first time? You know where she went first? She went to Toul Sleng because she was scared.[1] She thought maybe that was where your grandpa died. That's where they took all the important people. She didn't want your grandpa to die there. It was not good to die there . . . terrible. She went to look at all the pictures. She wanted to see if your grandpa was killed there. She find out he was killed somewhere else . . . in the field . . . in the country somewhere. She so relieved. It would have been a terrible way to die, the worst. She glad he had died somewhere else.

Q. Would you want to see this place?

No, I'm too scared. I don't want to go. Bad memory; bad feeling. When you experience it . . . it's scary. You're young and you're born here so you can go and it doesn't scare you. You haven't lived through it. It's not a part of you.

Q. How has this experience affected you?

You don't forget. You never forget. [It's] always in your memory . . . in your head.

Q. What was it like in the camps?

Not good. Bad. Dirty. No food.

Q. Can you describe it a bit more?

What do you want to know? It's bad. You don't want to hear [it].

Q. No . . . but I do.

No. No, you don't. [Long pause.]

Q. Auntie, did you know that by definition the Khmer Rouge is not classified as a "genocide"? Because genocide is defined as the mass killing of an ethnic and/or religious group by the government.

So? What do you call it then? How many Cambodians [did the Khmer Rouge] kill? So many people died and it was just an accident? No. [Long pause.]

Q. What about the war tribunals?

Stupid. It was just all stupid.

Q. Why is that?

Because . . . because they are not enough. It not going to bring them back, all the people who died.

Q. You don't think it's worth it?

No. They're already dead. They are gone. They're not going to come back. Will it bring back my father? No! My brothers? Your uncles? No! It's stupid.

Q. But what about the perpetrators?

They're not going to get them. All of them? No. So many. A lot are dead too, already dead. They're not going to feel what we feel. They need to feel what we feel. How come [the war tribunal] doesn't get [the Khmer Rouge] and put them in the camp? [Long pause.] Like how Khmer Rouge did with us.

Q. So you're saying these perpetrators deserve the same treatment they gave the victims?

Yes. How you say . . . even Stevens?

Q. You mean an eye for an eye?

Yes. Yes!

Q. Do you think that's fair?

Yes, of course it's fair. They hurt me, so they need to be hurt, too.

Q. Is that how you saw it before Pol Pot's regime? Did you always think "an eye for an eye" was a good philosophy?

Yes, yes. It's fair, you know? That is what is fair.

Q. When did you come to this country?

Nineteen eighty . . . eighty-something. So long ago now; thirty years almost. It was so strange! I went to junior high . . . ninth grade . . . and then high school too. It felt strange. I just kept smiling in school. That's what people always told me. It's how I look. They told me, "Navy, you are always so happy."

Q. And were you happy? Being in a new place?

I don't know. Better than [in Cambodia]. Over here, I don't need to . . . I don't lie.

Q. But you lied over there to survive.

Yeah. I don't do that here.

Q. Would you go back, Auntie?

I already go back one time. I go with you. We all go.

Q. But would you go back and live there?

Are you crazy? No. We have a good life here. I can't live there. No more. Not any more. It is so hot there, too.

Q. Is that the only reason you wouldn't want to move back?

Everything's bad there now. It's not safe.

Q. How does that make you feel?

I'm okay. It's better here than over there. The Khmer Rouge is gone. They took everything already. The communists are gone, and the Cambodians . . . they're gone too.

Q. I don't understand. . . .

It not the same Cambodia. No, not the same. No more Cambodia from before. The Khmer Rouge destroyed the land and the people. We're not the same anymore. [It's] not my Cambodia anymore. I hate them.

Q. The communists?

Yes, I hate them. They take from me. They steal and kill. Communists! So bad.

Q. Okay, okay.

We finish now, right?

Sara cut off the interview from here, ending it rather abruptly even though I had more questions to ask.

NOTE

1. Toul Sleng is a genocide museum located in Phnom Penh, Cambodia's capital city. Originally a high school, Toul Sleng was used as a prison and interrogation camp, notoriously known as Security Prison 21 or S-21. It housed between 17,000 and 20,000 people.

10 SOMEONE LOVING ME

Kimberly, on the Khmer Rouge

Q. What was your life like growing up? How was your relationship with your parents?

We had a great relationship; our family was very close, bonded. I had a total of nine in my family, and I'm in the middle. We were born and raised in Cambodia, in Phnom Penh, in a business family.

Q. Was there anyone, in your family or a neighbor, who was an influential role model?

Yes, my dad. He is my role model. He is my mentor. He is somebody I look up to. Who I am today is because of him.

Q. When you were younger, was there anything about you or your family that set you apart from the rest of your community?

No. Until the age of thirteen it never crossed my mind something would happen in Cambodia. Unfortunately, it did happen, and I was devastated. I was lost. I was thirteen when war began. April seventeenth, 1975. I had been born and raised in the city, in a very educated family, a business family. They took us from the city and made everyone go to the countryside. We go back to zero. They wiped out all education, all doctors and professors. That way we could all be laborers and work on farms.

Q. When things changed, what was the first thing you noticed?

We knew what was beginning. There was a bomb, and all over the place shooting in the city. The worst part is I lost a sister when the Khmer Rouge came and took over the city. When we escaped to the countryside I saw many dead people on the road. At that time my grandmother lived in the countryside so we were able to go to the town where she lived. When we got there, as a young child I said, "Hey, no more school. Freedom. No Mom and Dad to tell us what to do," and we were free. In less than two months the Khmer Rouge decided to break us apart and form age groups. I was thirteen and in a group of thirteen-year-old girls. My mom was in a group with women her age. The same thing with my brother and sister. Slowly, only a few months later, we realized what's happening. We knew we were not going to be able to have a family anymore. Your family is who they told you would be your family.

Q. You said your family was really close; how was it when you realized you weren't going to be able to have a family anymore?

I was devastated. In shock. I was . . . I . . . [shrugged]. At that time they were teaching and training us. Their philosophy was: "Any kid can walk and eat. You are independent, and you have to take care of yourself." When we broke into groups the youngest ones could stay home, but home was with a group of, here you call them nannies, but there you didn't really have a nanny and you still pretty much had to take care of yourself. When they took me away from my mom and dad I could not even go home. It came to the point where you could not even call your father. You had to act as if he is a stranger. They taught us to hate. You pretty much had to survive on your own. There was no emotion involved. You could not even look straight at the people you were talking to, including your own parent.

Q. Were you able to keep your sense of self or family?

Yes, but as a young child only thirteen, my dad is my role model. Growing up we had everything. We were always taught we were lucky. We did have a maid; we had a cook. My dad would discipline us so that if something happened we would be able to cope, be responsible, and take care of ourselves. At the time, all that my dad was teaching us, it just went over my head. But you learn as you go; you learn to adapt to the environment. What the leader asks you to do, you do without question because you learn to be aware of what's around you. You learn who is your friend, who you can talk to, and who you can cry to. I got by through God's grace. I can say this. At the time the teachers showed no morals. No peace. No. I forget the words *love* or *kindness*. You swallow it; you keep it inside of you. At the same time I did know, deep down, that my family was always going to be my family, regardless who's telling you what. So I keep that in my heart and say, "I always have a family."

My father cannot be with me or talk with me, but I could hear the voice of my dad. He said, "Listen. And follow. If you are in the city live as in the city; if you are on a farm, live as a farmer." Those are things that stuck with me in my head. At the time I learned how to survive, to adapt to the people who were the leaders.

Q. Is there any particular memory that stands out?

Trust and love. That really stayed when I felt lost. It was almost four years. They took us in April 1975 and gave us the code-name, different from code names of people in the country. They called us April seventeenth. As soon as you had that code name, regardless how they knew you in the town, they kept you in a different group; they treated you in a different way from the people from the countryside. You are the last one to get fed. You are the first one to get up on the battlefield regardless of rain or shine. You had nobody. Basically you were alone and had to know how to take care of yourself. If they put you to work, and if you complained or were not working, then you would either die from them killing you or from starvation. I did lose some family: a brother, an aunt, an uncle, and my cousins.

Q. Were you ever presented with a moral choice, or told to do something and had to decide to go along with it or not?

That's a great question to ask. You probably already know from learning history, people often go back and say: "Why did you make this choice? Why didn't you fight back?" At the time, you're all alone. They singled you out. You didn't know who was your family, who was your friend anymore. In front of you there is an apple and they say, "Here is your apple. Whoever catches it first will be alive." But if they give you a choice between a gun and an apple, do you grab the gun first or the apple first? If you grabbed the apple first and the other person grabs the gun, apple may not be of use to you. So therefore, why didn't we fight back? We couldn't. I questioned myself the other day. There was only a young kid that held a group of twenty of us. We were bigger than him; why give him more power? Because we weren't worried just about us; we were worried about our families as well. We hoped, yes, that one of these days freedom would come. But at the time you lived to obey. They told you to shuck and you shucked; they told you to get up and you got up. They tell you not to eat and you weren't to eat.

When you asked this question, I thought of the time I was crawling to find my dad. I got a punishment for that. I just had to ask him,

"Are we still father and daughter? Or are we going to be enemies like they are telling us?"

My dad said, "I'm still your father; you're still my daughter, for better or worse, no matter what." That gave me a sense of yes, I do have someone loving me to keep me going. But for a stranger to come, could I fully trust him? No. Because as a young girl you wind up in bed and the person next to you, she could make just a comment, and she ends up disappearing.

Q. So you lived in fear you would do something and disappear?

Yes. Even the way you talk, even . . . they pretty much tell you up front. Each day you had a task to do and a field to go to. Let's say during harvest you have to harvest twenty thousand pounds of corn. But then in the field that's close to you there's not much corn so you have to go a little distance; you have to go farther and it takes longer. If you don't get there and back you miss the meal. You know this. Does your friend go before you and bring you the meal? No. You are all alone. Are you going to go to your parent and ask for a piece of bread? No. If they give it to you, they get punished as well. But my mom, when she'd walk by me, she was able to sneak a piece of salt. She'd put it in my pocket and say, "Here's a piece of salt. When you eat a potato have a piece of salt with it." So it's love for family. That's why I'm saying that bond is really important in the family. Regardless of where you're at, your family is a comfort. You will always have this – how do I say this? – opinion. We always had our own opinion. It was different from what they taught in our camp; what we saw and what they saw was different. Your family is there no matter what's going to happen. My family and I are blessed, and thank God for it! Thank God my family is there and that they did have a way to find me. The Khmer Rouge taught us to kill our own family, but we would rather take the punishment and let the person go. We don't sell our family out. I think that's the most valuable message to try to send; no matter what, or who you become, your family will be there for you. There's something I heard from the English: "Blood thicker than water." That's true. It depends on your upbringing, what kind of culture and value you see in family. I saw that clearly as a child growing up; you have everything, and your dad is telling you things. You say, "Don't tell me how to do things." That's how you think, until somebody else comes along and tries to be your parent but teaches you a different way. Then you say, "Oh, this is not right." So the bottom line is to trust somebody, to love somebody that much. As you grow, you taste it, you feel it, and that sticks with you. I saw that through my entire life.

Q. You said they tried to get you to turn against your family, to kill your own family members. But you had a strong sense of family. Did you see other people do that?

Yes, in my own family. To give you a little story. We lived in the city. The Khmer Rouge code-named us educated people "April seventeenth." At first in the war they were killing anybody educated; my older brother was the first one to go. The reason we survived as long as we did was because my grandparent was well known in the town. The leader, toward my brother and me, gave a little slack, I guess is the word I'm looking for, but not much. If we were able to live until the next day, he said that's okay, but without food. So my brother they took away from us. My uncle was married to a Vietnamese so there was no exception to keep him. They said, "You married a Vietnamese. You're not Cambodian. You're supposed to go." My grandparent asked if she could keep the kids. They said no because they were not pure Cambodian. "If you want to keep them then you will die as well." My grandmother only had two kids: my uncle and my mom. My grandmother had to decide: "Do I let them all die? Or do I sacrifice the ones that really stand out first?" She had no choice, really. She had to seal her lip, close her eyes, and let them make the decision. So I lost five cousins, an aunt, and an uncle right in front of us. They just took them away. They disappeared. We knew the Khmer Rouge killed them. And they took my brother.

Q. Have you ever been able to make sense of what happened, of how people could do something like this?

At the time . . . [paused] you go back and say, "Why? How can you allow this to happen?" It is easy to react at the time when it happens. Does it make sense? Do you have time to think what tomorrow will be? No. What you think about is: "Will I live the next minute? Or the next hour? Or am I going to get food?" You wake up the next morning, you feel your body or your co-worker – not a partner or a friend – but someone in your group, are they still next to you? If you said, "Well I'm still alive today," regardless of who disappeared, do I question where that person went? No. There is no time even to think. Put it this way. If you see a fire and then touch it, the way you react to it by taking your hand away, that's an instant reaction. They control your emotions. They control you physically. Everything; you don't even have time to think. To be honest with you, I think I was brain dead, if I think back on it. Did I say: "What am I going to eat tomorrow?" No. Will I be able to get up tomorrow? You try to cope and sleep, to just have enough energy to get up when they tell you to get up. If you don't get up you pray somebody will come along who is not too harsh. But that person who gives you slack, that person you know will get a punishment. There was a time when I was sick and my parents thought I was going to die. A person who owed a great deal to my grandparent because she was raised by my grandparent, this person told the leader that it was her fault. She took the blame. They ended up punishing her. They killed her. So I got to live because of her. At the time, as a thirteen-year-old it didn't make sense. If somebody did something wrong they could be gone, disappear; therefore you learn how to be strong. The only things you could say were "yes" and "no." It wasn't about how you felt anymore.

Q. How did you finally get out? Were you rescued or did you escape?

Yes. In [pause] I want to say, January seventh of 1979. In I believe September they planned to have a meeting where all of us would die, including themselves. They had a bomb ready in September. But somehow, due to the season of rain they couldn't hold the meeting. There was something with the leader not getting it right. The next thing I knew, some message was sent to Vietnam. At the time I was camping at the borderline of Vietnam, working in the rice fields. My mom was at the same camp and my dad as well. But my older brother and my older sister lived way down in Battambang, in what they called the Dead Skull Island.[1] You were sent there to die because you could not survive the weather and there was no food. That night there was a boat on the river, flashing back and forth. The next thing we knew we were hearing gun fighting. With the gun fighting we knew either they were shooting some of us or the leader was killed. I knew every night when I heard the music that meant somebody was going to die. That night it was different. There was no music. My mom knew and she said, "This is not internal war; it's external now. Somebody is coming in." So we braced ourselves. This time we don't need to listen to the leader. When the gunshots started it was about two o'clock in the morning. I went crawling, looking for my mom because I knew where her camp is. She said, "We need to stay together now; they're not going to come and break us apart because now it's a different war." Just like the beginning in April 1975, so therefore you can escape. We got hit first. This all took place in the middle of the night. By the time the sun rose we saw a field of bodies; also the leaders were banished. We were in shock. We just stood there and said, "We cannot go anywhere in case they come back and tell us what to do." The next thing we knew we heard different voices and smells. They were not Cambodian, not the Khmer Rouge leaders anymore. We knew it was a Vietnamese accent coming, so we knew another war began. We were able to escape. From that moment, up to town from the farm where the Khmer Rouge had put us. My mom said, "This is the war; we are going to live through this one." In the battle the Vietnamese were shooting us. The Khmer Rouge were also shooting us, so you trusted nobody again. The person in front of you, do you think this person is a leader of another group? They could shoot you. So you camouflage yourself. If a person talks to you, you answer them whatever they want to hear. You just follow! We followed a person who said, "I'm not a leader. I'm going to the hometown." When they mention the hometown, you think, "Okay, we're going home." So do you trust this person? You learn to survive by the minute. You move to the next step, then to the next town, then to the next road. You were lucky if you could cross a town without anybody killing you, or without stepping on a bomb or a mine, that kind of stuff. I lost a sister on the way because she couldn't duck down fast enough. The gun was shooting and I couldn't grab her. The bullet went right through her stomach.

Q. After the Vietnamese came in and you left the country, how much of your family was together?

It was just me and my dad, and then my youngest sister who survived. We went to town and the next thing I knew I found another sister at a different town by talking to an older person. The town where we were, everyone knew my grandparent and someone was able to guide us back home.

Q. Home is where?

In the beginning of the war when the Khmer Rouge took over the city, we went to the land my grandparent owned. The leaders were guiding all of the people and the people followed the leaders wherever they went. My mom told us we could look for food at the same time because we had to gather things. My youngest sister was able to come back and we found her. My older brother was still on the line walking with the leader. My mom told me, "Go grab your brother." So I took him and we escaped. My sister is another story. She lived in Battambang and she didn't know where home was. But people from our town were going back to the town where my sister was, and they took her the message: "Yes, your parents are still alive. You can go back to your hometown." If you didn't know where your hometown was you hoped that by following everybody else you would get to your hometown. That's what my sister, my brother, and I did. Because when you were in the camps they swapped you. You stayed in one place for only about a month and then moved on to another place and then another place. If you're in line to be killed, then you are sent to the land to be away. My older sister and my brother, that's what they did with them.

Q. What was it like after you got back to your hometown? Was the war still going on?

Yes. In the hometown at the time, you're still a nobody. You've just got to survive. You keep it low. Lay low. Your house is not your house anymore. Whoever is there first, that's their place. So again, my parents taught us morals were important in our family. It's funny to talk about this because I just talked to my sister about this earlier this morning. Dignity. I'm not quite sure I used the right word. In English I don't know how you say it. How I grew up, your name, it is well known who you are. Your last name and passing it on with care through generations. When they say, "This is Mr. Smith's daughter," and it gets passed on from my grandparent, that's what you carry with you. Even the people my grandmother raised and fed became leaders and forgot who they were. After the war, do we go back and think we are going to get our home back? No. My parents said, "Let's live day by day. We won't forget who we are, and we won't let anything take away from who we are. Even though we are living in the water or in a shack, we are still who we are." In order to survive we asked people in our hometown if we could have a bottom part. Because in most of Cambodia, where my grandparent lived, families lived in houses on stilts. They built the property on stilts in case of high floods. We asked them if we could just have the bottom ground, a small square. We survived by that and, I guess, by hunting. At first around town you were able to find food: rice, and grain, and salt. Later on it got thinner; you had to go extra far to find stuff. My family, we all stuck together. What we ate we all shared, among all of us so no one in my family would go hungry. My parents always made sure we got fed first. Now I look back and realize sometimes they did not get food. I guess the way it was is that if you were older you passed food to the younger ones. You had less because the younger ones were going to need more.

Q. When did you find peace?

We didn't have any peace until 1979, almost 1980. That's when we knew there were no more leaders of the Khmer Rouge. We knew we needed to follow guidelines because we saw the Vietnamese all over the place; they were the ones in control. At the time though, we could start building our own home. All of the family could live together. That was January 1980. I started seeing the leaders disappearing from the towns, but there was still a war since the Vietnamese told us we had to be in groups in the town. Each group in so many square feet had to have a watcher and my brother ended up being the watcher. I remember one night I thought, "Hey, no more leaders." Next thing we knew, they all came from the riverside and from the small side of town. They came and tried to get all of us. That night my brother was the watcher and there was a gunfight going on again. In the end we found about ten of the leaders – who had come to try and take all of us again – dead in a pit. So when did we really find peace? I'd say probably in 1980, in February or March. We were able to go back to the city then and could go claim the property. Whoever found it first, it was your home. So February or March 1980.

Q. After all that, how did you adjust to going back? Was it ever normal again?

Normal? Not really. You always lived in fear. Every day. Fear of who you talked to. Especially at a young age when they told you to remember that nobody is your family and you were taught how to hate. Your parents are not your parents; they just had their own good time and then you happened to be born. It took me a really long time to trust, to know who I'm talking to. But at the same time it also gave me the discipline to know how to adjust myself to the nature of people. I knew that after everything that happened, Cambodia was very corrupted. When your country is turned upside down corruption will make the rich get richer and the poor get poorer. Even when you do business there is always a duty. My parents grew up in a business family. Afterward we were able to build up a small business again by doing things for a cup of rice. We would ask for a cup of rice and ask if we could do anything for them or fix anything. After the war some people were able to hold on to some of their things or get them back because not everything was destroyed, like their gold from business, and they became the wealthy people. For my family, when we went back to the city where our home was, everything was destroyed and some people were staying in our old home. We asked them if we could just go there and help them out, clean up their house and whatever, fixing things for rice and stuff like that. This was what my family and I did until the Vietnamese left the country and we had our own president. Even then, with the internal corruption from the war, things never went back to being the same. It was always there; you always watched your back and wondered who was behind you. Because you were not just fighting a different country. Do you know what I'm saying? Suddenly you're fighting your own people. You don't know who's your family and who is your enemy. There was corruption by buying off; if you're liked enough then people will pay you off. And there is no freedom. There was no freedom of speech. There were no human rights. Even today, as we speak.

Q. When did you leave Cambodia and how did you end up here in America?

I skipped the part in the story about my uncle who knew the country was going to go down. He was a pilot; he worked for the government. He got to pick only one family to fly to the United States because he was a pilot between the United States and Cambodia. He worked for the government with the embassy. He wanted to bring out my other uncle's family because with a business family the Khmer Rouge would give you a little slack and weren't going to kill you first even though they knew you were smart. But anyone who worked for the government or was a professor would go first. So my uncle wanted to take my other uncle's family, the one that worked for the government. That family ended up dying really quickly because they were sent to the land of skulls and ended up dying. So after the war, well after 1979 when the Vietnamese came over, some of us were searching to find any family still alive. We thought my uncle was dead. When the war started, Pol Pot knew some people had escaped. In 1979 the Khmer Rouge sent letters asking people to come back saying, "We will spare you. Our country needs you. If you are in Thailand, come back. If you are in the United States or anywhere, come back." We thought my uncle went back. We heard a rumor that many people died in the end. But he didn't go back. He sent a message to the Thailand government saying he still was looking for family. Funnily enough, someone was in Thailand reading the list of names on the board and saw our names and that we were still alive. They wrote a letter back to my uncle in the United States saying some of his family were still alive. Then my uncle sent my other uncle as a messenger from Thailand to Cambodia.

He was between Thai people that try to kill you, the Khmer Rouge that try to kill you, and the Vietnamese that try to kill you. But somehow he was able to get to the city and he found us.

I've gone through three wars. The city had come back alive and we had even gone back to school before I escaped to Thailand. My uncle said we had to leave everything. Bring nothing with us because we were going on the dead road, and if we survived, if we were lucky, then we would get to the United States. Crossing the border, you might not survive since there were three groups of people shooting at you. Because the war was so devastating for our family, my dad decided we needed to flee the country. Home is where family is. If you don't have family then that's not home. We ended up deciding to take the offer from the messenger from my uncle. My uncle had to pay him seven hundred dollars. I thought it would be just hopping in a car or on a plane and coming, but that's not it. We had to walk at night with shooting in every direction. We had to try to cross the border to Thailand with the Thai people killing us. Then we couldn't go back and we had to go forward. My mom almost was killed; I saw many people killed, either from that or the mines and other situations. You had to walk in a straight line through the mud and rain. You could only walk at night and you barely had any food.

So we came to Thailand and stayed at a refugee camp in Khao-I-Dang with help from the Red Cross.[2] We stayed in Thailand and endured so many interviews. I asked my dad, "Why did we come here? We're not going anywhere. We're stuck." Everyone was so corrupted. It was all about money. If you didn't have enough money or give the right answer to a question you would stay another year. Somehow, bless my uncle, he was able to work and pay the government. He guaranteed that our family was not a communist family and that we were not people who would go to America and be on welfare. Stuff like that. We stayed in Thailand for almost a year. I was nineteen in Thailand. We would live and sleep on the ground. Every day we feared for our lives. You didn't have a sense of, "I'm a girl." You were all boys. You didn't have a sense of, well, anything. You thought about how you were going to live through the next day. Nothing more material than what you were going to eat the next day. Once we were in Thailand, we couldn't go back. If we went back, the Khmer Rouge would kill us because we ran away from the country. Even if we were lucky enough that the Khmer Rouge didn't kill us, other people would kill us. So we stayed in the camp.

So to answer your question, it was my uncle who sponsored us. We went through a lot of headaches and it took away a lot of our dignity.

For me, as a young girl of nineteen, they stripped you, and they, you know. . . . [Long pause. She could not continue.] There was torture. We never had enough water to drink and to bathe. But as I look back I tell people: what I've gone through in life is an experience, and I thank God every day for this moment. With Him also it inspires me to say there is somebody out there loving me, and with learning how to trust again. It took me a long time to be able to trust somebody. I knew I could trust my parents and my family, but with anybody else I pretty much acted like a servant. If they asked for a glass of water, whatever they wanted you to do, you just do it without question. For myself, I look back and realize I've been through three wars: The war of your own people killing you. The war of the Vietnamese coming over. And the war of trying to escape from your own country looking for freedom, for a decent life again and something to call a family.

Q. When you finally ended up in the United States, was it difficult to adjust to a different culture?

Yes. It was very, very difficult. At first you were an outsider. You didn't speak the language and American culture was different from ours. Americans were mistreating us, including myself. In that environment no one wanted to hire you. They made fun of you. It was not that easy for us. One thing my dad always said was that we would do whatever it took to survive and not let pride take over. We will always be who we are. So we were going to live day by day and do whatever it takes to survive the next day. When I came to America my uncle was providing for us financially. We went and lived in a town, and what do you call it? The S.S.I.? They were helping to find us a place to stay and give us a fridge. It was the worst place ever, in Compton. Now I look back – I was twenty – and thought, "This is not heaven. This is not freedom in a new country. You cannot even open the window without someone shooting at you." We could not even go to school because we didn't have transportation. My dad had to ask, "Where am I going to go work? Okay, labor work." He picked strawberries; he spent all day working and brought twenty dollars home. I don't know how we survived here, to be honest with you, but we did. We shared breakfast, because that's all we could have, a piece of bread and half an egg. I came to America in 1981 and worked by mopping people's houses. A good friend showed me I could go to school at night and work in the daytime. So then I worked at a Winchell's Donuts. I had a great man supporting us and a neighbor who was a fisherman provided us with food. He would always bring us fish. We had a small one-bedroom apartment and we slept in the living room. Not all my family was here. Half were still in Cambodia because we were separated after the Vietnamese came over and some of us went back home and some to the city. I thought my mom was going to die afterward, but she didn't. At the time it was only my older sister, my dad, and me who came to America. When we came to America I said, "This is not heaven." There was a barrier between the language and education. It was a blessing that our neighbor taught us. They brought my family into their house and told us what we could do, and we did it.

I went to school and in 1983 I got married and was able to buy a house. At the time, when I first went to work, I acted as my dad said to do and didn't have too much pride. Just do what you have to do and it's not you, it's them. When I worked at the donut shop, I used to cry every day because I couldn't speak English; as for today, I'm all self-taught. When we first got here my dad said I need you to go to school to learn the basics: how the United States works, how the money works, and then go from there. That's what I did. I took an accounting class and a business class. Word of mouth is very important; who you associate with. My dad would say it doesn't cost you anything to speak up. If people make fun of you, then take it in. You can learn from that, and I did. People called me names; before I was married people thought I was Vietnamese. They called me all sorts of names. "You Vietnamese people come to our country and you try to take over." We came here legally! We came here and worked with our own hands. We didn't take any government money. At the same time, there were people who treated us like we were aliens. Like we didn't even exist. Like we weren't even human. Even now, with my son growing up here! It makes people not love themselves. Maybe when people are subjected to that treatment, then they show more kindness to other people. My dad taught us the first thing you can learn is to take an experience for yourself and then use it. So if people hit you in the head, you don't hit them back. You step away from it. Who can you talk to? My dad always told me to ask directions. Your mouth is what's going to get you where you want to go. He's right. It just gave us an opportunity to learn a lot by interacting and asking the right questions to the right people at the right time. You don't stop. One person might not answer your question and might call you a name, but that's okay. Go on to the next person.

I remember when we didn't have a vehicle and we didn't have transportation to go anywhere. We used to ride a bus. We didn't know where we were going, and sometimes we'd end up in a different town. My dad said, "Don't worry. Sit on the same bus and it will bring you back."

I learned a lot from him, especially later on. I was a little devastated because as I was growing up I had everything and then we didn't have anything. Then when I became a teenager I said, "I'm a young girl. I want to go out and I want to have fun." But at the same time all of that would come later in life. That's why when people say they've had a bad life, I say, "You don't know what bad is." As long as you have your freedom and you have control over the decisions you make and nobody comes and holds a gun to your head, if you're just concerned that you need to eat and that you need to sleep, then it's not that bad. You make the decision. If you want success, it's out there. That's what my dad taught us. Go. Go get it. It's out there. It depends how badly you want it. Some people don't really know what they want, and it's true that, deep down you have to really know what you want.

The thing that really gave me the ability to survive, to live through all of this, regardless of whether we had food or clothing, was to think there was somebody out there, especially a parent, that loved me. That bond is strong. It is so strong that nobody can break it apart. Physically they can break you apart from each other but emotionally you can hear your dad's voice or your sister's voice and you think of the memories of the good times. Even though it was so devastating at the time, I could taste that little piece of salt [my mother gave me], like chocolate. It's all how you interpret it in your own mind and it gives you the inspiration and the strength to say, "Yes, I can live the next day. Yes, I will see my mom tomorrow." Even if you know you're not going to see her, but again I'm not going to show any emotion to this leader because I know they're going to punish me if they see me happy. This philosophy, my dad taught me. This I still believe today. If you get one chopstick you can break it. If you get two chopsticks you still can break it. Three chopsticks it is a little harder. Four is a little harder. Five chopsticks, you cannot break that. The communist philosophy worked by taking that away from you. They put you in different places and put you against each other. But it's how you handle it from the beginning. I know some families that don't have that. Most likely these are government families where their kids go to kids' care. Even in the environment in America I see the same thing. Some parents are good. They know the value of family. Ethics are from home. That's what I believe strongly today. Thank God I had my parents as my parents. They taught me discipline and what life's all about. That it's not all about you.

Oh, I can go on and on. While I was talking to you earlier today, you may have noticed I got a little bit emotional because. . . . [Stops to regain composure.] Dad, when we came to America, once in a while we would get together and talk and he'd say, "Close that chapter. It's already passed. Don't believe the history." But in America you want the history to stay alive. He told us that if you can avoid it, don't you tell them. Even when I'm alone, every day I sometimes hear his voice. Who all do I trust? I'm not just saying it because we're at the church, but Father S___ is also my mentor. I can hear his voice in the middle of my day. I trust in God. I have faith in Him. He gives me strength. At the same time my dad was telling us you don't want to relive the history because it is so painful. Some people tell me, "You can write a book." A book would be good if somebody could really see into it. I do read certain books and what happened in those books really happened in the real life of that person. But we don't want to see it. We don't want to hear about that time until later on and we decide to write a book. In that moment you don't think about it that way. I listened to ex–Secretary of State Condoleezza Rice on a show talk about her book. She said who she is, beginning when she was growing up, her mom always told her to practice the piano and stuff like that.

I can add something else. "What are you going to do tomorrow?" People always ask. Tomorrow can bring nothing. It's what you are going to do today. All of those things already happened to us. Like today when your mom teaches you something and sometimes you think, "Well that's you, Mom; that's not me." But when you get older you're going to get wiser and think, "Oh. That was taught to me already but I didn't realize until somebody else wrote a book and I thought, 'Oh, wow.'" Do you follow what I'm trying to say? I taught my kids that all the time. Books, when people write them, it's their experience. It's already happened to them. But it depends on how you take it. Did you really see it? Did you understand it? Or did you just read through it? When you read a story it's different. When you're in it, it's a different story. A funny thing is that my daughter, my younger one, she's nine. She loves reading books. She was reading a book and one morning she told me she found peace. She felt the character as she read that book. I said, "That's good. That's the way it should be. You need to sense it and feel it and taste it. Feel what it's like." When I tell this story it's not just because I heard it. I experienced it. I'm not just saying it to tell someone's story. I tell my story because I'm passing on my knowledge. I've been there. I've felt it. It's your choice to decide how to use it. You will find there is one road that will get you where you're going, but this way will take you longer and you have to make a choice. That's why I am who I am today. My dad was always telling me, "You have to believe deep down in yourself first and then everything else will follow and you will succeed. If you don't know what you want, nobody else can give you anything." So you have to believe in yourself first and then you can do anything you want.

Q. Is there anything you left out you still want to share?

I know that a lot of people will ask "If you could go back and change things, what would you change?" I would not change anything, to be honest with you. Everything happened for a reason. For who I am today, what happened to me made me stronger, a person with a kinder heart. To see the world and find peace in a different way, a way that people don't normally see; to see what life is all about. Yes, I do hate that time. Yes, I lost my brother, my grandmother, and my uncle. But an eye for an eye? There were those who said, "You kill my brother, so I'm going to kill you back." With revenge, what does that make us? We're no better than that person who killed in the first place. It's hard. It's hard to say it now. But then I wouldn't have become who I am today. I know who the leader was that killed my brother. He stayed at our house. I told my mom, "It wouldn't take a lot to kill this guy. Just get the cleaver and kill him."

She said, "Does that bring your brother back? No. Does it make you feel better? Or will you have to live with that for the rest of your life?"

You don't need to go to school to learn that. It's what experience brings to you. You just have to take, see it, and feel it. She's right. I'm not going to bring my brother back. Does that make me a better person than that person? No. If I kill him then somebody will come and kill my father. So hate will go on and on and not stop. That's why Israel is happening today. We have to forgive things that are out of our hands. Would I go back and change time? No. I accept that this has given me the knowledge to understand that we are all human. Some of us understand that better than others. Some can forgive better than others, and some people have more hatred than us. The war and living through a society like that, you learn how to end up on your feet so you have to find peace in yourself. If you don't have that, you cannot have peace. So no, there is nothing I want to change. I am blessed for what I have. I thank God for what he put me through; that I was able to feel it, see it, taste it, and now I know what life is all about. There's always a light shining on this side. You know how people say the grass is always greener on the other side? No. It is green here and happy here. It makes me humble, what I do here every day. I'm happy.

NOTES

1. In Battambang province in northwestern Cambodia.
2. Khao-I-Dang Holding Center was 20 km north of Aranyaprathet, Thailand.

11 COLLATERAL DAMAGE AND THE GREATER GOOD

Doc, on the Iraq War

Referred to as the Second Gulf War, Operation Iraqi Freedom, or the Occupation of Iraq, the controversial Iraq war began on March 20, 2003, when the United States and the United Kingdom invaded Iraq. Before the invasion and following the bombing of the World Trade Center and the Pentagon on September 11, 2001, the United States and United Kingdom claimed their security was threatened by Iraq, especially by Iraqi weapons of mass destruction (WMD). UN Security Council Resolution 1441, passed in 2002, called for Iraq to cooperate with UN weapon inspectors sent to ascertain whether Iraq possessed weapons of mass destruction and cruise missiles. The United Nations Monitoring, Verification, and Inspection Commission (UNMOVIC) was granted access by Iraq but the head of the weapons inspection, Hans Blix, was not allowed to complete his investigation and thus could not verify whether Iraq actually did possess such weapons. General consensus holds that the Bush and the Blair administrations misled their citizens and it later appeared Iraq had ended its biological, chemical, and nuclear programs in 1991. After the invasion, remnants of pre-1991 chemical weapons did surface but these were not the type of weapons used to justify the invasion. The charge that Iraqi President Saddam Hussein had harbored and supplied al-Qaeda also was found to be false. In the end, the Bush administration justified the invasion as part of a broader policy of bringing democracy to Iraq. Saddam Hussein eventually was captured, tried, and executed by the new Iraqi government but partisan fighting between Iraqi Sunni and Shiites continues and any al-Qaeda in the area simply relocated. Statistics vary but most authorities hold that by 2012, over 500,000 Iraqis had died of war-related causes and the displacement crisis is the largest in the Middle East since the Palestinian flight of 1948. An estimated 4.7 million refugees (some 16% of the population) had fled by 2008, with 2 million abroad, 2.7 million internally displaced, and 5 million children (35% of all Iraqi children) orphaned. The current (2014) refugee situation is confounded by the 2 million Syrians who fled their country, many escaping to Iraq, leaving Iraq's humanitarian situation among the most critical in the world, according to the Red Cross. Although the U.S. Department of Defense claimed US efforts had improved security and economic indicators, Iraq currently (2012–13) ranks high (between second and eleventh) on the Failed States Index. This is the war in which both "Doc" and Sebastian fought, with quite different memories.

I am twenty-nine years old. I am currently a Federal Agent for the United States Department of Homeland Security. I work mainly in San Diego County near the U.S.-Mexican border. I primarily deal with intelligence and terrorist threats against the United States from our southern border.

Q. You were in the Iraq war. Can I hear your story?

Sure. I was part of Operation Iraqi Freedom, in 2003 to 2005. I was in the United States Navy from 1999 to 2005. Four years in active duty and two years in the reserves. The two years in the reserves, I was activated, and served one term of about one year, including six months in Iraq.

Q. Where were you stationed?

At the Naval Marine Corps bases in San Diego, California. I trained to be a corpsman at the Naval Hospital Corps School, Great Lakes, Illinois. After corpsman training, I began to work with the U.S. Marine Corps, as they are a division of the Navy. A corpsman is the field medic.

Q. Do you have any nicknames?

Most people called me "Rai" or "Doc," since I was a medic.

Q. Are there any stories you would like to share from Operation Iraqi Freedom?

I guess we can start with the conditions we had to deal with in Iraq. We lacked sleep and proper sanitation. Endured numerous sandstorms, and a lot of fighting. Nothing out of the ordinary at a time of war.

Q. Would you consider these inhumane conditions?

No, not at all. It was definitely not a four-star hotel but Iraq is nothing like America. It's a huge sandbox. The terrain is quite different from the United States. It's still mainly rural and Third World. We dug holes when we needed to take care of business and showers were a luxury. Sleep was another luxury. Even though the Republican Guard was not as trained as the U.S. military, they fought vigilantly day and night. The Republican Guard is Saddam Hussein's personal National Guard force. Rocket-propelled grenades, gunshots were normal sounds at night. There were twenty-four-hour watches over our campsites and bases nightly. The noise, you learn to ignore it after a while but Red Bull definitely helped on long nights. We were not deployed in Iraq. We were deployed in Kuwait and entered Iraq through Kuwait. I entered with the First Marine Corps Reconnaissance teams as one of the first few military convoys into Iraq for this mission. We spent some time in Kuwait and waited to hear word from the Sergeant Major, to enter Iraq or not. When Saddam did not approve inspection for weapons of mass destruction, we entered. My team, my battle buddies, consisted of a group of eight men. But we were in a larger platoon of about one hundred people, consisting of several other teams.

Q. What was your route like heading to Iraq?

It was a sandbox but some of our main stops were Camp Matilda, Nasiriyah, Baqubah, and Baghdad.

Q. Any stories from any of the cities?

Generally the same story, different day. The general mission was to review each city for hostile people and hostile buildings. The bigger cities were the toughest because civilians generally left so there were plenty of empty buildings to ambush us from. It was definitely danger-ous and the Republican Guards were tricky. They would hide weapons and attack from schools, mosques, and so on. So when we did find weapons and evidence of military sites, we generally blew the building up. We also joined the U.S. Army Main Invasion Force in Nasiriyah, Iraq. The Republican Guards were pretty well armed. They had AK-47's, rocket-propelled grenades, bombs, and so on. But they were not well nourished, and I would have to say the same for most of the unarmed civilians leaving many bigger cities.

Q. Do you feel you were disrupting the infrastructure of Iraq?

In a sense, yes, but it was a means to the bigger picture of Iraq: freedom from oppression. We will help rebuild Iraq. In any war, in any state there will always be collateral damage.

Q. Was the war worth damaging the public service infrastructure in Iraq?

We did not intentionally bomb every school or mosque we stumbled upon. It was tactical and only when we had proper intelligence. The United States plans to support and help develop the new government and economy, as we have in the past. We did not drive around looking for schools and mosques to bomb.

Q. Was there any methodology to your actions and orders?

Honestly, tactically my team did not head straight for Baghdad but the troop's focus was always Baghdad. We used scare tactics to misdirect and trick the Iraqi army but that also meant we invaded and sometimes destroyed smaller cities en route to Baghdad. For instance, in the Baqubah region, where we watched the north flank for the main force entering Baghdad, we did reconnaissance missions in several smaller towns to detract focus from Baghdad. As much as we were gathering intelligence, the Guards were doing the same. When we finally entered Baghdad, the U.S. Marines and Army had already entered Baghdad city and Saddam's palace. In the beginning there were not enough supplies, armor, or armor on vehicles. During our first reconnaissance missions we had very few supplies and at times traveled day and night. Sleep was sometimes hard to get. On some missions we were joined by the Iraqi Freedom Fighters; we would fight and assault cities together.

Q. What would happen if you ran out of food or supplies?

We did run out of food and supplies in the beginning. We were doing reconnaissance missions and were the first to head into Iraq. The arrival of regular supply trucks was not available. We would generally ration and make do with what we had but there were times we bought our own supplies and/or commandeered supplies from the locals.

Q. Was there anything you were worried about in terms of Iraqi civilians?

Of course. At first many Iraqi people welcomed the United States into Iraq or were confused as to why we were there. We conducted missions where shots were fired and bombing campaigns, so civilian casualties did occur. It's called collateral damage but we tried to minimize it. At the start, the Republican Guards [Saddam's supporters] were all in uniform but now they hide and dress like civilians. Also, the development of more aggressive rebel and terrorist groups in Iraq, those established after Saddam's regime, had to be taken down. We were never there to fight innocent people but we had to protect each other. We were not able to help or save all civilian casualties but we offered medical attention they might not be able to receive locally.

My battle buddies are like my brothers. We spent day and night together. We fought together. I owe them my life and we watched over each other. I did not question my team leader because he knew information we did not. Our team leader was like a big brother to us.

Q. Were there incidents you regret?

No, because we always tried to follow protocol. There were definitely instances where innocent civilians were hurt. But we never tried to ruin anyone's livelihood. The problem is we had very few translators and most of us did not speak Arabic. But we tried to help civilians through several different humanitarian missions.

Q. What kind of humanitarian missions were you involved with?

Since I am a corpsman, I was involved with medical humanitarian missions but there were food and water rationing missions, educational missions, and so on. We provided whatever field medical attention we could to people harmed during military campaigns, sick people, et cetera. We did not have a full military medical unit with us so medical help was limited. We did try to stabilize and give medicine to those we were able to. We mainly helped children. The children were scared and I do sympathize with them. War is tough on adults but even tougher on children. I don't think they fully understand. They can't comprehend what is going on during war. We did not want to create future jihad-American-hating people. I do think these humanitarian campaigns were helpful and helped develop relations and trust with the Iraqi people.

Q. Do you feel the Iraqi people were good?

Yes, I do. I have learned that in war there are three types of people: good people, bad people, and dead people.

Q. Do you think that is a normal state of mind?

At the time, yes. War is tough. You have to be tough and follow orders and standard operating procedure. But the majority of people are good. There were definitely mixed feelings among the civilians but there were more people thanking us than condemning us. The military were used as a scapegoat oftentimes. It ranged from "We didn't do enough" to "We do not belong there." We killed innocent people but never intentionally. We were there to help revolutionize and free the Iraqis. For example, when we put checkpoints in the cities, it was to protect us during reconnaissance missions, to stop people from entering dangerous zones, and to help assess whether people entering and leaving the city were civilians or hostile threats. We had humanitarian missions bringing people free medical aid, clothes, and water. The United States is also not the only opponent of Saddam's rule; there were several citizens and rebel groups we stumbled upon while collecting intelligences.

Q. Can you tell me about checkpoint duty?

Sure. Our protocol was to fire warning shots or smoke grenades towards oncoming cars that were not slowing down or not stopping while entering the checkpoints. When the car did not slow down or stop, they were considered hostile and dangerous. We would first shoot out the tires and engine but some injuries and deaths occurred to civilians who did not stop. We always followed protocol. I am sure you heard of suicide car bombers. They do exist. We had to protect our missions, and ourselves.

Q. Would you consider suicide car bombers evil?

Not evil per se but definitely the enemy. If someone wanted to kill you and you had the capacity to kill them first, wouldn't you? I mean, we have to protect each other.

Q. I guess you're right, I would. Do you feel overall you were doing a greater good in Iraq?

I do feel we were doing a greater good in Iraq. We are helping the politically oppressed and are suppressing an opposition. Many people in Iraq under Saddam faced tough punishment and bullying. Tough interrogations and cruel and unusual punishments. So many civilians told us they were glad we were there and that Saddam's reign was harsh and severe. He did not help the people or give medical attention to his citizens. He stoned, killed, and harshly interrogated people. Sure, some civilians did not understand checkpoints and therefore were unintentionally hurt by us. We always let them take their property after we searched their vehicles and deemed them nonhostile.

Q. Were the civilians mad that you damaged their property?

Sometimes, generally not. The way Saddam ran his government actually helped us at times. His cruel and unapologetic approach to his citizens made them mentally used to property damage and savagery occurring. The civilians usually apologized when we shot their cars to pieces. The people in Iraq definitely mourn differently than people in the United States. If someone shot my car to pieces in the United States, I would definitely file suit and it will probably be on the nightly news. People there live a simpler life but a hard life.

Q. Do you feel you got a good picture of the Iraqi people?

I do. They are generally good people, mostly content with their simple livelihoods.

Q. Was it necessary to relieve them of their government?

Yes because we can help them better their living standards. They are generally a Third World, rural country. We can help bring industry and a safer infrastructure. I truly believe you should not be afraid of your government. I appreciate all the freedoms I have at home in America. I truly think the United States will help with the balance of power in Iraq.

Q. So overall do you feel Operation Iraqi Freedom was a success?

The campaign I was involved with was and is a success. We removed a tyrant. We are trying to instill stability and trust, and develop a fair government there. I am not saying we are done there. It is a process that has yet to be complete. Operation Iraqi Freedom will finally be a success when they establish their own government, constitution, and so on. There are still Marines there but they're fighting rebel groups trying to gain power, not Saddam's Republican Guard. Also, the army has a more active duty to help stabilize. The CIA, the masterminds, are still continuing intelligence projects. They are really the masterminds of it all. I'm just a grunt.

Q. Is there more violence now or when you were in Iraq?

Definitely more violence after the siege because now you rarely ever know who you are fighting. It's almost guerrilla warfare against different rebel groups fighting to take power over Iraq. Military rebel groups hide with civilians, dress like civilians. Luckily they are still hiding weapons in the same places: schools and mosques.

Q. Was there more you could have done?

We were looking for hostile forces. We were not there to ruin anyone's livelihood, regardless of whether it was legal or not. We saw subculture activities like drug use, prostitution, et cetera, but we were there to free the people from their government. We could not micromanage every city; those were not our duties at the start of the war. There were points where we discovered Republican Guard weapons but we could not always stop because we had our orders to complete another mission, which was usually to review the city for hostile people and hostile buildings, not to destroy weapons or their caravans on the side of the road. We were there to free them and then help stabilize the country. After that it was *their* role to democratically establish their society. You know we took Baghdad in forty-one days. It took a little over a month to take over an entire country! I personally am surprised. It's a supreme accomplishment.

Q. It feels much longer than forty-one days since we are still over there.

Well, I pretty much left after the siege but the United States is still there because we have to protect the people. It would not be fair to leave Iraq with another dictator. Our hard work to overthrow Saddam would be a failure if we allow that to happen.

Q. Why do you think U.S. forces had such an advantage over the Republican Guard?

We were definitely trained better and better supplied. We were like highly tuned, exotic cars and they [the Republican Guard] were Hondas or Toyotas, just semiskilled. Many Republican Guards abandoned their units. Many simply walked home from their stations. Some were armed but they always surrendered. They were not in the war to fight; they had no passion or drive to fight. Many of the AWOL Republican Guards were fighting for the money. Some were forced to fight once Republican Guards took over their city. They just wanted to return to their families. Many deserters asked for help. They wanted assistance and protection to return home because if found, they were generally killed for treason. We were unable to protect most deserters and after they were interrogated, we let them continue on their way, usually to where they were from, with some water. If an individual had beneficial intelligences we would send them to Abu Ghraib Prison.[1] If they really knew a lot of intelligence then they would get sent to Guantanamo Bay for further interrogation.[2]

Q. Could you relate to these deserters?

Honestly, after so many years of training and the bonds I have made, no. I could not imagine leaving my battle buddies because I knew if I didn't protect my brothers, who would? Who would protect me? Trust was the most important thing to us. I may not talk to most of them now but I am forever honored and grateful to them. I cannot forget anyone in my team. To be honest, war is very political, internally and externally. The lifers, this is their career. They are trying to move up in the ranks. Also the stigma of war, the array of public opinion, et cetera, but you always have to believe you are doing the right thing because when you stop believing in yourself and your team, there is no coming up from that. War is brutal but there are good things; I'll never forget my battle buddies and the humanitarian missions where we got to meet the people of the towns.

Like I said, the civilians there are not bad people but there *are* bad people there. For example, the kids, they really touched my heart. I went into the war single, with no strings attached. I had personally planned it that way. I didn't want to leave a widow and children if anything were to happen to me. But during the humanitarian missions I realized children are so innocent and grateful and I knew after my term was up I'd want to start a family one day. I wanted some *tabula rasa* rascals of my own. I wanted to live and I felt that doubt and worry would only hinder my future goals. We also received care packages from children in the United States. They were mainly letters and pictures kids drew from elementary schools. It helped.

Q. How did you spend your free time, if you had any?

I spent most of my free time playing video games, mainly Call of Duty, and trying to return to a somewhat normal life.

Q. What do you mean by a normal life?

Mainly just a routine. Wake up, shower, groom, eat, play video games and football, eat some more, play more games, watch a movie, maybe read and write a letter back home and sleep again.

Q. This sounds different from being on the front lines. It must be nice to take a break. Did these breaks help keep you sane and maintain your humanity?

Yes.

Q. Did you get into other activities to keep you sane?

Yes, I would go talk to the pastor or priest in our unit and occasionally join in on a prayer circle, but mainly I tried to stay mentally prepared and played a lot of first person shooting video games, like Call of Duty and Halo.

Q. Would you say you are a religious man?

I would not but I do find comfort in it because I was raised Christian.

Q. What helped keep you sane on the front lines?

One, being prepared. My other nickname was "Tactical" because I carried everything. A small armory and tons of gadgets for anything and everything. I guess you can say I was fully loaded. Also music and the downtime we had helped a lot. Just rapping to gangster rap with my boys on long caravans and playing Xbox and PS games when it was available. Movies, talking and being open with issues helped with building the team.

Q. So when you returned to the front lines, would that mean more Red Bull?

There were definitely moments where sleep was a luxury. Mortars weren't going to stop falling because it was midnight. A lot of the action happened at night. Since we were generally better equipped, we won more battles even though they knew the terrain. Many luxuries were lost at the front lines. Sometimes even the use of toilets was nonexistent. We always carried adult diapers with us for instances like this. Most other times a dirt hole was your toilet. It sounds crude but it's a normal occurrence, especially with snipers.

Q. Did lack of sleep help deal with the fighting?

Yes and no. No because you always shoot better with a clear vision, mentally and physically. Yes because you were so sleep deprived shooting people felt more like a game. And I must admit I was angry. I couldn't sleep because of them so if we finished them off for the night, hopefully sleep would follow. We definitely had a lot of Red Bull and Five-Hour Energy drinks; it was necessary.

Q. Did you rap and sing with your buddies a lot?

Every chance we got. During some night watches and some reconnaissance missions we would be streaming hard rock and rap through our radios. It would amp us up, give us a boost of adrenaline.

Q. You said you've killed people. How does that make you feel?

That's a tough one so let's start from the beginning. Before entering Iraq I wanted to shoot everyone because in my mind, everyone was bad. I was somewhat excited; it was like a real-life video game. Then while I was in Iraq I became kind of numb. There are so many variables. I did what was appropriate protocol for the given situation. After the war, I realized if someone was shooting at me, then I must shoot back. I did not want to hurt civilians but that is a negative consequence of war. Regardless of where the war is located, collateral damage will occur.

Q. You compare shooting on the field to video games. Would you still say that now?

Yes. Training consists of playing video games. Shooting games depict a somewhat realistic scenario, in a setting that looks like the environment we were in. Also it trains the reflexes. But of course you don't die when you get hit in a game. You notice that difference in a live battle.

Q. Do you still play games?

I do. I play almost every day; you can almost say I am addicted.

Q. Do you feel like the games you play remind you of the battlefield?

Actually, no, which is kind of funny because the battlefield reminds me of the games. I have some of the best aim in real life and in games. A campaign through a city in Iraq is similar to a game because in the game there are these hidden shooters, both faceless and nameless enemies. It is kill or be killed. Traps, bombs, et cetera are set for us. You can say the same in a game.

Q. Do you feel war desensitized you?

In a sense. I still would be shocked if a tank was rolling down the block in front of my house but I can probably deal with blood better than an average American civilian.

Q. Do you feel games desensitized you?

Yes, when I raise my gun and shoot at the enemy, I almost feel no remorse. It has built an almost inherent reaction to want to shoot at the enemy automatically.

Q. Does that scare you?

No. Not during battle. I would not run around San Diego wielding a gun shooting people or looking for "the enemy."

Q. How do you deal with seeing death?

After shooting people and seeing dead people, they all start to look the same. There are only so many maimed, wounded, and dead people to look at. A gunshot to the head or the loss of an arm, they start to look the same.

Q. Did you go to therapy sessions after the war?

No, I did not, but there was a mandatory post-conflict counseling session. I mainly keep my sanity by talking to people and being open with what I have done. I believe secrets will eat you up.

Q. So you have told your wife and kids about your actions during the war?

I told my wife. As for the kids, I have not. They're too young. Maybe I will when they're older and ask. I have pictures in my uniform and plaques with Navy insignia. I am also in Homeland Security; I think it would be hard to hide my role in the war. I have many of the same friends from high school and college that I am very open with. It helps to have supportive family and friends.

Q. Are there any effects left from the war?

I do not have PTSD. No nightmares. No flashbacks.

Q. Do you have any friends or colleagues with PTSD?

I have seen and met people with PTSD. I think it is more of a mental preparation for battle. I had a choice to go into battle and I mentally and physically prepared for it. I was trained with the possibility of entering into a war zone. I came prepared and was knowledgeable. I was in the Navy for over four years at this point. I talked about what happened on the field, and when there was downtime, I kept it light. Some people are not made for war. I mean, Iraq is a giant sandbox. It is not lush and beautiful. It can be hard to escape memories and thoughts. My theory is that most people with PTSD questioned orders and protocol. I generally followed orders and protocol.

Q. Do you feel there is a choice to abide by orders? Is strictly following orders best for the greater good?

I do have a choice and I choose to follow orders because there are rules and orders which must be followed. I do strategically follow orders because every move is strategic and there is a reason for what we do. In war I do not know every variable so I follow orders from someone who is more knowledgeable than I am. I trust my commanding officers to keep me out of trouble because the threat was not always apparent. People were not targets. Threats were targets.

Q. Were people the threat sometimes?

Yes, but we would try to get accurate intelligence. For example, the Republican Guard would try to blend into the general population. So we would do reconnaissance missions to find where the Republican Guard will be hiding, sometimes with civilians, or sometimes hiding as civilians.

Q. Did you see acts of genocide or ethnic cleansing while in Iraq?

No, but there was tension between the Sunnis, the Shiites, and the Kurds. In the cities, especially Baghdad, Sunnis, under Saddam's rule, had more power. But they were all more like small bands of street thugs that looted and stole from the general public at this point. Civilians generally asked for protection, security, food, water, jobs, and to stop violence at night by the street thugs. We tried to enforce a curfew at dusk to assist the general population but that was not our main objective. Our main objective, after Baghdad was taken, was to stop new rebel forces from forcefully taking control of the country and to do further reconnaissance missions.

Q. Did you feel like a bystander, rescuer, perpetrator, or victim?

None. But if I had to choose, a rescuer because we were there to help liberate Iraq from a dictatorial rule. Now I feel like a knowledgeable bystander since I know what I saw and what was done in Iraq. I still support the U.S. endeavors there.

Q. Did you see any extreme acts of abuse from the war?

No.

Q. Do you feel there was something the Guards could throw at you which you would not be prepared for?

Well, there was always a chance of nuclear, chemical, and biological warfare. I mean, a gas mask can only do so much.

Q. One more question. Is there anything you regret from the war?

No, I take everything as a learning experience. All the decisions and actions I took were protocol and have helped me in my current career.

NOTES

1. The Baghdad Correctional Facility at Abu Ghraib is where U.S. Army and governmental agency personnel committed human rights violations of Iraqi prisoners
   via torture, physical, psychological, and sexual abuse, including the raping and
   sodomizing of prisoners after 2004. The Abu Ghraib scandal was a public rela-
   tions/human rights disaster in the United States, one still not fully resolved.
2. The situation for prisoners at Guantanamo prison remains controversial, with
   civil libertarians concerned that the prisoners are not being accorded full rights
   under international law.

12 EASILY THE WORST EXPERIENCE OF MY LIFE

Sebastian, on the Iraq War

I'm from a small California town where the community is very close-knit. You grow up in an environment where your neighbors and friends become your family. Everyone knows who you are, where you are, and where you're going. I had a very loving family; they were my support system, always encouraging me to strive for more. My older sister was a big part of my life, always giving me advice and helping me through any situation, whether it was good or bad. Going through high school I guess you could label me an overachiever; I was involved in just about everything you could do. I took the most rigorous courses, played sports, participated in student leadership, and even volunteered locally. I was always optimistic and upbeat. In my eyes, the world was a good place.

The United States had never previously been in a war that affected me. I was 18, which allowed me to vote and be in the military. Following the September 11 attacks, I was very distraught. On that day I can remember exactly what I was doing. I was getting ready to go to school. I remember walking into my parents' room. The television was on, which was odd considering my parents should have been at work. Looking at the television screen, I thought my parents were watching a trailer for a new movie. The twin towers were engulfed in smoke and flames with damage done all outside the buildings. It looked fictitious. Unfortunately, it was real. As talks of war started to develop, I wasn't sure what to feel. I thought the war could potentially be justified but it seemed more like an opportunity to enter the region and retaliate for what had been done to us. Initially I never saw the United States as a malevolent actor. In fact, it wasn't until my service and my subsequent education that I started to realize our role as a "superpower."

Q. What compelled you to serve?

My father is a retired army colonel. He dissuaded me from the military but I joined anyway since I was accepted at UC Berkeley out of high school and could not go because of financial reasons. I had all my money saved up in stocks. PG&E was the company and all at once they started to have financial issues and went bankrupt. It didn't leave me any options. I had no money for college and I didn't want to get trapped living in a small town so I enlisted in the military to get out and experience things I would not have experienced otherwise. I would have had to start working again and save up more money for school. I felt joining the military would give me a lot more opportunities or at least let me do something different.

Q. So your decision to enlist in the war had nothing to do with your obligation to your country or even your sense of duty to protect the ones you love?

No, I never really looked at it that way; it was mainly just an opportunity for me to do something different. The driving factor was ultimately finances. Certainly the terrorist attacks had an effect on me, but I would be lying if I said that's why I enlisted.

Q. What is your perception of the war now that you've seen the situation there?

It's still the same as when I went. My take on it is that although they [Iraqis] could use our help, we weren't there to necessarily help them. We were there for other purposes. We were there for the oil and to have control in the region. It never was about helping the situation in Iraq. It was a guise for promoting democracy and molding Iraqi politics and more specifically the Middle East; maybe it was even motivated by greed.

Q. Your perspective of the war resembles what we see here through the media. Do you agree with how the war was portrayed in the media or what the popular perception is here in the United States?

It's difficult because the media portrays the negative things that occur in Iraq strongly, while neglecting a lot of the positive things that occurred. They're also not allowed to cover certain things because of the government and that kind of shit, so we can't really get a full picture of what is actually going on over there. For the most part, I do agree with the idea that it never really was about anything other than money and power.

Q. Was it a matter of protecting national security or promoting ideas of democracy to a country that was oppressed by Saddam's regime?

It was more of a forced projection of that area of the world and the procurement of oil. I don't think it had anything to do on a global level with spreading ideas of democracy, but I'm sure national interest played a part. It was after 9/11. Even though the popular idea was that it was in the best interest of national security, I never bought into the idea that our national security was ever threatened.

Q. I know you enlisted in the military to eventually go back to school. Do you ever regret the decision to enlist, whether while you were serving or now, looking back on it?

I don't know. I learned a lot from my service and my time in the military so I don't regret it. I experienced a lot of things, both good and bad, that I would not have been able to get anywhere else. Overall, I think it opened my eyes to how the world really works. Of course I regret certain instances and certain things I went through. But that's pretty much it.

Q. What did you do in Iraq? Specifically what was your role as a soldier?

First, I served as a driver on convoy security. I drove an armored Humvee and then I was a gunner. Basically, whenever someone needed something, mainly protection, I would drive the armored Humvee with my unit and take people who needed help from point A to point B.

Q. What would a normal day be for you?

Wake up around five A.M.; get all your gear ready. Probably do physical fitness stuff, eat, and then start getting ready. Weapons check, ammo check, check your vehicles, load your vehicles, double-check maps and orders, drive out the gates, proceed with the convoy, and drive wherever you're going. The drives weren't just normal distances; they were probably five- to ten-hour drives. Then once you got to where you needed to be, we would stand down in reverse order. Next day you repeat the same process. It was very monotonous. Most of the time while I was out there it was incredibly boring. Occasionally we would spot some tanks but that's it. You never got to accomplish a large goal or anything like that. It was more that we got orders and would basically put all our efforts to making sure we got it done. Other than that, there never was any larger picture.

Q. Is there an incident you feel comfortable discussing regarding a difficult moment in your service?

There were some units engaged in prisoner transport. Things like that. They weren't always treating the prisoners properly. So I tried to contact the division headquarters about it and report what was going on. But when I did, I didn't get any response from them. It was a bit shocking that things like this really didn't matter to them. I probably should've tried harder, or shouldn't have taken a blank stare as an answer in regards to some of these things. They were prisoners, enemies even, but they were still people. They shouldn't have been treated like that. It's inhumane and defies almost every tenet of international human rights.

Q. That must've been difficult to receive such an apathetic response. But from your answer I'm assuming there was a connection between you and the Iraqis, even if they were prisoners who I'm assuming would be your enemy. How did you feel about the Iraqis?

I actually made a lot of Iraqi friends while I was there. I liked them a lot. I got the opportunity to take the time to get to know them. I felt pity for their situation because they had economic problems which we caused. We were supposed to be making their lives better by coming and being liberators but it was just as bad as before, if not worse. But I did make a connection with them. I did what I could to help them as individuals. I gave them most of my paychecks. I gave them things that were sent from home, like food and books for the children. Things like that. So I had a lot of friends.

Q. Is there anything else you would've done differently if you could've?

Personally, I would not have gone with the unit I was with, just because they were military police and they were basically fascist. Really, not good people at all! I didn't agree with how they handled things but what can you do? I got my orders.

Q. What was it about them that made you feel this way?

The people I personally served with, they were the military police battalion. They were pretty fascist. Mean people. They were really out to get people. They just wanted to find people to pick on and I couldn't approve of that. I didn't think it was right. They were always out to prove something and it was always at someone else's expense. Aside from them, everyone else was good people. They were trying to do the best they could with the circumstances at hand. They tried to follow orders as well as they could.

Q. I know you made a connection with the Iraqis, but you're still an American. How did you perceive yourself being a foreigner?

We didn't know the customs. We were constantly doing things the Iraqis viewed as crude or mean because we didn't know the customs. It was quite humbling until we learned what was acceptable and what was not. We spent so much time there, eventually we adapted to the environment. I can't say we lived amongst them, but it did teach me a great deal about differences in cultures and environments. One Iraqi I knew well liked us a lot because I took the time to get to know him and learn from him. However, each village we'd go to had a different behavior towards us, even when they were right next to each other. For instance in one village they'd come out running and would hug you and kiss you. The next village they would throw rocks at you.

Q. Did they actually throw rocks? Or is that a figure of speech?

No! They actually threw rocks.

Q. Did your time in Iraq seriously change your perspective on yourself or people in general?

Yeah, it definitely did. It made me a lot more wary of people. I also have a lot of concerns about the state of the world. It affects my everyday dealings. I think it's changed me, made me become more closed off and a bit skeptical of people. The things I experienced definitely changed how I perceive people.

Q. Before you enlisted in the military how did you perceive yourself?

Pretty happy, outgoing, and trusting. In retrospect, that's naïve. But of course I didn't know that then.

Q. So as a result of serving are you a different person now? Or has your personality changed?

Yeah . . . All of the above. Like I said, I became extremely closed off. I accept a lot less bullshit from people and the world around me. So I'm a little more demanding, a little colder. Probably a little more angry too, in general.

Q. I can only imagine what you experienced there. Do you think your actions in Iraq were influenced by any factors in your life prior to war?

Absolutely. I really believed in justice and doing what was right. There were a lot of circumstances where I didn't engage people and didn't do things I was supposed to, given my orders, because I didn't want people to get hurt. People needed to get certain help that I wasn't supposed to give them. But I mean, they needed help so I did whatever I could.

Q. How is the war perceived in Iraq?

Things have changed so my perspective is a couple years old. At first Iraqis saw us, or at least I think they saw us, as liberators. Slowly, things didn't improve in the country because we were so slow in rebuilding their infrastructure that they then saw us as a pain in the ass. They figured we were just another Saddam regime. The soldiers at first were pretty excited to be there and after the war, we made that quick transition to seeing ourselves as being there to help the Iraqis. Eventually a lot of people started resenting the private military companies because they were so slow getting us supplies and helping us rebuild. It kind of fell apart because of that. It was difficult. We wanted to do all these things but our hands were tied because of people outside the military. There was a sense of frustration that we can't really do anything about.

Q. Just to get a time frame of everything, when did you enlist? And when did you get released? Did you choose to leave?

I entered the military service in 2001 and I got out of active duty in 2005. I was serving until 2007 in the reserves. I got out on honorable discharge; I was actually medically discharged out of the reserves because of injuries to my legs from the war.

Q. Okay. What do you take away from the war? Specifically your perception of others and how they feel about each other pertaining to groups and cultures.

As Americans in general, we are unaware of culture and history. Personally, it changed me a lot because I think people are quite naïve as to the real world and how things actually work. It's hard for me to engage people and just make small talk, because I always have these things in the back of my mind. It's difficult to connect with people now even if it is on a very basic level. My trust of others has diminished greatly. My social interactions have also diminished because I won't talk to people.

Q. It's so weird to hear this from you because I know you as a friend and I know how you are socially. When I hear this, I try to imagine how you were before, because to me you're still a fun person to be around and a lot of people would agree with me in that assessment. To me and to others you are a pleasant person, but when you talk about yourself you have a very pessimistic outlook on it.

It's hard; I have to force myself a lot. [Sebastian paused.]

Q. I remember you mentioned you still have that injury. Were there ever any thoughts that you might lose your life in Iraq?

Yeah, definitely. Before entering Iraq I was assigned to guard a fuel tanker, big trucks with gas and jet fuel. I was really afraid it would take a hit and just blow up. I was really afraid. I just decided I didn't have the will to live with a very short life expectancy. So the way I managed dealing with that kind of stress was debilitating, sitting there thinking "I'm gonna die, I'm gonna die, I'm gonna die." So I was like, "Fuck it, I'm already dead." So I can just stop worrying about that and just worry about what I have to do. Writing off my biggest fear made it much easier to function and react to things rationally.

Q. What allowed you to continue, knowing what could ultimately happen to you?

I didn't have a choice. The people next to me needed me, and I needed them.

Q. Did you lose people close to you during the war?

Yeah, I lost a couple of friends.

Q. Does the result of that change your feelings about the Iraqis?

No, I don't think so. At first I was angry. When I came back I was angry but it wasn't because of that. I don't have a negative opinion. They have different values and that's fine. That's life.

Q. Was there something you wanted to accomplish in Iraq?

Personally I wanted to make a positive impact in the lives of people I encountered. I did my best. I provided food and water, money to help them out. They taught me Arabic; our friendship was based on me being a provider. I just didn't want to go there and not do anything positive.

Q. Would you ever consider going back?

No. I actually have a cut on my back to remind me never to go back. I fundamentally disagree with everything going on there. It was easily the worst experience of my life. It's where the worst experiences of my life occurred. I had a profound sense of powerlessness and fear and pain. So it's still something I wrestle with and I don't know how well I would be able to manage. I don't think I could go through all those feelings again. It's difficult not being able to change things.

Q. If you could say one thing about your experience in the war, what would you say?

War makes you grow up really quick. I went from being a high school senior to putting my life on the line. I matured and learned a lot. Like any situation in life, it had negatives and positives.

Q. After everything, the hard experiences and ultimately the turmoil of war, do you think it has affected your ability to care for others?

No. It definitely wasn't that. I mean, I connected with the people and helped them out as much as I could. Whoever needed help, I tried to help them. I think my actions there show I still care for people. The thing that changed the most is probably my perception of people. The trust and the social interest, it just isn't there anymore after seeing what I experienced.

Q. Do you have any closing thoughts?

Believe whatever you want but keep it to yourself. Intolerance and hatred have ruined too much.

Note: While willing to sign the consent form and agree to an interview, Sebastian was uncomfortable and unwilling to speak about many events. His name and critical descriptions have been changed to protect his identity.

PART FOUR

CIVIL WARS AND GENOCIDES, DICTATORS AND DOMESTIC OPPRESSORS

13 GRANDFATHER HAD HIS HEAD CUT OFF

Rose and the Armenian Genocide

The series of events considered the first twentieth-century genocide took place against the Armenians before the word genocide was coined.

The Armenians emerged as a people in the sixth century BCE *in Eastern Anatolia. One of the first national groups to convert to Christianity in 301, Armenians had an independent country until 1375. Thereafter, Armenia was part of the Ottoman Empire. On most indicators, Armenians were a loyal minority in the empire until the late nineteenth century, when Christian minorities in the western part of the Ottoman Empire used Great Power support to achieve autonomy and independence. The first attacks on Armenians came in 1881, when 100 thousand to 200 thousand Armenians were killed – many in 1895 – and others were forcibly converted to Islam. The period between 1895 and 1922 is the controversial period, with dispute focusing on the genocidal intent of the Turkish government.*

The core of what is classed as genocide by most scholars – while vehemently disputed by the Turkish government – began April 24, 1915, and emanated in Turkish fears of Armenian separatism and disloyalty toward the Ottomans during World War I. Armenian intelligentsia and civic leaders were deported and murdered. Armenians in the army were put to death. Military units attacked communities in the Armenian heartland. They killed the men, raped women, then kidnapped and raised children as Muslims. "Delegates" (murahhas) organized and supervised the deportation and massacre of departing Armenian convoys, usually in the deserted backlands, with "Special Organization" (Teskilatl Mahsusa) bands in charge of the killings. Armenians who survived the initial onslaught were subjected to further forced marches into the Syrian desert, where they were frequently killed. The total number murdered is estimated at 1–1.5 million, but the destruction and obliteration of cultural institutions, art, manuscripts, churches, and cemeteries, along with the deportation of an additional 1.1 million Armenians, makes the toll of the genocide much higher. Unlike the Holocaust, the Armenian genocide was surprisingly well reported in the contemporary American and European press. It is still considered a crime to describe these events as a "genocide" in contemporary Turkey.

I was born in Aleppo, Syria, in January, 1910. My family is originally from Turkey. My two oldest brothers were born in Turkey but the oldest died when he was just a child. The others were all born in Syria. There were six children in my family. The second child was a boy, and he was sent to Persia as an interpreter, but I barely remember him. I was about your age. He couldn't get out of Persia. They wouldn't let him out of the country. They would find out he was Armenian and kill him. We never saw him again. He stayed there. He found an Armenian girl. By now he would not be alive because he was much older than me. I'm the youngest. My next brother is seven years older than me. That was John. He was going to come to California, but he died. For seven years my mother didn't have her period and she thought she was going through the change. Then she found out she was pregnant with me. She was forty-eight or forty-nine years when she had me. I had an aunt who worked in an American hospital as head nurse. She wanted to give me an American name so I was baptized as Rose. When I came to America, I knew four languages: Armenian, Turkish, French, and Arabic. You have to learn these in school because when you go shopping you have to speak Arabic, and some places you have to know French since Armenia was under French mandate. Armenian I learned in the house. We had Turkish neighbors; I was always over at their house. When I came to the United States I learned English. So I knew five languages. I'm forgetting the other languages because I don't use them anymore.

I went to Catholic school when I was little. We didn't have an Armenian school. It was during the war. They didn't open the Armenian school. I had to go to the Sisters. They were only a block away. It was World War I. I was a little girl – five years old. The Catholic school was only a block away so I walked. I went for five years, until I was ten or eleven. Then the Armenian schools opened. My parents thought I should learn some Armenian so they sent me to Armenian school for one year. Then we came to America. I was twelve. They didn't know what grade to put me in when I came here. They gave me a book to read and I could read only French. So they put me in fourth grade. But I was the best one in arithmetic. In a couple of months I learned English. I went through elementary school. I didn't go to high school. Elementary school was up to eighth grade. But I was in a rapid advance class so I graduated in about seventh grade instead.

Q. What did you do after you graduated from elementary school then?

My parents were old. My sister Maggie was working in a factory. She got me a job there. In the old country they believe girls are going to grow up and get married. They don't need lots of education. I thought I would work in the factory until I got married. I worked in the factory with Maggie. She was a head operator there. It was a knitting factory. She made the samples. We made sweaters, scarves for men, dresses. I learned everything in that factory. I got so I had a good job. To go to high school we would have to take the bus and my father heard sometimes men fooled around with young girls on the bus.

I was born in a Christian home. We don't have a testimony. We were always going to church. We saw our father and mother. They never talked back or yelled. We thought everybody else was like this. Others get up and give their testimony. They were drunkards and had bad lives. My father wasn't a pastor, but when he preached, it was better than a pastor. We saw nothing but love in the family. Years ago in Urfa, Turkey, he had a variety store. He used to send things to other cities. If you want something, go to his store. He had from soup to nuts. My father's name was George. After he got to Aleppo, he had gotten older, so he worked for an American Bible Society. He sold Bibles. They went door to door selling Bibles and Christian literature. My father wanted to get married and he wanted a Christian girl. They gave him a list of girls' names. So he put his finger on the list and prayed that God would put his finger on the right one for him to marry. He put his finger on my mother. My mother's name was Susan. My mother used to be a teacher before she got married. When she married my father, she became a Protestant and became born again. When she was little, she used to sing Gregorian hymns with the children in her neighborhood.

I never saw my mother and father fighting. The only argument they ever had was that my mother used to cook salty and my father didn't like it. My father didn't have much of an education. He was the only son and he had to help support the family. He had a sister but over there, the girls don't work. He educated himself. He read the paper every day. When he used to write, his writing was like shorthand. Nobody could read it. Only Maggie could read his writing. He would sit down with educated people and talk and he knew as much as they did. He didn't only read religious books. He read all kinds. He had a bad foot because he walked a lot selling the bibles, and he didn't wear the right kind of shoes. He had corns and calluses, and he died from that, too. His foot got gangrene. This rich man who was in the rug business used to come and he would say, "You have bad feet and good brain, and I have good feet and bad brain." He knew lots of stories. He had a light complexion and blue eyes. He didn't look like an Armenian at all. His skin was like velvet. He didn't have much hair.

My mother looked like an Armenian. Darker complexion with black eyes and black hair. My father got gray early, like me. My father was humorous, too. He would crack jokes and was very popular. He had a lot of books. Books and papers. His room was filled with them. My mother used to say she couldn't clean his room because there were so many books and papers. He said to her to close his door when they had company. My mother was a homemaker. She lived in this world but she wasn't a part of this world. She had Bible studies every Wednesday. She would pray and cry. Every time she prayed, she would cry. They left Turkish Armenia because there were always problems there. My father had this variety store. Every so often the Turkish people would come to the stores and steal and break everything. My father used to go to other cities sometimes to do business. One time he wasn't there and my mother was worried because there were riots. He had closed the store and boarded it. After the riots stopped, my mother went to look and see if everything was there. The next door neighbor was a Turk. He saw her peeking through the boards, and he said, "What are you looking at? As long as I am here, nobody is going to touch your store."

We moved to Aleppo, Syria so we wouldn't have to live under fear. It was under French mandate, not Turkish. It was in Urfa, Turkey, where my grandfather had his head cut off. He was my father's father. My grandfather was very simple. My father told him he was going to have his picture taken, so his grandchildren would be able to see him. He didn't want to have his picture taken. He thought if you had your picture taken, then something would come out of you. Finally, my father convinced him it would be good to have his picture taken. So he went to the photographer. My father told him to stand still and not to wink because if he did he would spoil the picture. He said he would let my grandpa know when it was done and he could move. When they finished, the photographer and my father went into the darkroom, and forgot to tell my grandpa he could relax. He had tears coming down his eyes because he wasn't blinking. My father comes out and tells him, "Pop, it's all finished." And my grandpa said, "Oh, I'm finished too!"

Q. When you moved to Aleppo, what was life like?

Aleppo was an average city, not expensive and not poor. We went to the bathhouse once a week. They had people at the bathhouse who would scrub you if you wanted. My mother always washed us instead. We had a toilet on one side of the kitchen. We would have to draw water from the well to flush it. We ate Armenian food growing up: *sarma, kufta, dolma.* We didn't have a refrigerator. If you bought food, you had to use it the same day. Some of the things that had to be kept fresh, like butter, we kept in the basement where it was cooler. The butchers over there only sold what they had that day because they had no way of keeping the meat fresh. They didn't put anything on ice in those days because they didn't have any. We had very simple Christmases over there. Apples, oranges, balls made out of rags. No fancy decorations. My mom would make me a doll out of rags for Christmas. I got a new dress for Easter every year. That would be my good dress. I would wear it on Sundays when I went to church. I wore a skirt and a blouse to school every day. The boys would wear pants and a shirt. *Tunder* was the word we used for the low table we sat around to keep warm. Hot charcoal was in the center in the frame of the table and a comforter was spread over that for everyone to share. We used one of these tables in the wintertime. In the summertime we slept on the roof. The roof was cemented and had a railing around it. We kept our beds up there. It never rained in the summertime, only in the winter. We could see the moon and count the stars. We didn't do much entertaining. My mother was busy. We used to play jacks, marbles, jump rope. We did a lot of reading.

I was twelve when I came to the United States. We went to Marseilles, France, first. We had to take a boat from France. We stayed there one week till the boat came. We stayed in a hotel. We had to come with the "quota." Every year they would only take a certain number of people from each nationality and not anyone with health problems. If you miss the quota, you had to wait seven or eight years to come to the United States again. You had to go through Ellis Island in New York, and they checked you for health problems. I came with my parents and my sister. My two brothers came to the United States before us, two years before us. We came with two other ladies. My uncle who came with us wanted a bride from the old country and said he trusted our judgment. My father sent him a picture of a lady and he liked it so they were engaged. The trip on the ship took about five or six days. My mother and I were seasick the whole time. We took a train from Syria to Marseilles before we got on the ship. It was one overnight before we got there. The boat's name was Brava, Cunard Line. I even remember its name. I didn't like that boat because it wasn't that clean. It was a cruise ship. We had our own room but my mother and I were always in bed throwing up. We were at Ellis Island about a week until we were called. We rented an apartment. My mother had conjunctivitis years before she came to the United States and it was healed before she came. Conjunctivitis is contagious. When we came to Ellis Island, she cried easily. She was going to see her sons who she hadn't seen in two years. When the doctor examined her, he saw that her eyes were red and watering and said she needed more treatment. They sent her back to Marseilles to wait for the next quota. She didn't know French so my sister had to go back with her to France so she could find a place for my mother to live while she waited and got treatment for her eyes. My sister then had to come back by herself because my father was old and he couldn't work. So at first it was just me, my dad, and my uncle's wife. My two brothers lived in Rochester and Pennsylvania, and they came later. Fortunately, my sister found an Armenian family in Marseilles for my mother to live with. When my sister came back to the United States and began working, we would send money to the family she was staying with for her room and board. I was twelve and had to go to school. My mother had to stay in Marseilles for seven years because the quota had already passed. Finally my father became a U.S. citizen and went to Marseilles to get his wife and bring her back to the United States. He brought her back to New York first class. She didn't even get treatment over there for her eyes because the doctor said she didn't need it. The doctors didn't even have to look at her.

Q. Living for so long without your mother must have been hard. How did it affect you?

My mother didn't get to see me graduate from elementary school.

Q. Tell me about the man you ended up marrying?

My marriage was arranged. Our families knew each other. My husband-to-be's mother said to him to be a man and marry me. That's what they said in the old country. I was eleven and he was four and a half years older than me. My husband's mother was going to come to America but when she was in Beirut, she got terrible diarrhea. My husband had a younger sister and we lived together. I learned to cook from her. She was a good cook, two years older than me and we got along very well. I didn't know how to cook when I got married. When you entertained in the old country, children stayed in their rooms. I didn't see my husband-to-be very much. He stayed in his room when we came over. He was shy, too. My husband's family was very wealthy. His family was from Antuk, Turkey. His sister, the one I lived with, used to talk about their velvet sofas. They were the only ones with a velvet sofa. The Turks took everything away from them. The father died of a heart attack. It left just the mother and the kids. They had to run for their lives and leave everything behind. They came to Aleppo. I was twenty-one when I got married. I was almost twenty-two. I got married in December, and turned twenty-two in January.

Q. And you had two children, correct?

My first child, Frank, was born when I was twenty-three. Connie was born two years later.

Q. How did you end up in California?

We came to California in 1948. We had a candy store in New York for ten years. Then we came here and bought a store that was bankrupt. We struggled. It took a while for us to build up a reputation in a small town that our candy was good. At first when my husband came to America he was seventeen and he didn't know what to do. He tried photo engraving, and he didn't like that. He tried watch making and he worked for my brother. You have to have a lot of patience. If you lose one piece on the floor, you have to look for it. This one company was looking for a candymaker, and eventually the boss died. My husband's family liked to cook and that's what he liked to do, too. When the boss died, the wife tried to run the business but she didn't know how to run it. So eventually he decided to open his own business. Everyone said, "If nobody had enough money to buy bread, who's going to buy candy?" But that's what he wanted to do. We couldn't afford a candymaker at first so we did it all by hand. I needed to help out in the store so I just brought the babies with me to work. When the business finally picked up, our lawyer said he thought we'd do better if we moved the store, so we moved it to Mission near the bank, on Fair Oaks. We were in business in California for sixteen or seventeen years altogether and the same in New York.

When my husband died, I sold the business. He went to get his driver's license one day and I got worried because he was taking so long.

I was in the shop, and the next thing I know I see my son there. I was surprised to see him at that hour. He never usually got home until seven or eight P.M. He told me that dad got sick. He didn't tell me that he had died. I wanted to know what happened. I had cleaned his glasses before he went to the driver's test. He was happy. He had just been to the doctor's office the day before, and the doctor was happy with him. His blood pressure was down. His weight was down. Gradually they told me what had happened, that he had died of a heart attack. Connie came with the guy she was dating at the time. They put a sign on the door that we were closed due to a death in the family. All the neighbors were stunned! My son went to pick up his father's car, and it was so funny, he hadn't even locked the door. He always locked the door even if he was only going to be gone two minutes. He had heart problems and diabetes, but they were under control. He was a big worrier. He had a very quick temper. We used to work a lot of nights, until eleven or twelve at night at Christmas, and then I would have to come home and do the washing and ironing. I never answered him back. But one time around Christmastime he went on and on and I said, "Listen here! I work here, too. I make lots of sacrifices, too." He didn't know what to do. He went into the chocolate dipper room where it is very cold and he said to the dipper, "My wife is mad at me." He was like a pussycat after that for a while. He never praised me in front of me but he told other people when I wasn't around that if it weren't for me, he wouldn't make it.

Q. Do you talk much about the massacres committed during the Armenian genocide?

What good would it do?

Note: All names were changed. My great-grandmother did not want to speak about the genocide itself, noting only that her grandfather was beheaded by the Turks for refusing to give up his Bible. It was Rose who saved the bloodstained Bible.

14 A RESISTANCE TO KEEP YOU ALIVE

Ngũgĩ, the Mau Mau, Anti-Colonialism, and Home-grown Dictators

The Berlin Conference (1884–85) divided the African continent, making what we think of as Kenya a British colony. After Kenya became its protectorate, the British used "divide and rule" to play off the ethnic groups in the new country, thereby both creating and solidifying perceived differences among various groups and allowing the British to introduce a settler class – akin to the British landed upper middle classes – to establish and export cash crops. British colonists benefited from colonial policies producing unequal legal rights, punitive labor laws, identity cards, and native reserves. To stifle African resentment at this ill treatment, Britain banned all African political groups, allowing only the formation of organizations concerned with "people's welfare." Disturbed at these injustices, Kenyans staged an uprising from 1952 to 1960. The uprising enjoyed mixed public support and pitted a Gĩkũyũ-dominated anticolonial group (the Mau Mau) against the British Army, auxiliaries, and anti–Mau Mau Gĩkũyũ. The Mau Mau rebellion set fracture points that endured into independence, creating long-standing divisions within the Gĩkũyũ community. In response to demands for independence, the British grudgingly allowed formation of political parties. Two main parties – the Kenya African National Union (KANU) and the Kenya African Democratic Union (KADU) – were established in 1960. Kenya achieved independence in 1964 but remained effectively a one-party state, ruled by the KANU and a Kikuyu-Lui alliance under Jomo Kenyatta from 1963 to 1978. Kenyatta's successor – Daniel Arap Moi – held power until 2002. Pressured by the United States to restore a multi-party system, Moi did so in 1991 but won the elections in 1992 and 1997, with political killings involved on both sides. Moi's involvement in corruption and human rights abuses led to his disbarment from running in the 2002

election, an election won by Mwai Kibaki. Widely reported electoral fraud
continues.

   Ngũgĩ's life was caught up in the anticolonial fight. His father had
multiple wives and the family was divided during the Mau Mau rebel-
lion, with brothers fighting on both sides and Ngũgĩ's mother report-
edly tortured at the Kamriithu homeguard post.[1] *Ngũgĩ attended schools*
in Uganda and England, publishing his first novel (1964) in English.
His second novel takes the Mau Mau rebellion as its background. Ngũgĩ
later renounced English, Christianity, and his given name, arguing that
all three reflect colonial repression. The political aspect of Ngaahika
Ndeenda (I Will Marry When I Want) antagonized then Vice President
Daniel Arap Moi, who ordered Ngũgĩ arrested. While in the Kamiti Max-
imum Security Prison, Ngũgĩ wrote the first modern novel in Gĩkũyũ,
Caitaani mũtharaba-Inĩ (Devil on the Cross), on prison-issued toilet
paper. An Amnesty International Prisoner of Conscience, Ngũgĩ was
forced to leave Kenya and live in exile, returning only after Arap Moi left
office in 2002. Ngũgĩ now lives in California.

I am Ngũgĩ wa Thiong'o. "Ngũgĩ" means "son of Thiong'o," which is
my father's name. I come from Kenya, East Africa. Kenya was a British
settler colony from 1895 to 1963. There are two types of colonies in
Africa. One is a settler type where a number of settlers came, particularly
from Europe. There were other types of colonies, where there were no
sizeable European settlers. An example of the latter would be Nigeria,
Uganda, Ghana. An example of a settler colony would be South Africa,
Algeria, Zimbabwe, Kenya. These are interesting settlement patterns,
and very different histories. What is common to all settler colonies,
whether they are French (like the settler colony of Algeria) or British (like
Kenya, Zimbabwe, South Africa) or Portuguese ones (like Mozambique
and Angola) is really the question of land, which is an issue in all the
settler colonies. Another interesting feature is how these countries came
to get their independence. In all the protected colonies – like Nigeria,
Uganda, Ghana – independence was won through organization and
negotiations. In all the settler colonies there was armed struggle. That
is, where people fought to get their independence – as in South Africa,
Kenya, Mozambique, Angola, and Algeria – they went through armed
struggle because land is such a contentious issue. You can say America
belongs to the settler colony type. America, Canada, New Zealand,
Australia, all are different types of settler colonies but all had Europeans
who settled and worked the land in the colony.

Q. But Canadians didn't have to fight to get their independence.

Yes. That's true; that's true. But in Africa this was common in all of them. Of course these are older settler types, an old settler system. What America went through when it fought for independence, Canada didn't have to, nor did New Zealand. But one can also argue that in such situations as Canada – even America, or New Zealand and Australia – the indigenous people, the *original* indigenous people were the ones who were colonized really. Their colonial status was never really resolved. It's true with New Zealand, Canada, Australia, and so on. Where it was actually resolved in one way or another, like in Africa, they went through a phase of armed struggle. This is because of the land; the land became a very contentious issue.

In Kenya the 1952–62 armed struggle was through an organization called the Mau Mau. Independence came in 1963. The reason I'm mentioning this is because I was born in 1938 on the verge of the Second World War and I grew up and went to school through the first of the struggle. I meant to bring my book, called *Dreams in a Time of War*. It tells of that childhood, through having dreams. It is relevant to this group because we are talking about war on all sides. In World War II some of my brothers fought for the British in places in East Africa but also in the Middle East, Asia, and so on. Yet when they came back they could not get jobs. It was their European counterparts – the ones who settled – who got jobs. The armed struggle itself against the colonial rule I have talked about in my book, where I tell how my own family was torn between brothers who fought in the mountains, in the guerrilla army, and others of my brothers who were on the side of the British. I came from a large, polygamous family, a family of five wives. My mother was the fifth wife of my father, so it was a large household. In a war some members of the family fought on different sides. This touches on a fundamental issue in ethics – loyalty toward biology and loyalty to ideology or beliefs. My family, all of us really, are caught in between. This is the atmosphere in which I grew up and went to school, during the war against the British. In *Dreams in a Time of War* I've talked about those tensions that come in a family. My biological brother is fighting against the British and my other half brother is fighting with the British. I have another half brother who works in a factory near home; he lives in a particular house for the workers. Both brothers who were fighting each other didn't know that each one of them was going to visit their relative, this third brother, but at different times. On one occasion they both decided to visit their half brother. The workers quarters has a main gate. At the entrance of the gate these two rival brothers come face to face with each others. They looked at each other and just ran away from each other in opposite directions. This is because they know that as fighters, it is war. In a war it raises ethical questions as to why and with whom are you fighting. Should I do this, or that? Or some other option?

Another episode from the book is when I have gone through school and have done my exams. I am waiting for results to go to a prestigious high school, prestigious for Africans. Schools in Kenya were segregated. Some schools for Europeans only, for Asians only, for Africans only, et cetera. One school was famous because it was very competitive. It's like University High School as the only high school in Irvine or the entire Orange County. The best. I do the exams. Then on the day I have to sit the exams, I got to the train station but I'm not allowed to board the train. Why? Because people of my community – many Africans in Kenya – could not travel from point A to point B without a pass. It was like going from Los Angeles to San Diego, you have to have a pass or a travel visa. That kind of situation. That kind of a law. I didn't have one. This is the only chance I have because it is so competitive. This is my only chance. I've never been on a train before. Some of the students from ___, I saw them standing on the platform. The train goes and I'm literally crying. As much as I have been trained that as a man you don't weep or cry, I am standing there with tears going down my face. Then another ethical issue comes up. A railroad official, British or European, with an assistant who is an African, came up to me. How, I don't know, but he came to know my situation. He told me not to cry. "Let's see what we can do."

He waited for the right train. There are passenger trains with nice coaches and so on, but these went away. The other trains are only for carrying goods, only goods. I don't know who he talks to but I am smuggled into the car that has all the workers' tools. Jackets with sweat. Tools. Things like that. So I'm there. That's how I got to high school, smuggled in a cargo train.

Writing continuously raises those ethical dilemmas. Everyone has to face them in some kind of an encounter. In my life I have gone through so many things! We can't go over everything right now. Just let me give you one more example of these ethical problems one faces all the time. This story shows one way I had to decide what to do. In December 1977 I was professor of literature at the University of Nairobi of Kenya, where I come from. I chair the department. I had published three novels and I was working on getting known nationally and internationally. The United States and the University of Nairobi had generated a group to work in the community theater. This theater in the community was in our own language. English was our dominant language in Kenya but that is not my language. My language is Gĩkũyũ and Swahili. If you really want to work with the people, you have to use the language they use and yet this was not the norm. We went to work in a village in the Gĩkũyũ language. We produced a play, which you can now find translated into English, called "I'll Marry When I Want." The play opened in November with a troupe in the village; the troupe was made up of the working people in the plantation nearby and in the factories in the nearby villages. Working in all languages is very exciting. Working with the language of the community, it is really great. It opened space for me mentally. We were all happy. We think we are doing a good thing. But lo and behold, the newly independent African government thinks to the contrary. They say what we are doing to the village wasn't very nice, especially performing in an African language. So the play was stopped. On December thirty-first, 1977, at midnight before the New Year, I was surrounded by armed police. They came to the village. I was taken to a maximum security prison. There was no trial. I have recorded someone's experiences in my prison diary called "Detained." The key thing was that I was not put on trial. I was only questioned by the police. It was punitive. In a maximum security they wanted you to confess but since you didn't know what you were accused of you didn't know what to confess. I remembered when the judicial review came. There were high court judges with books of law all piled up all around. I go and I sit down and the first question was from them. "Can you tell us why you have been detained? Tell us what you did to the government that brought you here."

"But I wanted *you* to tell *me* why I am detained!" I was very cross. I don't know what I said. I suspect I said something not very nice. The point is that after being there for some time, you always question yourself. Should you tell a lie and invent something so you can get out, although they didn't say "If you say this you are gonna get out." You don't know what you actually will do. You don't know what can save you or not. You are always confronted with those questions. "If they ask me to lie, would I actually lie to get free? What would I do?" Every single day; every single night, you ask yourself another important question. "Do I succumb? What do I do to survive?"

You can do two things. One, you can moan and think about, "Aaww this is terrible!" Especially if you are an intellectual and you are used to writing and you have no books. No pen. You don't have a name. You have to sit there! "Aaww, this is terrible!" That won't help. Or you can start to find forms of resistance that keep you mentally alive. With me, I chose to write in Gĩkũyũ language. I wrote the first book in my language, translated as *Devil on a Cross*. This book was written on toilet paper. I can show you in my office. That is a decision that nobody can teach you. You have to dig deep in yourself and find a form of resistance that can keep you mentally and spiritually alive. For me it was writing and writing in my own language. Both are important. I was put in prison because I wrote in my own language. I worked with Gĩkũyũ people and without getting paid. We just volunteered. We had to drive from the University of Nairobi and then go one thousand kilometers into the village and then walk there. So you feel good about yourself. You are volunteering services, doing things. You are helping them or they are helping you, in this case.

I started thinking about the language issue very seriously, about the relationship between European languages or colonial languages versus non-European languages. I wrestled with these thoughts in prison and I came to this conclusion. There is a close relationship between the colonial and the African languages. Languages also were colonized. People, particularly educated people, have been brought up to think there is a great distance between themselves and their own languages. There is nothing as terrible as that, to be made to feel uncomfortable about your own language. Then you're already a prisoner in your mind. That's what I think, anyway. I have become a prisoner. I came to think it is normal, that you become a prisoner of the English language – or whatever language the colonial language is – and you think, "Oh, it is normal to become a prisoner." Then you look at your own language and ask, "What is that language? I don't know." Or, "I don't care. It's not useful." Whereas in reality, if you know your language very well, then add to it other languages, including English or a number of European languages, *that* is empowerment. You are more empowered because not only do you know your own language very well but you are also a master of another language. In that sense you are more empowered. But the colonial system is a way of making people think the other way around. They don't see having more than one language as empowerment but rather as something uncomfortable. They become uncomfortable about their own power. Their own empowerment. They become uncomfortable about it. I talked about this and looked at the colonial relationship between languages and looked at India, French-African languages,

Portuguese-African languages, and so on. The result of all this thinking is in my book, *Decolonising the Mind*. It talks about some of these issues. In prison, we weren't allowed to write. We don't have pens. We don't have paper. That's why I had to use whatever we got freely or very limited, and that was toilet paper.

Q. What did you write with if you didn't have a pen?

You had to say you were going to write to the tribunal about your case. You must say you are going to write a confession to the tribunal. Then the authorities will give you a pen so you can write confessions. I would say, "I'm writing confessions. Give me a pen." But I was writing my literary work, on toilet paper. Writing was important to me but more important was the question of resistance, which came as I was writing in a language that was my own. That was the best that came from the time of incarceration. So I am defying that imprisonment, in my own way, by actually in prison, even though guarded there, by writing that language, using material given by the state, including pen and paper. So you see there how the act of writing was itself a defiance. You feel good about it. You are writing, guarded by them as it were. So writing in an African language, Gĩkũyũ, became very vital. Not only because I was in prison because of putting on plays in Gĩkũyũ but also it was vital because from that whole confrontation came my ability to look at the relationship between languages in a new way. There was also no book that was novel-length written in my language. Ever. So I was writing a novel-length book in Gĩkũyũ for the first time. All these things you draw upon constitute an inner strength called formal resistance.

Q. I'm fascinated with what you're saying. I am reminded of stories about Anwar Sadat when he was imprisoned by the British for his anticolonial activity. He said it was important for him to put his mind someplace else. He said you can at least be free in your mind even though you were incarcerated. I'm intrigued by the response you have to language; one could see quite easily how you could come to the point where refusing to write in the oppressor's language was an important expression of both resistance and the inner freedom Sadat talks about. Yet that was not the route you chose to take. You chose to go to multiple languages. I assume you're fluent in more than just two or three languages.

No, I wrote in English for the most part. In prison I wrote in Gĩkũyũ. I made the decision after that prison experience that all my novels and plays were to be written in Gĩkũyũ language. They're available in English. I have done some translation myself; other works have been translated by somebody else. My reason is like this. There is nothing wrong with any language. Any other language is as good as any other language.

Decolonising the Mind deals with this issue of languages. When I go to India, or anywhere outside the developed world, or even places like Ireland among indigenous intellectuals, even here in America, the most questions I get on *Decolonising the Mind* concern my arguments about languages and the power relation. I am very interested in power relationships between languages. What is wrong isn't the languages but rather the power relationship between languages. If you look at the world today, you look at the United Nations, the official languages are about five European languages and another one outside the European languages, which is Chinese. All the others are Russian, English, French, Spanish, not German.[2] They are different languages. The tendency has been whether, here in America or in Africa or some other places, to confuse education with mastery of the dominant language. The people who come from nondominant languages sometimes feel uncomfortable about their language. They confuse being educated with simply having a mastery of the dominant language. Sometimes they go a step further and see that they must distance themselves from the language of their community. They don't see what they are doing. They are denying themselves a legitimate base of their power.

There is what you call the language of power. It is a language which enables you to negotiate your way into university. You use it in the marketplace of power so obviously whatever is the language of power, whether it is English or French or another language, you have to master it because it is the language of power. Without it you won't survive in that marketplace so it is to your advantage to master it very well. But the false equation has been that the mastery of the language of power must necessarily go with distancing one's self from the language of one's community. The assumption is that the two are mutually exclusive. That's not true. They complement each other so you become much more powerful than ever before. If English is the language of power and you want to come to University of California Irvine [UCI], you have to master English. You can't say you want to come to UCI and don't master the language. You must master English to survive. But here's the false equation: thinking that when you elevate one language in order for that language to be and to remain the language of power then other languages must be denied their legitimate place in that society. That's the problem, not the other way around.

Q. So you're in favor of multiple languages, not one exclusive language.

Yeah. I'm not a believer of that. It's practical. My children like the idea that they work in English but can turn around and speak to us in Gĩkũyũ language. One daughter is in Spain now. She is chattering in Gĩkũyũ and then reverts to Spanish or whatever language she is speaking. I like that. Let me put it in another way. If you think of languages, think of treasure. I'm sure all of you like to read novels like *Treasure Island*. Books with stories of how children get lost somewhere and look for treasure. I think of languages like that. You are in a room or a house with several rooms. Each room has treasure, and each room has a key. Language is a key to a treasure house. The more languages you have, the more keys you have, the more easily you can open doors and see what's behind. The one who does not have that key can only stare. If I am in a Spanish-speaking environment I must learn Spanish to know what people are saying. If I don't, I'm completely shut off the moment they start speaking Spanish.

Q. Have you ever done any writing with a mixture of languages, in both English and Gĩkũyũ ?

No. There are some people who come from a three- or two-language situation. What you find in Kenya is that we have a three-language situation. Every person speaks their own mother's tongue and then Swahili as the lingua franca, then English. So I mix Gĩkũyũ and English. In my family we do this all the time. We are speaking in English and then switch to Swahili. I like using several languages but it's not good to mix them that way. Someone who knows Swahili can follow what I said as one sentence, one unit of speech. But someone else who doesn't know Swahili would understand some of it and then all of sudden he or she is cast off. So while you can have a conversation with three languages – you just mix them up – I don't like it as a concept. I think it's a bad thing, but I do it.

Q. Why did your government find your writing Gĩkũyũ threatening?

It's a colonial thing. It's an African government but it followed colonial thinking. That's why we need decolonization of the mind. I can reconstruct how the colonial thinking goes like this. You have been brought up to think there is something negative about your language. Even an African government makes a policy not necessarily to ban the language but at least not to encourage its use. Now there are more governments that are more open to African languages. It varies from place to place. But the insistence comes from the mind. The policy makers are people who have been to school, who have been educated, and taught to use the colonial language. The problem of mental colonization is not among the working people. Mental colonization takes place in school. The people who come from the university are the ones making the policy. They internalized the negativity toward or indifference to African languages. When they come to make policy they see how important languages are. They've got to normalize the situation of African languages and learn that avoiding African languages can be in the way of progress.

It's not unanalogous to the time when the West moved from Latin to the vernacular. Dante started writing in the vulgate as the language of the people. This made a powerful statement that you don't have to be an educated person to count. You don't have to go through the socialization processes that elites go through in order to understand and communicate. So putting the Bible, for example, in Italian or French as opposed to Latin, meant even an ordinary person can understand it. That is a very powerful statement towards equality, isn't it?

Q. As you think about the resistance to colonialism, do you find there are ways to resist that are immoral or dishonorable?

I've done some things where you can say neatly that "This was moral; this way is immoral," and so on. I presume these situations arise with some of the ethical questions one confronts every day. When you are in other situations – such as a war situation – if you don't believe in killing anybody, things get more complicated. What happens when you confront another human being on the other side of the fence, so to speak? What do you do? You are confronted with the same question, "Do I kill or not kill? If I don't kill I will get killed." Those human questions are still there no matter what you do. That is why people have their own psychic wounds even when they are left victorious.

Q. So your response to that, I am guessing, would be your earlier statement. You have to dig down deep within yourself to find out what can keep you mentally and spiritually alive. Maybe sometimes it is better to even be killed yourself than to live with the knowledge that you have killed somebody. Is that right?

Yes. One has to find one's own path. I may be wrong here but the question of morality sometime has no easy answer. As a novelist you write about characters who find themselves and who have to make decisions one way or another. Some of those decisions do not necessarily end up benefiting them. If you think of literature, literature really is the dramatizing of the moral questions we face every day, in different kinds of situations. I want to be very clear. I don't think I can say there is one moral route. We always want to assume that. For example, during wars people make rules. So you weren't allowed to kill women or children. Even though it is a war situation, if you killed women and children – for any reason – you lost all respect. You have done something terrible. One German writer addressed this. Soldiers are praised for one's killings done in war. Everyone says, "You've done great." But if the same soldier kills during the period of peace, he is baffled by the fact that he is now being tried for having done something very, very bad. But he just did exactly the same thing he had been doing before and for which he was given medals! The war resumes the following day and now he's supposed to kill again. He has been tried for something he did during a peaceful period – yesterday – then the war resumes the following day and it's back to killing again.

Q. Let me ask you, then, about contemporary war. You talked about not hurting women or children during war. Yet what about the increasing frequency of having child soldiers? These children are being deliberately recruited, brutalized, trained as killers and they're nine, ten, eleven years old. At the same time, we find rape being used increasingly as an instrument of ethnic cleansing in war.

Yes. It's terrible. This isn't how we used to think of wars. We didn't think of wars in terms of rape, in terms of killing the defenseless. But then the question is: Is war ever really moral? People seem less horrified when one soldier and another solider fight and kill each other than when someone who isn't armed gets killed. That's a different moral calculus. It involves different questions and ways of thinking. These are problems writers deal with all the time. You put characters in different situations and the characters go through moral crises to answer certain questions one way or another.

Q. Were you involved as a freedom fighter for your country?

I actually didn't fight myself.

Q. But in your own way you fought. You can fight not just with a gun but with a pen, in your case.

I agree. I was once falsely accused. They had a sweep and I became a part of that. It happened to me when I was waiting to go to college. The policeman was armed to the teeth, saying he had to restrain me cause I resisted arrest. All I did was ask for a lawyer. I have been taught at home and at school – I went to a very Christian school, a missionary school – that the idea of lying was something you don't do. You don't lie. I'm sure people lie here and there, but not a very serious lie. I was taken to a courtroom under the false accusation that I had resisted arrest and as a result some very important prisoners escaped. They said I was fighting, which was absolutely not true. I was more scared than anything else. There was a lot of pressure in the courtroom for me to say, "Yes." In which case, I would be fined a couple of dollars and be free. "If you just say yes we will reduce the sentence." That kind of thing. In the end one has to say no but the temptation is there. You feel, maybe, maybe, maybe, and then another, don't, don't, don't, so the two are fighting all the time.

Things are complex during war. I would never say that all lies at all times are immoral because there are situations where we have to lie. There are situations where if you don't lie it's immoral and situations where it becomes more immoral for you to lie. If you are hiding a person who is in danger do you think it is more immoral to say, "Yes, I know where he is. He's hidden there. Can you see?" In that case, I'm telling the truth but it's immoral. When it comes to morality there are really no easy answers. It's not mechanical, like a robot. You use your own judgment. Maybe we should bring in the question of judgment, the question of morality. You have to make that split-second decision. How do you make that decision? On what basis do you make that decision? That is why I'm a writer. It is impossible for me to write without these questions. This is why we write novel after novel. Because there are questions you try to raise and you think you have answered them with one novel, then you find, no, once you finished you have a new set of questions. So everything you finished gives rise to another set of questions. Then you want to write something else hoping that you come to grips with that question and it goes on.

Different writers have different approaches, obviously. People work very differently. When I meet with other writers I'm always curious how they work. How do they set about writing? Different writers have different approaches. The ideal thing is to be able to explore. Some of the best novels or poems are the ones where the moral questions arise out of the very actions and feelings and emotions of all the characters. Many readers are sensitive to anything they feel smacks of moral preaching. The best works are ones with imagination. Plato's *Republic* writes about all these ideas but at one point Plato uses a parable or a myth to explain certain complex, moral issues, like the "Allegory of The Cave." In Christianity, the Bible has Jesus preaching, then he tells a story. Those stories become interesting in their own right. So every writer tries to strive for a story or an image that becomes its own statement. That's why we still enjoy these fables, or any story: because they work at the level of image and they let the image moral speak.

When I've written a story there is a satisfaction I can never get from my more academic explorations. It's very different from writing *Decolonising the Mind*. I liked that analysis very much but it doesn't give me the completeness I got from some of my very simple stories.

Q. When you personally have had to go into yourself and dig down deep to see how you feel about something, is there any principle that guides you or is it just how you feel at the moment? Do you simply have a strong sense that this is the right thing to do?

There is a mix. Things aren't always one or the other. Some may be just emotion or just reason, but the two aren't necessarily mutually exclusive. Some may be interwoven judgments. Judgment isn't simply a mathematical equation or theorem, where you say if X is true then what follows is Y. Reason comes into it but so do emotions. Feeling, intuition, intuitiveness, imagination, these all come into writing. Imagination is in everything. A scientist accumulates data. But there's also that imaginative leap where you feel now you've discovered something, this is new! Even if it is an idea, there's still the whole Eureka moment.

Q. You talk about stories. You talked about how we learn morals and deep truth better through stories, and you mentioned Plato and Jesus. Do you find something spiritual or sacred or religious that communicates to you in your own life?

Spirituality to me is what is human. What makes us different from animals is the way we come to a moral decision. You can get angry at a lion for killing somebody but you don't feel it has been immoral. You can probably kill it but you don't judge it in terms of immorality because morality has to do with choices we make. If you can't make a choice, if you are programmed to do one thing rather than another, then there's no moral dimension to your existence. If you are programmed to have no fear then the question of your being brave or a coward does not arise. You can go through a forest full of danger but do you call that bravery if you are programmed to go? But if you are scared of going through that forest and yet you make a choice to go and rescue the other people on the other side, then that brings a moral dimension to that decision. You are showing bravery – or cowardice – because of the moral judgment you bring to it. That whole area is what I call the spiritual dimension.

Now let me come to religion because it is quite important. All religions respond to this spiritual dimension of the human. They're trying to get at the spirituality and find ways of enhancing it or giving it meaning. Unfortunately, what most happens with most religions is that they end up with ritual. To show that you are really thinking, you have to drink the water before and then meditate. Or some such thing. Although initially the ritualistic acts are a means of expressing something else, this ritual itself becomes more important and it becomes the actual expression of the spiritual. The reason you find so many religious people fighting each other is because they each say my ritual of drinking water and your way of drinking become two different rituals. We both are trying to get there but we're arguing about the means of getting there. Then both of us hold to our own way. We say, "To be spiritual you have to drink the water the way I say so." Then you start fighting but in the end what they're fighting about are rituals. A particular ritual becomes symbolic of an expression of where you are going in terms of spirituality. That is how I look at religion. All societies have a higher being. That higher being is an expression of this spirituality. But people fight cause they think that their god can favor one person over another. "God favors me! I spoke to him last night in a dream. What you say he told you he did not tell to me." So we start fighting, you and I. But really spirituality is what is important. People can learn from all these different rituals if they want, but not the rituals themselves. That's my little bit about spirituality.

NOTES

1. This is according to Nicholls 2010, 89.
2. The official languages of the UN are Arabic, Chinese, English, French, Russian, and Spanish. Two are non-Western, three if you count Russian, four if you count Spanish.

15 STUCK IN THE MUD IN THE MIDDLE OF A CIVIL WAR

Fabiola, the Nicaraguan Civil War

The Sandinista Revolution (1974–79) protested the Somoza family dictatorship and the long-standing latifundio system that favored a select few while fostering overall political and economic inequality. An earthquake exacerbated the problem in 1972, with foreign aid funneled to allies of President Somoza. By 1974, the Frente Sandinista de Liberación Nacional (also called the FSLN, Sandinista National Liberation Front, or Sandinistas) began kidnapping government officials. Violence and nationwide strikes forced Somoza from Nicaragua in 1979 and brought the Sandinistas to power. They faced massive problems, from debt to environmental disaster and American hostility and in 1990, Violeta Barrios de Chamorro won a surprising victory for a coalition opposing the Sandinistas. Chamorro's own family reflected national divisions during the conflict, with two of her children Sandinistas, two opposed to the regime, and her newspaper-editor husband assassinated in 1978 during Somoza's dictatorship. Her campaign – emphasizing her desire to heal the rifts in the country as she had within her family – resonated with a country tired of fighting. President George H. W. Bush lifted the embargo and the United States has continued to work with the Nicaraguan government even after a Sandinista leader, who broke with many of his compatriots, won the presidency again in 2006.

I was born in December 1967 in Nicaragua. After escaping with some of my family at the age of twelve, I relocated to the Midwest, then eventually California in the pursuit of a new life with and for my family. Since then, I've lived a moderate life with my husband and two children as a city employee.

Q. You mentioned you had not spoken about your experiences as a child in war-torn Nicaragua. Why is that? Why wait so much time to confront the issue?

There wasn't a need to talk about my past. My family coped with it at the time and as unpleasant as it was, it wasn't necessary to relive. We wanted to refocus and move on with our lives, especially during my teen years. Now is as good a time as any to begin talking about it. Until recently my children didn't even know the major details about my family's escape from Nicaragua. I wanted them to be more mature to receive the information better. It is my job as a parent to protect them. Now that they are older, this protection is not as necessary.

Q. Can you tell me about your experiences as well as you can remember?

I grew up and experienced childhood in the city of Estelí, Nicaragua. Life in Managua in 1966 was simple. I lived with my father, mother, and my sisters Letitia, Lucilla, and Maria. Lunch and dinner, prepared by maids, were the times the entire family joined together for a meal. Breakfast was eaten quickly because everyone rushed to get to either work or school. My father was chairman of the Physics and Math department at the University of Managua. My mother was an accountant. The men of the family, since the late 1800s, were intellectuals who had studied abroad in France and Portugal and returned to Nicaragua to be military leaders and politicians. One became president of Nicaragua in the early twentieth century; others became businessmen, entrepreneurs, and some established the first radio broadcast through Nicaragua. All of these factors contributed to the family's wealth, which enabled my father to travel, study abroad, and learn from a greater perspective. My parents divorced when I was eight. The separation was very difficult for my sisters and me, especially after the earthquake of Managua in 1972 devastated the city, forcing us to relocate to Estelí, a city two hours north of Managua. In Estelí, I lived with my mother, grandmother, and three sisters. My grandmother was the head of the household. She set and enforced all family rules regardless of her very mature age. She was strict, but we respected her.

I went to school not because I was forced to, but because I desired to. Education was heavily emphasized in my family since both my parents were highly educated with college degrees. Therefore, my sisters and I were placed in the most prestigious and highly regarded school that money could buy. My Catholic boarding school, taught by French nuns, was intended only for the upper-class citizens of Nicaragua. Education for women wasn't definitely promoted but my family had the money so we attended. My years at that school would create some of my favorite memories, and be the start of my nightmares, the day the revolution found its way to us.

Q. Was it a particular day or event you remember?

"Boom, bang, boom, bang!" "Bourgeoisie!" was all I heard. My heart was racing. I peered around with a panicked expression only to find twenty other students with panicked faces as well looking right back at me. There were so many angry faces glaring at us from outside our classroom windows. Sister Elise hesitated before turning to us to give us instruction. "Hurry, to the basement," she commanded while trying to keep a controlled demeanor. All twenty students rushed to the basement to get away from the mass of leftist university students who invaded our school in support of the revolution. The revolution was coming, and we all knew it. The liberal party, called the Sandinistas, consisted of young adults in the lower economic class who felt they were being oppressed by the then President Somoza. Most of the country was ready for change, most except a few, including my family.

Q. How did the revolution against Somoza affect your family?

During the couple years leading up to the revolution, my father had become in charge of all electrical power in Nicaragua. This was one of the most important factions of the government. He was well liked and well respected for his intelligence and progressive thinking. I hardly visited him since he remained in Managua after the divorce of my parents while the rest of the family moved to Estelí. During the revolution I needed a strong figure, a father to feel protected from the chaos. Of course, now thinking back, that would've been extremely difficult since he worked for the government and the government was being revolted against. But then, I just saw him as my father, not a part of the revolution. Now I wish I had been more mature and understood the circumstances.

Q. That's understandable. Can you tell us your firsthand experience of the revolution?

In the mountains just north of our city, Estelí, we could occasionally hear guns firing during the night. We knew the rebels would be coming through the northern mountains. It was only a matter of time before the rebels would invade our city. That time came at five A.M. I was eleven years old in 1978. Every half hour was a gunshot that got louder. Voices, which soon became decipherable commands, were right outside my bedroom window. The gunfights and unexplainable fear kept us and the town confined to our houses. There was a sense of security within our house because our house was made of concrete blocks, then finished with stucco, which in turn made our houses nearly impenetrable to bullets. The less fortunate downtown residents had houses made of wood. They were fragile against the piercing bullets of the guns. The fighting came in waves for a period of two weeks. Each time the fighting subsided, we'd leave the safety of our homes to check on our neighbors. Sometimes, the news was good, but most often it was sickening.

Even though I was a child, I had a pretty good head on my shoulders and I wasn't too young at the time. I had been educated. So I was able to deduce that something very serious was happening to my friends and family. In fact, I lost some friends and many neighbors from the town to the violence of the rebels and the military. Resources also became unavailable sporadically throughout the two weeks. We were lucky to have one of the few houses that never lost access to water or electricity. Residents from the downtown would knock on our door, bringing with them any sort of container that could carry water from our kitchen faucet back to their homes. As I remember, residents of Estelí were instructed to evacuate the city. The Nicaraguan military had orders to kill anyone who remained in the city, to terminate any rebels in the city with no forgiveness for innocent residents. The military would be firing by airplane, in which case even our concrete house could not protect us. Everyone packed up any belongings they could carry and started their journey away from the city on foot.

My grandmother was very old. She said she would not be forced from her own home. A kind of sick, nervous feeling in my stomach expanded and inched up to the inner parts of my eyes, where an unforgiving stream of tears flowed down my face. "Why can't we stay?" I thought to myself. The realization of what our fate would be if we did not leave settled into our brains as we packed whatever valuables we could into a pillowcase and filed into the car to leave behind our beloved city.

We decided to travel to Managua. Most of the area was war-torn and it was incredibly unbearable. When I speak of unpleasant memories and times, it was this time of travel that I refer to most. It was the most unsure I have ever been about anything my entire life. Our two-hour journey to Managua on the main road started with all eyes on the lookout for military planes. Our trip to Managua was halted on numerous occasions, the first being a military stop. Three armed Nicaraguan military personnel stopped us for questioning and inspection. I looked out the window and saw an old jeep pierced with uncountable bullet holes and two motionless bodies lying next to the vehicle. One of the soldiers continued to ask my mother where we were going, why we were heading there, and where we were from. I watched from our car as one of the other soldiers lighted the motionless bodies with fire. The smell of burning flesh was unavoidable and unbearable as it entered the car and seeped into my lungs. I noticed my hands had begun to shake uncontrollably as I brought them up to my face to block out the unpleasant smell. I thought for sure, this was it; we were not going to make it out alive. Eventually we were cleared to continue on our path. The soldiers advised us to avoid the main road but we had no other way to Managua.

Q. Was that your first experience with death? How do you cope with that feeling?

You know now, looking back, the feeling has not changed at all. I remember every detail of that moment. The two bodies, motionless. I remember everything about how I felt, down to the white dress I was wearing and how scared of dying I was. I never felt so unfairly treated or oppressed in my entire life. And I wasn't even one of the people who lost their lives that day! It was definitely a moment that scarred me for life.

Q. What happened after that incident?

We continued. The next obstacle we encountered was a section of asphalt road that had been removed so cars could not drive on it. Our only option was to drive off the side of the road, around the missing section of asphalt. It had been raining earlier in the day and as a result, the dirt off the side of the road was extremely muddy. The car proceeded to sink into the mud and there we were, all five of us females, stuck in the mud in the middle of a civil war. Our attempts to push the car were useless. I felt as if all hope had left my body, not a trace of prayer left in my soul to plead with God. Then from off in the distance, a young man appeared from out in the forest and proceeded to help us. All he carried with him was a backpack. The young man found scraps of wood and wedged them under the wheels so we could get the wheels of our car back on the main road.

Q. A complete stranger? Sounds like something from a fairy tale or movie.

We were in disbelief too. We had no choice but to accept the help. Of course we as a group were incredibly wary of anybody we met for fear they were rebels. But we did not have a choice. Once we were back on the road and past the missing section of road, my mother asked the young man where he was headed. He said to Managua. Since we were grateful to the young man for his help, my mother offered to provide him a ride there. He accepted. We never asked the young man a single question during the remainder of the car ride, not his name, his occupation, or the reason why he was by himself on the road. He became more of a mystery as we approached Managua. The military personnel increased and security became tighter. Every time our vehicle approached a checkpoint, the young man showed his identification card and the soldiers simply allowed us to pass. "Was this man a member of the military?" I thought as I stared at the young man from the backseat. When the young man told my mother to stop the car and to let him out, we did so and never saw him again. The young man was mysterious, but a blessing in disguise. He was the one who had allowed us to enter the city safely.

Q. What was the city like? How did your family survive the oncoming rebellion?

Once in Managua, my sisters and I saw our father. I missed him so much! At this point, my family did not know the future of our family, or Nicaragua. "Was the violence going to end and our life be restored to normalness? Or were we going to have to make immense changes?" My mother decided that my sisters, my grandmother, my mother, and I were moving to California. My father chose to remain in Managua. My family was granted work visas in the United States upon boarding a plane headed for Los Angeles. We had relatives with whom we were going to stay while the turmoil in Nicaragua settled.

I soon realized my mother had no intentions of returning home. I was only twelve then but I knew my mother was not going to let me make any sort of major decision. Frankly, I did not want to leave. I wanted so badly to stay with my father. Being reunited with him was one of the most amazing feelings I have ever experienced! Until this day, I still remember looking for him in the city, sitting on a bench with my sister and seeing him come up to us to hug us. That memory is as fresh as yesterday. I will never forget it. So no regrets but mostly because I was not the one making decisions. Sadness, yes. I did consider myself very fortunate.

I wanted so many things for the people of my city of Estelí. Now, in the back of my mind, that place seems so small, so vacant. When I visited, I felt a disconnection. It's strange. I always thought I would consider it home.

In Los Angeles, I did not speak or understand any English so I was enrolled in "English as a second language" classes in seventh grade. My class placement made my sisters and me immediate targets for teenage teasing. I did not start out in a good position. My sisters and I had to find our niche, something we could put our focus on to ignore the negative judgment and allow ourselves to incorporate into a normal teenage American life. Upon entering high school, my sisters and I joined the cross-country and track team together. Letitia and Maria were older than me, as well as slimmer and more athletic. Yet I was willing to give running a try. "Left, right, breathe in, breathe out, almost there, one more mile," was all I could think about as I finished up my seven-mile run for cross-country practice. Running and studying became the center of my daily life. The cross-country and track team members became my lifelong best friends. My teammates on the cross-country and track team were smart, friendly, hardworking, but most importantly, indifferent to the color of my skin. My sisters and I were " brown." We were more what I call "light brown" but anything that was not white was inferior. Alhambra High mainly consisted of Caucasians who often asked me if I was a wetback. At the time I did not know what that term meant, nor did I know it was intended to be offensive. Classmates would interrogate me as to how I entered the country, if I was legal, whether I had to swim across the ocean to get to the United States. Confused at the questions, I would simply, but honestly answer, "I came on a plane."

Q. Having gone through what you did as a child in Nicaragua, did you feel especially different? Did you feel misunderstood?

Different yes, misunderstood not so much. That was because I never felt the need to tell them all the details of my life. Even to my own children I kept the details of my childhood and escape from Nicaragua's revolution very private. I consider that part of my life was defining, yes, but a part that is extremely personal.

Q. Did your "escape" have to do with your family's wealth and your father's prominent political position?

Oh, most certainly! That was why we were able to leave. A lot of people tried to leave but couldn't. Without my father's position and the wealth we had before, we probably wouldn't have been able to afford anything we used to get out of the country. Much less the car we traveled in. Being called a wealthy person was at that time a bad thing. We were targets of the revolution. That was why I was extra scared. I knew I had something other people wanted. The revolution focused on those in the lower economic field.

Q. Then was the revolution a result of the government or more of those revolting?

Both, but probably mostly the government. Had the Somoza government spent more time bridging that poverty gap, then perhaps the revolution would not have happened at all. I would have never learned English and come to America. A lot more people would be alive today.

Q. What happened to your father?

My high school years were when I began to wonder about my father. Was he okay? Why hadn't he called us? He must not care. I wanted him to find my sisters and me. I wanted him to leave Nicaragua and join us in California even if that meant still living separately. Not knowing at all about his safety was the most painful part.

I heard sobbing one day coming from the kitchen. It sounded like my sister, crying at our dining table, covered with legal documents. I came to find out what the matter was. On the dining table was a Nicaraguan newspaper article. It was about my father. The Sandinistas imprisoned him after they came to power in 1981. My father was a political prisoner and the communists were locking away his freedom. One could only imagine why a mother would not tell her daughters their father was a political prisoner with a slim chance of ever seeing freedom again. My mother was using the articles on my father and other documents to assemble a case of political asylum in the United States. That's why these documents were out. When we found them, my sisters and I cried together all morning.

We had been able to escape but my father was being imprisoned because of his connections to his government. There was no doubt in my mind that if my father had chosen a different occupation he would not have been in that position. His association with Somoza captured him.

Q. Did you see him again? What was your life like then?

To answer the latter, I graduated high school with excellent grades and an intense passion for running. College was in my future but I was inexperienced in the entire application and scholarship process. My dream was to attend UCLA. I thought it was the most prestigious college in California. Then to my surprise, I was offered a full scholarship to Brown University. I did not have a clue as to the rankings of universities, did not understand that Brown University was an Ivy League university. In any case, I was not able to accept the full scholarship because I was not a United States citizen at the time.

As for my father, it was not until I was twenty-three years old, with a college degree, married, and with a one-year-old son that I was able to see my father again. My father had been imprisoned for eleven years, until the Sandinistas were overthrown and a new president established. I was overjoyed to see my father once again, in the United States, away from any political turmoil, but I was also saddened for I was not the little girl he last saw in Managua. I was a grown woman with an education and family, a grown woman whom my father did not have the opportunity to shape firsthand. The strength of my father, however, even from afar, inspired me to be the person I am today.

Q. How did the loss you experienced shape the person you have become?

The friends and neighbors I knew in Estelí, who did not make it out of the city, who never had the opportunity to reach their potential, motivated me to make the most of the opportunity given to me. A part of me always felt guilt that my family survived the revolution without any casualties, that during the two weeks under fire in Estelí we continued to have water and electricity; that my mother owned a car to escape Estelí when most of the city fled by foot, and that we had the wealth to leave the country on an airplane. Leaving behind a country of my people who did not have the option of freedom led to guilt. My guilt served as fuel to my ambition and discipline for hard work. I am a professional, a wife, and a mother, but most importantly I am Fabiola and I am proud to say I am Nicaraguan.

Q. Proud even after having experienced what happened to your father and the revolutions and the government? You said yourself that perhaps the blame lies with the government.

Yes, but I'm not thinking of the government when I say I am proud to be a Nicaraguan. There was a spirit to the people, a spirit that united all Nicaraguans. Even those who revolted, as drastic and desperate and violent as their actions were, they felt a need to reform their country and be a part of it.

Q. How has relating this story to your children affected you? Do you feel happy they don't have to experience the same turmoil? How has time affected how you feel?

Telling Andre and my daughter, who is named after me, about my experiences was not as difficult as I had originally thought it might be. They received it very well and were actually incredibly surprised I had never shared that information with them. So to be able to share that information now, so openly, and freely, to someone who isn't even my child, means I've accepted it as part of who I am. I don't know when that happened but it must have happened sometime when I discovered who I truly was as a person.

Q. Do you wish to go back to Nicaragua?

Oh, I've since been back plenty of times. I travel there to visit extended family. My father now resides in Miami and the connections are as close as they can be without impeding on everyday life. Having that experience as a child has made me a better mother, I feel.

Q. Were there any coping mechanisms you put in place? Seeing all that death around you and being so terrified, that journey to Los Angeles resembles a movie.

It didn't feel as if it were a movie at the time! I just remember the rawness of it. The coping mechanisms I used at the time, even being just eleven years old, was to tell myself that death would not be that bad after all. I saw death as perhaps a release from the turmoil around me. Saw that if my family and I were to die, then perhaps it would not be as bad. Looking back, of course, I know this to not be true and my life has been full of happiness and memories. It is a sad thing to admit that at such an early age I came to such a comfortable level with death. Once you accept that your death is inevitable, and that perhaps it is better than living, death does not scare you as much.

Q. That is a very mature thing to have concluded at such a young age. I feel sorry to hear you felt death was the only way to cope with the hardship.

It wasn't the only way. I had hope in my family and in humanity still. But it seemed so impossible that day, especially after having lost neighbors and personal friends and having seen the dead bodies. All that death must've put death in my mind. I just naturally compared it to myself, and saw that perhaps the same would happen to me.

Q. Well it did not, and I am so happy it didn't. Your life is the American dream.

Thank you so much for saying that! Thank you for asking such in-depth questions. It really made me relive a moment in my life.

16 TOO MUCH WAS SEEN

Marie, the Lebanese Civil War

Raging from 1975 to 1990, the Lebanese Civil War was complex and multifaceted. Estimates suggest between 150 thousand to 230 thousand civilians were killed, with roughly a quarter of the population (one million) wounded. As Marie's story illustrates, a further one million people fled Lebanon, with the postwar occupation of Lebanon by Syria driving into exile more of the Christian population, especially the leadership. Assassinations were random and not uncommon. Little consensus exists on what triggered the Lebanese Civil War. Perhaps the most widely accepted explanation is one emphasizing the breakdown of the fragile institutional and political arrangements designed to maintain balance despite underlying sectarian divisions. This breakdown was precipitated by unequal birthrates of the diverse communities within Lebanon plus the influx and militarization of a large Palestinian refugee population, especially the arrival of Palestinian Liberation Organization guerrilla forces. The result was a militarization of feudal militia and a resulting arms race among the diverse Lebanese political factions. The war involved shifting alliances and great political uncertainty as much of Beirut lay in ruins during the 1980s.

My name's Marie and I'm eighty-two. [Marie smiled and winked.] I had five children; now I have four. I lost my eldest daughter a long time ago. During the war in '75, I was living in Beirut. During the war, they were all shooting at us.

Q. What did the government do to make you feel safe?

Nothing. The government *was* the war. The war was with the parties in politics, and the parties were divided by religion. One party would come around collecting money, saying they were using it for protection and they promised they'd protect us. But nobody protected us.

Nobody. Nobody gave us any sort of protection. My husband and I would stay up all night, every night. We would sit up all night on the balcony, watching and waiting. Watching the house, looking from the balcony. The neighbors in the building across from us would shoot at us.

Q. Your own neighbors were shooting directly at you?

Yes, our neighbors. They would shoot bullets directly from the building. Right there! They would shoot bullets! Some fifteen bullet shells I picked up from the balcony one morning. I threw them away. It was all for show. Stupid! They were with a political group. In our building there were a lot of Druze people.[1] The neighbors thought we were helping the Druze. [Shrugged.] We did help [the Druze]. But we don't have any blood on our hands. No hate. My husband and I never hurt anyone.

Q. How did you hear what was happening during the war?

We didn't watch the news. My husband hated newspapers and radio. We never looked at anything. He would tell the children to never get involved with political parties. He would scare them and they'd listen. They were good kids, always listening to him.

Q. How were the Druze part of the war?

They had their own political party and would ally with another Christian party.

Q. Were you and your husband on good terms with the Druze?

Yes, of course. Our whole town was filled with Druze and Christians. Friends; we were all friends.

Q. When the war broke out, where were you? What was happening in your life during that time?

It was terrible. My daughter was sick. She was a schoolteacher in the nearby grade school. A newlywed, only married three years when she got sick. She was living with me at the time. She had just given birth to a baby boy. I was left to care for and raise her little boy. I raised him like my own child. Even breastfed him when she got sick. I breastfed him for a whole year.

Q. So when the war started you were in Beirut. How did you know the war started? Did you hear anything?

Of course! The noise was too loud to ignore. The whole house would shake. You would hear the gunfire hitting, breaking windows. Thank God we lived on the higher floors of the building. My youngest daughter Amira could not stand the noise. She took her mattress and put it under the kitchen table and stayed under there. It was terrifying for a child. I wasn't scared. I had to pretend it was going to end soon. I had to be strong. But my daughter could not bear it. She would scream every time. Ohhh, it was all very loud! We heard rockets and gunfire. Horrible. Then when my eldest daughter Sonia got really sick, we had to take her to the hospital. It wasn't far from the house. One time we had to take her to another doctor an hour away. They bombed close by but we had to keep going, God willing. The doctor told us to stay the night and he'd perform the surgery on her in the morning. Her husband did not like the idea. He wanted to take her back down to Beirut and consult his parents. So we came back to Beirut. God help a mother's heart, my daughter was so beautiful! She was beautiful and smart. She was at the top of her class.

Q. It must have been hard to care for her and be cautious during the war. How did you manage?

It was so, so hard. I would stay with her at the hospital and then when it would be safe to walk home I'd rush home because at home, I had a whole family to take care of. Everyone was waiting for me.

Q. During the war, how did you manage to bring food for your family if there was firing?

It was hard but the neighbors would help. Whenever there would be a small cease-fire, we would rush to the store and buy what we could carry and cook small meals. It was hard feeding a family and caring for my sick daughter in the hospital and trying to raise her infant son at the same time. I helped my five children a lot. When I would work, when I first started to work, I had only Georges. Before I had Georges, I would knit. My husband was playing cards and gambling, and I knew I had to make money somehow. I said to myself, "I need to work."

There was no money. I would knit. I knitted everything. I would work with artisans and work for shopkeepers. No one knew. Nobody had any idea. I would stay up late until one A.M. and wake up at five A.M. This was before the war. During the war, I would make clothes only for some people, not for shops. I would buy yarn and fabric and make clothes in bulk: sweaters, shawls, and blankets. I would take orders from neighbors and their friends, and I would just make clothes. It helped with money. When I got money, I would spend it on more clothing material and, of course, food for my family. During the war whoever had the money and needed clothes were still buying clothes. A lot of people quit their jobs. During the war it was hard for everyone, hard to make money. But not everyone quit. Some people would risk it and some would not. Some children would go to school, and some wouldn't. It all depended on the area where you lived.

Q. How old were your children during the war?

In their late teenage years. My older sons were working. My oldest son Georges was studying in France. My son Bechara was working at the airport. And Hamid was at university.

Q. So some things remained somewhat normal?

God willing. War was on and off. Sometimes there was school and sometimes Amira would stay home for a month.

Q. Were there ever close encounters with gunfire or fire with you or your family members?

Yes, my son Bechara was nearly shot. The bullet came right past his right ear. He heard it zoom by. I was thankful to God.

Q. Was the city ever too dangerous to stay in?

Yes, especially for my oldest daughter Sonia. She wanted to move. We all decided to move to a safer city. She contacted her husband's relatives and they found us a home in another city, Byblos.

Q. Was it dangerous to leave?

It was scary. My son-in-law arranged the driving. Sometimes we would drive down a road and right after we passed, it would get hit. Right after we passed the road! Sometimes the road would get hit right in front of us as we were driving. A rocket would strike and the light would be so blinding. We always had to find detours. We arrived like a miracle. We didn't bring anything with us, only a few clothes and few basics. But my daughter Sonia brought all her things. Everyone who was living at home moved with me. My son Bechara would be working at the airport and would stay there for nights at a time because it was dangerous.

Q. So your oldest son, Georges, didn't see the war?

No, he got lucky. But when my daughter Sonia got worse, he would call and say bye to her.

Q. When you moved to your new place, was the situation with the war better?

It was better because of the people, not because of the war itself. We would go to the rooftop and see all the rockets.

Q. How were the people different?

We felt so comfortable so fast. When my daughter passed away, they arranged the whole funeral. It was sad but so comforting. Even during the war, I felt we weren't alone.

Q. Where were your relatives during the war?

Some of my sisters moved far away and some lived in close cities. In Byblos, we would stay in shelters below the buildings, with all the neighbors. One time a bomb fell into the backyard. Smoke and debris filled the shelter and we had to run to the next building for shelter. We had nothing with us sometimes; barely bread or water. There were hundreds of us crammed in a small room. Dark, damp, dirty, smelly. It was horrible. We'd be stuck there for hours until the noise stopped. It was so sad. We would see young men being dragged out of their homes. We used to see men being dragged behind a car. They would tie their feet and drive off. The men would die by being dragged around town. It was so sad. One time we saw this car with three young men get stopped by one group. The guys swore they were not from any political parties. They cried out and the men just drenched their car with gasoline and lit the car on fire. We heard them screaming as they burned. We watched from the balcony. We couldn't do anything. You'd see their mother screaming and running out the house. Someone grabbed her. She couldn't do anything! Or they'd put her right there with them!

Q. That sort of thing doesn't erase from memory. How did you feel after that?

I saw so much during the war. I saw a lot because I was the one going and coming. Sometimes I would get stuck; I would just wait. I would have to wait until dark and then try to rush back home. I had to stay strong. I knew I just had to.

Q. How did you find food when the war was very bad?

You would always find something. Everyone would help each other even if it was just some bread from here, cheese and yogurt from there. You would always manage to put something together. You couldn't go home without something to eat.

Q. So there was kindness between neighbors, even during the war?

I will never forget the people of that city. They weren't like people in Beirut. We got closer because of the war. Our city was mostly Christian but there was no hate against the others. We would find common ground. All the women wanted to bake. They thought I didn't know what to do because I was from Beirut, the "city."

Q. They didn't accept you right away?

I had to prove myself. I was proving to my family that I could keep them alive, and next I was proving to the women in the neighborhood that I could bake amazing bread. They didn't believe my mother hadn't taught me. I learned how to cook and bake by myself.

Q. When the war first started, did you automatically feel responsible to be the leader?

Because my husband was in the army, I felt I had a bigger responsibility. I would even cook for soldiers from the army. I'd cook big dishes for them. I'd wait by the road and they would pick it up. They knew who I was and they were thankful. No one else did that. No one else cared to.

Q. How did you stay safe and keep your humanity at such a tense time?

I had many connections because of my husband; he had relatives who were in the army. His uncle was a well-known general. He said if I ever heard a knock on the door and felt scared, I could dial one number. Only one number. I would have to press and he would send help. I knew many people, top people.

Q. Did you feel safe with your husband with you during the war?

Yes. When he was around. He would gamble. I wasn't allowed to say anything about it. To get money for food, I would knit. I would make covers for furniture, as well as clothing, sweaters, and blankets. It was something to do and a way to get money.

Q. How did this make you feel as the breadwinner for your family?

I didn't think about it like that. It was money. Money meant food. During the war, my husband wasn't in the army. He was retired but would get a pension. He was working at the hotel at the time. When he would get paid sometimes he would give money to his workers to go back to their homes in Syria. He took all his money with him when we were moving and he never saw his boss again.

Q. So he saved money for the move?

Yes, but every month he'd drive an hour and a half to collect his pension. One day he didn't come back. He passed away on the drive one day. Not because of the war. He had a weak heart. It was a few months after Sonia passed away. She passed away three years after giving birth. She was too weak to continue. She got sick after she gave birth. Then six months after she died, my husband died.

Q. So you had to deal with war, the death of your daughter, and then the death of your husband?

Yes. All in the same year. I didn't even know when my husband died. I heard the story later. They were on the way to the city to collect their pension, he and a few friends. His relatives lived in the city and tried to help him get to a hospital. But it was too late. I was so depressed. My daughter passed away; my husband had left me. I was in the worst shape.

Q. How did you manage to continue to provide for your family?

I had my sons who helped me a lot, but this wasn't something I was taught about when I was younger.

Note: Marie continued to discuss the time in her life where she felt most helpless. She shared personal stories of sadness and mourning which are not included in this book out of respect for Marie's privacy.

Q. How long did it take you to come to America after that?

There was an opportunity for Bechara to meet Georges, who was studying in France at the time. Bechara moved to America, and then your dad soon followed. I wanted them to leave. The airport was closed; they all drove through Syria and flew that way to France. In France, Georges took care of them. I didn't feel abandoned. I wanted them to go.

Q. Did you ask them to take you with them?

No. They didn't have papers for us.

Q. Were you alone . . . just you and Amira?

It was me, Amira, and my son-in-law Gaby, who was taking care of us and we took care of him after Sonia died.

Q. So you never asked your sons to take you with them?

No. I wanted them to go for themselves. I wasn't worried.

Q. Did you want to leave Lebanon at the time?

Yes. I had nothing to lose. I wasn't healthy. The place was ugly. I didn't want to remember anything anymore. There was no moving on. Too much was seen. From what we saw, nothing will be forgotten.

Q. Have you been back to Lebanon since the Civil War?

No.

Q. Would you want to go back and revisit?

No. I don't plan to. I've been asked and begged by my sons and grandkids to go back and visit. But too much changed. Nothing is the same over there. The people are different now. Now there are more Europeans. There's no more traditional Lebanese. It's all flashy now.

NOTE

1. Marie defined the Druze as people who belong to another religion in Lebanon, a minority religion that is neither part of Islam or Christianity but an entirely separate religion altogether. Our readings suggest Druze are members of a monotheistic religious community, located in Lebanon as well as Syria, Israel, and Jordan. They first are noted in the eleventh century and have a somewhat eclectic belief system that includes elements of Abrahamic religions as well as Gnosticism and Neoplatonism. The Druze refer to themselves as Ahl al-Tawhid (People of Unitarianism or Monotheism) or al-Muwaḥḥidūn (Unitarians, Monotheists). The formal name of the sect is al-Muwaḥḥidūn al Dururz (The Unitarian Druze). Although a minority, the Druze played an important role in the formation of modern Lebanon. During the period Marie discusses (1975–90), the Druze favored Pan-Arabism and the Palestinian resistance represented by the PLO. Many Druze supported the Progressive Socialist Party under Kamal Jumblatt's leadership. The Druze fought with other leftist and Palestinian parties against the Lebanese Front, which was constituted mostly of Christians. After Kamal Jumblatt was assassinated (March 16, 1977), the Druze community was led by his son throughout the sectarian bloodshed that lasted until 1990. In August 2001, Patriarch Nasrallah Boutros Sfeir toured the Druze Chouf region of Mount Lebanon. His positive reception signaled reconciliation between Maronites and Druze and underscored Lebanon's multicultural identity.

17 CARE ABOUT OTHER PEOPLE

Okello and Idi Amin's Uganda

From 1971 to 1979 Uganda was ruled by Idi Amin Dada, a military leader in the British colonial regiment known as the King's African Rifles, where he rose to the rank of Major General and Commander of the Ugandan Army before taking power in a 1971 coup. Idi Amin was one of the most notorious of the post-independence dictators in Africa, called the "Butcher of Uganda" for his brutal, despotic rule. Estimates of the carnage under Amin range from 100 thousand to half a million opponents killed, tortured, or imprisoned. Amin's rule was characterized by massive human rights abuse, ethnic persecution, nepotism, corruption, and political repression, including extrajudicial killings. Despite Amin's brutal crushing of opposition, dissent continued within Uganda. After Amin attempted to annex the Kagera province of Tanzania (1978), the Uganda–Tanzania War broke out and led to his downfall. Amin fled to Libya and Saudi Arabia, where he died in exile on August 16, 2003.

I am Okello, born in Gulu, Uganda, on August twenty-fourth, 1955. In my immediate family I have ten siblings. Six boys, five girls. I am number four. That is my immediate family. My parents are both dead. Three of my brothers and three sisters are alive; four are dead.

Life as a child was very exciting, very productive because we grew up as a family and as a community. That's why you say in Africa that it takes a village to raise an African. School was the most important thing. It's part of me. In my family, education was the most important target. That means you must wake up in the morning, you must take care of your chores; you must go to school. There are no ifs, ands, or buts about it. That's the rule. Just school, school, school, and study, study, study. That's basically what my parents taught me. My mother was a teacher. She was very strict about how you have to learn. You have to go to school. You have to be educated. Because she was a teacher she taught me how to read, write, how to do mathematics. She taught all those things to me. A typical day, you wake up in the morning. You take care of your chores. There is no grocery store, so you grow your own food. You wake up in the morning, go to the garden, take care of your chores, then before eight o'clock, you wash up and take a bath, not a shower. You take a basin with water in it, then splash the water on. You clean up very well. Then you have to go to school. That's the beginning of a school day. At school, there is no lunch provided. There is no food. If your school is near your house, you come home. Your aunty may have cooked some food and you come and eat lunch. Then, you rush back to school. That's just the way it is. You walk barefoot. We didn't have shoes and we walked to school. For me, the school for the first eleven years was half a mile to one mile away, very near. But for my last year, it was seven miles away. I walked every day. Rain or snow, I walked. [Okello laughed.] Rain or sunshine, I walked. There is no snow!

I went to a boarding school called St. Joseph's College, Layibi. It is exciting, just like an American kid going to college. That's the first time you are out of home, and that is your freedom. That freedom you develop – the euphoria of being free – without parental control, that is basically what boarding school is about. It's where you meet your friends. You develop a close-knit friendship with a group of kids who live in the same neighborhood. That's basically what I did. I had a very exciting group of friends from the same Gulu area. The senior secondary school absorbs everyone from all over the country so you might find somebody coming from one hundred or two hundred miles away. Then you form a clique, the group you do everything with. You study together. You try to do things together. You try to help each other.

It was a boy's school. There was a girl's school almost ten miles away. The school I went to was a boys' school. There was some other mixed school where boys and girls were together but the school I went to was completely boys.

The political world, when I was going to senior secondary school, was normal. In 1971, when Idi Amin overthrew the government by military coup, that's when everything changed. When he overthrew the government, he decided the politics at that time. Most of the people from my tribe – the Acholi tribe – we were in the military. We were known to be the best military people. So he decided to eliminate all of our leaders. That's exactly what he did for the first four or five years.

When he first came, he started by eliminating – in other words killing – all the military officers from my tribe. Some ran away. He got rid of most of them. I lost a lot of relatives at that time. Then after he finished that, he started going after the young men who come from my tribe. That's when I got involved in the politics, when the word came they were going to get rid of all young men from my tribe. We decided to run away. I left Uganda in 1976.

Q. Before you ran away, during this period of five years, what happened?

Idi Amin affected not just my tribe; he affected my family as well. My uncle was one of the people who was affected. One of the uncles was a colonel in the military at that time. He lives in Virginia now. He was almost killed but he ran away. His brother was severely beaten. They busted his testicles and eventually he died of that injury. There were a lot of people hurt. When they took us to Nairobi, they took us to different places. There was no refugee camp at that time so a group of us – about twenty of us – were put in a church. The church was the one taking care of us at that time. The church only provided where to sleep. The United Nations provided the money for us to eat. They give you very little money. But the church gave us a place to sleep. In the morning, in the evening, around six o'clock, they would allow us to go to that big church hall and we'd put our mats there and sleep and cook. In the morning at five A.M. we would have to wake up and clean everything because the church hall was also being used as a kindergarten. That's just the way it was.

We were there for a year. Fortunately, because most of us had some kind of education, we got jobs as teachers in Kenya. I was teaching Biology and Chemistry. That's how we got extra money. Extra money, just to survive.

Q. What language did you speak? Did you speak Acholi when you talked?

We speak English. From grade one. That's the first thing they teach you: how to speak English in Uganda. You have to. You have no choice. Uganda is an English-speaking country. Kenya is a Swahili-speaking country so everything was supposed to be taught in English. We knew science and most of us were educated enough, up to high school level. We knew all the science experiments, how to do them. They give you a book and we just start teaching out of that book.

I was there two years, then they ran out of money. But there was a visiting professor – a chemist – who is in private practice. He decided to take me home and pay for my school on condition that I go to a cheap school. I went to Metropolitan State College in Denver, and he finished paying for my school. I rented a small room with a kitchen – a studio; you would call it a studio.

Q. Did you have a job, or were you just going to school?

I ended up getting a job as a student engineer; that was part of the money that was helping me finish school. I graduated in 1983. When I graduated, I ended up getting a job with a suburban city in Denver. I worked there for about a year. Then I decided I wanted to look for work. There was a magazine that listed a lot of jobs in California. I wanted a warm climate. So I looked for Atlanta because it was warm. I was much better off than before. I had been in what were called Acholi Camps. You will find entirely displaced persons camps. You will see the horrible conditions. That is what genocide is really like. A genocide is when a whole group of people are put together and they are dying slowly, very slowly. Basically that's what happened.

Q. Were you able to save as many of your siblings as you could?

They had already left.

Q. So you helped get them out. It is 1985, 1986. You are a young man in Northern California. You didn't get the job interview. Where does that now leave you?

I came to San Diego in 1986 with my relatives. I went to interview in Northern California. But I see my relatives were over here so I started to look for work around San Diego. I got a job with the City of San Diego, where I worked about twenty-three or twenty-four years.

Q. How did everything you went through affect who you are today? How did it shape who you are today?

The thing is, nobody wants to leave where they were born and raised but in a lot of countries in the world, people are forced to. The only countries where you are not forced to leave are in the developed world, mostly Britain, Europe, and America. Nobody is forced to leave America but a lot of the other African countries and other developing countries, small countries – South America – you can be forced to leave at any time. It makes you grow up very fast because when you leave home and you are twenty-one, you have to learn how to take care of yourself.

Q. Now that you are here, I am assuming you are happy. At least you have more stability. You have more of a life here. What does that leave you, as a fifty-five-year-old man today? What's next?

Next thing is to continue to try to help the people who are still left there, people who are still suffering. Of course, secondly, you have to use your resources so the people and the organizations you know can help people who remain there. Then thirdly, of course, you have to be able to do things on your own – I do things on my own – to help people at home. It is very uncommon, of course, but I share all of my resources with the people at home.

Q. What about religion?

Religion is the pillar. My home was right next to a church and you [Okello pointed to his daughter, who was interviewing him] have been there. Church is a block away. Every Sunday you go to church. The church is right there. The church teaches you some moral values. Whether you grow up with it as an adult, that is your choice. But it taught you moral values. You have to be honest. You don't cheat. You don't act crazy and stupid. It teaches other moral values also. You have to give and help other people. That is what church teaches you. That is the religious part I grew up with.

Q. So you grew up with that religious aspect and implemented that into your life today. What about your siblings? Do they try to help Uganda or give back? Or are they distant and leave it in the past?

One of the values you grow up with is the value of family and community: your parents, your neighbors, your uncles. They teach you how to do things for other people. That is why I do things for people, and continue to do things, even today.

Q. What about having your siblings leave? Did that make you closer and more connected? Or have you remained connected?

When you are forced to leave, you always think about your siblings. That's what I did. I thought about my siblings and that's why I paid for eight of them to escape to London. That's why you have all those relations over in London. It teaches you that you have to care about other people.

Interviewer (Okello's daughter): *People often deal with events that become hard for them in two different ways. (1) They can talk openly, sharing their thoughts and emotions with those around them. (2) They* *can choose not to talk about their past, keeping their thoughts and emotions to themselves. Perhaps these people fear that if their painful past is brought forth, others might treat them differently instead of helping them move on in life. My father falls into the second category. My father never told his children what he had been through in Uganda or the events that occurred after he escaped. Before this interview, everything I knew about my father came from my mother or my father's relatives. This interview was the first time my father opened up and discussed these events with me.*

18 PEOPLE SUFFERED GREAT LOSS
Reza and Afghanistan under the Soviets

From December 1979 through February 1989, the Soviet Union supported the Marxist–Leninist government of the Democratic Republic of Afghanistan in a battle against the Afghan Mujahideen[1] and foreign "Arab–Afghan" volunteers. The Mujahideen received extensive military and financial support, unofficially and often covertly, from many countries, including the United States, the United Kingdom, Saudi Arabia, Pakistan, Taiwan, Indonesia, China, and Israel. As Soviet involvement dragged on, bleeding the USSR, the Afghanistan occupation became known as the "Soviet Vietnam." Russian forces withdrew from Afghanistan in 1989 but war then broke out among the various warlords and militia units, with the Islamic fundamentalist group known as the Taliban taking charge. After the World Trade Center and the Pentagon were attacked on 9/11, the United States targeted Afghanistan as a hiding place for Islamic terrorists. United National Security Council Resolution 1378, of November 2001, condemned the Taliban for "allowing Afghanistan to be used as a base for the export of terrorism by the al-Qaeda network and other terrorist groups and for providing safe haven to Osama bin Laden, al-Qaeda and others associated with them, and in this context supporting the efforts of the Afghan people to replace the Taliban regime." War ensued, led by the United States, which continues to have troops in Afghanistan in 2014.

October seventeenth, 1949, is my legal birth date but we don't keep track of the real birth year in Afghanistan.[2] For the past thirteen years I have lived in California. I was in college in 1974. That was my fourth and final year in the university. I was your age. Daoud Khan, the cousin of the King Zahir Shah, did a coup d'état and took power from the king.[3] The king was in Italy for vacation for some health treatment. This pattern is very common in the history of Afghanistan. The king has always fallen from power and another king has taken over. But for the first time, when Daoud Khan took power in 1973, he announced he took power as a president, not as a king. This was something new for everyone. At first we all wondered how one governs a presidency. People were somewhat happy there was a new presidency, especially the young generation. People in college were especially happy about the situation. But slowly things changed. Daoud Khan came into power by the help of the Communist Parcham Party [a faction of the People's Democratic Party of Afghanistan and one of two Afghan Communist parties]. He held power for six years despite pressure from Western countries and Middle Eastern powers, like Saudi Arabia and Iran. This all was around 1978 or 1979. I was about thirty. Daoud Khan went to Russia for a visit. The head of the Russian communists told Daoud he has to be friendly and careful with the communist parties. Daoud got mad and left the meeting. The Russians tried to convince him to sit down, saying they wanted to talk. But Daoud said, "No. There is nothing left for me to say because Afghanistan is a free country. We will do whatever we want. We are not servants of Russia."

A year later, the communists did a coup d'état and took power from Daoud Khan. That was 1978. The communists had two major parties: Parcham [usually Farsi-speaking people] and Khalq [Pashtoun-speaking]. Both were puppets of Russia. A year before the coup, Russia told them to unite to bring down the government. There was a big struggle and the last night of his presidency, Daoud Khan put all the heads of the Communist Party in jail. Before he could do anything with them, the Communist Party – which had a big influence on the army – took power. Of course the Russians were behind this. They were very active in the army. The Afghan army was under the influence of Russia. Ammunitions, teachers, everything was from Russia. The USSR had spies and took the power and gave it to the communists.

From there, a big struggle started inside Afghanistan because the Afghan people were not communists. They didn't like communism. They were Muslim and no matter what, they stood against the communists. There was a big struggle, especially in the countryside. Slowly people started to rise. The government started to fight them. But the government was weak and after the initial unity between Parcham and Khalq dissolved, within a year there was fighting between the two groups. The Khalq took power from the Parcham and sent them away, as ambassadors to communist countries, like Russia and Czechoslovakia.

Q. Do you remember what it was like when the Russians came, that first day?

When the Russians came I wasn't in the capital. I was in Herat, about one thousand miles away from Kabul. We were eating dinner. Radio Afghanistan announced a demonstration in the capital. They said people wanted to disturb the peace inside Afghanistan and the government took action and put all the heads of Parcham in jail.

The next day when we woke up, there was music on the radio. We lived with some communist people in our work area. When they got some phone calls and left, we got suspicious that something is going on. Our feeling was right because later we understood that the communists took power in Afghanistan and killed President Daoud with his family. Seventy-two people! Women, children, all killed inside the castle. The next day we still didn't know what was going on. We were wondering who had power. Was it really the communists, or was it the Muslim Brotherhood, the Muslim hardliners? By evening it was announced that President Daoud was killed. Then we knew it was the communists. They didn't announce who took power. They just said a revolutionary guard was controlling the country.

For two years the situation was like that. The communists had power, with Russia giving them lots of ammunition. Sometimes their airplanes bombarded the areas which weren't sitting quietly. But slowly the situation got worse for the government and some areas fell under the freedom fighters' hands. Russia had no choice but to go into the country with the army and fight the people there. Before that happened in 1980, we had no idea what was happening behind the curtain. But we saw a line of Russian army planes coming to the Kabul airport. People living in the area told us that all night and day lots of tanks were coming, and nobody knew what was going on.

There were two heads of the Communist Party: Hafizullah Amin, who was working in foreign affairs, and Taraki, who was the president. Amin was a keen guy. Both were Pashtoun. Amin got his master's degree in America, then suddenly he came to Afghanistan to work and establish the communist party.

One day my family and I were sitting at home having a good time; before lunch, my brother Hestahma was outside. He called and asked if Ghosh Tashi, my brother-in-law, was still there. I said yes. He said, "Tell him to go home as fast as he could." The situation was bad and there was a lot of commotion in the city, especially around the presidential palace.

My brother-in-law asked me, "What was that?" I said it was nothing. My mother was setting the table, ready to serve. I told my brother-in-law that it was nothing, just that Hestahma called and said there is some commotion inside Kabul and he wants us to be calm, quiet, and alert. Ghosh Tashi jumped up suddenly and put a pill under his tongue, because he had a bad heart problem. The whole family was down in the street behind him as we called a taxi. We heard gunfire and heard cannon fire. They jumped in the taxi and went home.

Meanwhile the political leaders, Hafizullah and Taraki, went to Havana. When they came back, Taraki went directly to Russia, and Hafizullah to Kabul. In Russia, Taraki was told, "Hafizullah Amin is someone we don't trust because he studied in America and maybe is CIA, so we want him out. We want to help you take care of him." Two, three days later when Taraki came, everything changed. The head of the Communist Party and Hafiz Amin were shot at but weren't hit by the bullets. Amin escaped uninjured because the person with him jumped in front of him and took the bullet. The next day the Russian embassy interfered. They told Taraki to tell Hafizullah Amin to come, that no one would harm him. When Amin came, they fired on him, but he survived. The next day he took power and put Taraki in the jail inside the palace. After a couple of days they killed Taraki with a pillow. Hafizullah Amin became the head of the Communist Party. There was mistrust between him and the Russians because Russia wanted him to get out and Taraki to have power, but Taraki was out. There was a lot of killing among the communists.

Q. Did you know anyone who was killed?

No, but one of my friend's brothers was the one who killed Taraki with a pillow and they put him in jail. This guy usually tried to convince us to join the Communist Party. We were very close friends. We worked in the same agricultural research farm and we joked about all this stuff. He said, "You should be careful. Don't say this stuff to other people. I know we are friends but it is my job to convince you to join the communist party. But if you don't come, please don't say anything bad about us to other people because it is dangerous." We slowly came to understand that yes, it is dangerous!

After Amin took power, in the four months he held power, he killed about fifty thousand people. All of them doctors, teachers, big people who were opposed to communism or actual communists who had had power. He was like Hitler in some ways. He wanted to have power and have no one on top of him. Russia knew if they put a little pressure on him, he would call for America's help. His cook put some kind of medicine in his food that made him sick. But before that Russia made him sign a treaty that said Russia would help Afghanistan with all means. Three days before he was killed, a lot of Russian airplanes came. One night, a week before Christmas 1979, there was fighting outside. We had a house in the mountains around Kabul so we rushed outside and saw, at the palace, a lot of rockets and fire.

The next day when we woke up we saw Russians all throughout the town. People were sad; they saw Russians for the first time, a foreign army. We used to work in the D___ farm. The next day we went there; half of our building was destroyed because it was just behind the castle. The farm was destroyed completely. The situation was grave. Everyone was wondering what else was coming.

Our family was sad because we were now against the Russians. That was a surprise for everybody. People were thinking the Russians were behind all the change one hundred percent but when they saw the Red army it was different. Slowly the people came and the Russians started destroying the suburbs because the Mujahideen were rising from that area. So there was a lot of bombardment, a lot of killing.

Q. Did you ever think of joining the Mujahideen or your brothers?

No. I didn't have that belief and I wasn't strong enough to join. We just said we couldn't join them. We knew they were fighting for their own benefit. But they were using the poor people to fight. Their leaders weren't people you should trust; everyone agrees on that now. Those people are not the puppets of America and they had the blood of a lot of people on their hands, all of them. They weren't good people.

Q. So what were you doing at this time?

I was working. I stayed out of the fighting. Pressure came every day to get involved. As the fighting came close to Kabul, there was a lot of killing. Prices went up. There was nothing coming inside the city. They said everyone should join the army, and this is why my brother Hestahma escaped, and Haider. They escaped to Pakistan. In Afghanistan everyone who was twenty-two had to go to the army for one or two years. Haider didn't go to the army after college because the government told him to work in the urea factory in Mazar-e-Sharif in the North. Urea is a fertilizer. After the situation got bad and there was no one to fight for the communist regime, they announced everyone would fight. This is why Haider escaped. They next announced everyone who was eighteen to forty had to join the army, no matter what. This time everyone was on their feet to get out of Afghanistan. I came home and talked to my mother. I said I had to go with Hestahma and couldn't wait a day. No matter what, I had to get out of there. I told her we would be in Pakistan. I told Ahmad Shah – my youngest brother – to sell everything and come after us. He was shocked.

He was in his last year at the university. Twenty-two, still young. He didn't know what to do but he agreed. When the government looked at the reaction of the people, suddenly they saw the entire ministry was empty. No one was there to work for them. So the next day they announced they didn't mean the people who had served already or had a bachelor's degree. These people were exempt. That gave a little break for me to get ready and sell everything. But Hestahma went. Ahmad Shah was in college; they didn't bother him. But you have to carry a document that said you passed your army duty or are studying or finished studying. I asked Ahmad Shah, "Do you want to stay two more months to get your degree and go?" He said no, because the situation was getting really bad. So we decided to get out. He never did get his degree. He has only two months left but he wanted to leave instead. We came to Pakistan in August 1982.

Q. How did you leave?

There were many ways to leave. Remember how I told you about that [half] sister who had come to my house? That sister had a son who was in college but wanted to get married to a girl, but because of the bad situation – the father had passed away a few months before from a heart attack – my sister called me and said she wanted to get Waheed out of Afghanistan. The problem was that he was in love with a girl and wanted to marry her. I said that was great and he should do it. But she said no, she didn't want anyone to know he was leaving and so she couldn't go out to request the marriage from the girl's family. She told me, "It is your job to go out and to arrange everything." I went and talked to the girl's father. I said I had a strange proposal. "These two are in love but my nephew can't stay here. He must get out. But he won't leave because of her. He wants to marry her and both of them should leave. It should be a very quiet ceremony; no one should know about this ceremony."

He told me his brother was his neighbor. How would he not know of the marriage?

I said not even he could know. Because there was a lot of talk. If the word got out that Waheed is leaving Afghanistan, the government would stop him.

Q. They were worried about people finding out he's leaving, not that he's getting married?

Yes. So finally, after a few conversations, they agreed. We had a small party inside their house and they married each other. Every night he took a cab to her house and then early in the morning he took a cab back to his house because no one could know that he wasn't home. We found somebody, a close friend of my sister's family, who would take us: me, my mom, Ahmad Shah, my nephew, and his wife. We sold everything and we left. We went to Ghazni and from there to Pakistan. The guy had a good car, a Ford SUV-type car. We sat there with some other families and went to Pakistan.

Q. When you were selling all your stuff, wouldn't people get suspicious?

Probably. No matter what, people know. The worse thing was that my sister had left a year earlier and part of their home – they had a huge house – the downstairs was empty when my sister left. They rented that section to two brothers who were big communists. Very big communists! And very rich people. Very young, too. My sister's mother-in-law, who was like a mother to me – she called me son – she brought them to the house. I was surprised. She told me not to worry, that they were good people. Even the communists knew people were leaving. So they came into the house and they were the ones who bought our stuff. [Reza laughed.]

Q. Did they know you were leaving?

Yes. They said not to worry. First the good stuff was sold to friends, family, and people like that. Then the stuff that was left we sold to the thrift store. And we were ready to go.

Q. Was crossing the border hard? How did you cross?

We went to Ghazni, and from there we went near the border, and stayed one night at the house of a person who took us in. The next day, we went to the border. That side of the country belonged to the Mujahideen so we had to have permission from the head of the Mujahideen. Maybe you can't believe it, but on the way there, there was a shawl on the back of the guy we paid to bring us out. We paid a lot of money. Thirty thousand Afghanis, which was a lot at that time. He had something on his back. When we got to his home, he said, "I'm going to get something from the leader of the Mujahideen to let us through the mountains." He came back very late and when we left, he said it had taken a lot of time to get that Mujahideen leader drunk enough to sign this.

I said, "What are you talking about?"

"Did you see that bottle I was carrying, the one that I told you was medicine? That was whiskey I brought from Kabul to get him drunk so he'd sign this."

So maybe every twenty or thirty kilometers we had to show some Mujahideen this paper. A lot of communists were escaping, too. It was an income for them because we had to pay them in every area. In Qamar al-been, the leader of the Mujahideen who used to be a sergeant in the army or something, whose house we came to, he told us to stay in that room tonight and he would see if he would let us go further into Pakistan. That was close to the border.

So we stayed there. We found out that room belongs to him and he wanted us to pay the rent for one night. In the bottom was a bakery. Early in the morning, there would be smoke in the room so you woke up coughing. The person who took us came and said, "Don't worry. He just wants some money, so give him as much as you can and tell him this is for the Mujahideen. Just make any excuse to give him some money."

Before he came to see us, we thanked him for his hospitality. We told him he was so brave, and that here was some money we wanted to give to the Mujahideen.

He said, "Oh, okay. Go ahead. Don't worry. You are such good people."

He didn't search our bags or anything. We sat in the car and went to the Pakistan border. We got there about ten P.M., got the bus ready, and were on our way to Peshawar. We were in a hotel for about twenty days until I found a friend who helped us find an apartment. We came to Islamabad and lived there for about eight months. It took about eight months to get our paperwork at the American embassy approved. They accepted our asylum application and we came here as refugees. Mr. Kashta's elder brother sponsored us. He's been in the United States two and a half years. He was working and had an American wife, so they sponsored us and we came to the United States. We came here on June fifteenth, 1982, to Chicago. After a month I found a job, and life started to grow here. It was an interesting history because of all this commotion and changing and fighting. There was a lot of sadness in our short lives. A lot of killing. The only person who lived to die normally was the king himself. Everyone else was killed by someone else.

Q. How did you keep your hope when you saw all the killing?

To tell you the truth, first, we had a strong feeling the communists would finally fail in Afghanistan. But we didn't know that when the Mujahideen took power there would be fighting, killing, and destroying the city. When the Taliban came in 1996, they brought a lot of good things. Like there weren't any killings in the areas they controlled. But still there was no hope, no happiness, and there was no college. Even in the six years they didn't establish anything to make the country grow or bring hope for the people. Just the notion that the ladies should stay home and girls couldn't go to school. Everyone was escaping because it was bad. There was fighting between the Taliban and the Northern Alliance. Communism wasn't accepted in our society.

My belief is that the Taliban had no idea that the Arabs who came in through al-Qaeda were going to destroy the buildings in New York, because the Taliban at the time were having a good life. A week before the attack they killed Ahmad Shah Massoud [the leader of the Northern Alliance].[4] In fact they had destroyed the entire Northern Alliance. It was easy for them to capture all of Afghanistan, and that's it! But I don't think they knew about the plans for the World Trade Center.

Q. They didn't know what they had planned for the whole world?

That's right. Now Afghanistan is free, but not really. Al-Qaeda still has influence. There is still fighting and destruction. But there is hope. Those who have Western influence will continue to fight al-Qaeda. It'll take a few generations until there is peace. There is potential that things will move forward and not backwards.

Q. When you were living in Afghanistan, did you see any killings?

Yes. They took people off the streets. There were kidnappings. The communist government wanted to fill the army no matter what. So they were searching the houses, the streets, the buses, asking if the people had documents to show they were exempt from the army. If you didn't have it, that was it. They took you before your family knew. My family had some kidnappings, too. My mother's cousin went to the army and didn't come back. His parents are still looking for him. They asked us to search America. Maybe they thought their son was here. It was really sad.

My cousin was killed by a rocket, one of the Mujahideen rockets in the market. He was torn into pieces. My uncle wrote a letter to us in America and said the only way to know it was Aref was by his mustache because half of his head was blown off. A lot of people suffered great loss. But fortunately, it wasn't really close family, like brothers or sisters.

Q. How did you keep your humanity when you saw all the killings?

First was praying. The second thing was helping the Mujahideen. No matter what groups were there, give some money. We also sent money to friends, family, and charity. It was a very bad situation, especially in the Taliban time. But what's coming in the future, I believe everything will turn good. But not soon.

Q. Do you think it will be a democracy?

Eventually. I know it is very corrupt now, from the president down to the people who work as a guard. It is very bad. The western ideal makes people hungry for the dollar; it drives corruption, to get to a level where they have something. The gap between the rich and the poor is huge.

We were never rich, and never too poor. The people were kept isolated from the western influence and education because the country was kept as a buffer for the region. No one wanted change there. It wasn't introduced to western ideas. Everything was locally based. People were comfortable. Even the king had nothing to compare with the people in Afghanistan now. The poor are really poor now.

Q. Do you think the Russians were crueler than the Taliban or the Mujahideen?

All of them are the same.

Note: Reza has never returned to Afghanistan and says he probably never will because he believes the situation had not improved since the invasion.

NOTES

1. Mujahideen means those who struggle in the path of God.
2. Names other than those of historic figures have been changed to protect privacy.
3. Sardar Mohammed Daoud Khan or Daud Khan was born July 18, 1909. Daoud served as Prime Minister of Afghanistan from 1953 to 1963. He became the President of Afghanistan after he deposed his first cousin and brother-in-law, Mohammed Zahir Shah. Daoud did not declare himself king, serving instead as

the first president of Afghanistan, from 1973 until he and his family were assassinated in April 1978 as part of the Saur Revolution instigated and led by the Communist People's Democratic Party of Afghanistan (PDPA). Daoud Khan was heavily involved in the politics of the region and is known as someone who followed relatively progressive policies for Afghanistan, including economic modernization and giving more rights to women.

4. A political and military leader, Ahmad Shah Massoud (1953–2001) was a central figure in the fight against Soviet occupation of Afghanistan. He was assassinated on September 9, 2001, possibly on orders of al-Qaeda.

19 RELIGION MIXED WITH POLITICS CREATES BAD THINGS

Leyla and the Islamic Republic of Iran

The 1979 Iranian Islamic Revolution overthrew the Iranian monarchy under the Shah Mohammad Reza Pahlavi, and replaced it with an officially Islamic Republic under Ayatollah Ruhollah Khomeini. Public demonstrations against the Shah and his repressive government began in October 1977. They intensified and erupted into widespread civil resistance – both secular and religious – with demonstrations and strikes that paralyzed oil-rich Iran from August until December 1978. The Shah left for exile mid-January 1979, and Ayatollah Khomeini returned within weeks, to a great welcome. Iran held a national referendum, voting to become an Islamic Republic and to approve a theocratic constitution making Khomeini Supreme Leader of the country in 1979. The Iranian revolution surprised the world, partly because it was precipitated without the usual triggers of revolution: defeat during war, a financial crisis, a disgruntled military, or a peasant uprising. The speed and the popularity of the rebellion further startled observers because it was the first time a modernizing monarchy was replaced by a theocratic state.

Things have not improved in Iran since Leyla left. The 1980–88 war with Iraq killed hundreds of thousands of people and cost Iran billions of dollars. The United States–imposed economic sanctions and emigration of 2–4 million skilled craftsmen, entrepreneurs, and educated professionals – such as Leyla – resulted in income levels below those of pre-revolutionary Iran. Mahmoud Ahmadinejad, the controversial president of the Islamic Republic of Iran from 2005 to 2013, was condemned for both his economic failures and his violations of human rights. His support for Iran's nuclear energy program and his anti-Semitic statements denying the Holocaust further isolated Iran and the current situation remains unclear under the present (2014) leadership in Iran.

During the Shah, a lot of people were not happy. Democracy was not perfect, but it was better than after the revolution. During the Shah's rule, you were free to move around, free to go on holiday. The Shah's government did not force you to do anything. Even your personal life, they did not interfere with. They had notions of freedom. Iran was one of the first countries that talked about human rights. The Iranian population has it in them. The most unfortunate thing about Iran is the location. It is in the middle of everything.

The revolution was in 1979. I was teaching social science at the Pahlavi University. We did not have a good situation. When you teach social science, social science is about everything, past and present events. The revolution was Islamic; they did not want to talk about politics. I was talking about human rights. I wanted to talk about social science and basic human rights but the government said I couldn't. More than ten times they warned me, "Do not talk about this. Do not talk about that!" Finally I realized I could not stay in Iran and teach social science. After the revolution, in the 1980s, there were a lot of educated students, especially in the fields of politics, who wanted to talk about things that went against Islam and its ideas. For a few months some of my students were hidden in our basement because the government was looking for them, just because the students were speaking out against the government's ideas. Three students, who were twenty-two, twenty-three, maybe less, maybe even twenty years old, were hiding in my house for three months, right in my basement. Nobody knew! Everybody was looking for them. We are Islamic so if you help somebody, they know you are faithful to them. After three months, the students told me they must go. They left my house. One of them was arrested and killed; two kept hiding and now, I believe, are still alive.

I always had very good relations with my students. They would frequently come to my house. We used to talk. We discussed everything. During this time a lot of young people were imprisoned, especially during the war between Iran and Iraq, from 1980 to 1988. More than five hundred thousand young people were killed! When the war broke out, I had a very difficult time teaching social science. My oldest son was thirteen years old, and they wanted all the young people, even children, to go and fight in the war. They passed a law, which meant no one above the age of fifteen can leave the country; they must stay and fight in the war. When I read in the paper that they were taking all the young people to war, I knew we had to leave the country before my sons reached that age. We were very lucky we could leave. My daughter was in junior high school but she experienced the gravity of it all. They wanted her to cover up, and they explained to her what she should be.

Oh, I have a lot of reasons for leaving: the inability of me to do my job properly, concern for my daughter, for my sons. I remember we had a huge pool. One week, I put all the books from my huge library collection, everything I had at my home, in the pool and burnt them. If the government knew I had those books . . . [paused] there was everything, books about politics, the real politics of Iran; one should not have such books! If the government knew I had these books I cannot imagine what they would have done to me. I would have been killed. This was in 1984, right before we left. The government would demand university professors be silent about this topic or that topic. What should I talk about, then? I didn't know much about Islam and I thought to myself, "This is my profession! It is my profession to talk to my students about all kinds of political events. What should I talk about to my students?"

"Just talk about Islam and the life of Ayatollah Khomeini," they said. "Go to some classes and learn about Islam, then you will be able to do your job. We should not talk about politics and human rights before talking about Islam." To them nothing existed before Islam. I could not stand it anymore! I left the country; finally, we went to England. Over there, we could live our lives! We moved at the beginning of 1984. We stayed in England for about three years.

I told my children about the fact that the government was restraining my ability to teach, and that they were not letting me properly publish my books. I remember when I published one of my books; they asked me to take eighty pages out of the book. It was a book about another religious leader in another revolution that happened before the Islamic revolution in 1979. What kind of book is it if you take eighty pages out of it? I was still able to work on two of my other books while I was living in England. I was able to come back to Iran sometimes, but after 1986, I stopped it. I think it was better for me then to stay with my children.

I have three sons and one daughter. I decided to do something else because still I had a bad memory of teaching social science. I did not want to be against them or with them; I would rather just be neutral. So I decided to do something else. I studied online to become a librarian.

Q. What influenced your decision to move to England? Was it mainly because you did not want your sons to be drafted into the military?

Yes, that was one of the reasons. Another was for my daughter's sake. She was so restricted. Not only did she have to be covered up, she loved sports and could not play them. A lot of professions were forbidden as well, agriculture, social science. . . . We had a lot of problems at the beginning of the revolution, especially for the women. For two years, they closed the University of ___. We had to change the whole system! A lot of people left the country then. I remember the prime minister of Canada gave a lecture. He said thank you to the revolution of Iran, because Canada got six thousand educated people from us. All the intellectuals, all the good teachers, they moved. I am happy I came here [the United States] because there is so much opportunity, so much opportunity for my children to study, to continue their education. They were very smart. My daughter got to pursue what she wanted; she got a PhD in it! All three of my sons have been very successful as well. I do not want anything else. I got my license as a librarian and I worked as a professional for seven years, until I got cancer in 2007. Right now I'm working as a volunteer at a home that deals with kids with cancer. I also volunteer at a home for people with Alzheimer's, activating their minds, to help them remember things.

Q. Did you have any trouble leaving Iran in 1984? Did they try to stop you?

They stopped me from teaching! They closed my university completely in 1982. At that time it was not easy to get a visa for the United States. That is why we decided to go to England and then tried to get visa for the United States.

Q. Earlier you described how you took in university students. . . .

Yes, in 1980. I hid university students in my house because the government was looking for them. They looked for young people who were against Islam. A lot of them were thrown into prison. I hid three students in my house for three or four months in my basement. Nobody knew about it. Not even our neighbors.

Q. Were you aware of the risk you were taking in hiding them?

I think everybody has a mission. It was the least I could do for my students. They were not just my students; they were my friends, and I love them. They are young and smart. They went into the streets to protest and they were arrested and killed. The army had no rules at the beginning. Even right now. A few years ago, do you remember? Did you watch it on television? A lot of young people were arrested and killed for speaking out against the undemocratic Iranian election. They had a symbol: "Where is our vote?" They all voted for someone else so they wondered, "Why did Ahmadinejad get elected?" They only wanted answers.

Q. So you had the opportunity to hide these students because the government trusted you?

No! The government certainly didn't trust me! They didn't think, they never considered, they never knew I was hiding these students! I knew if they found out, they would have killed me. I know that for sure! Not only me; they could have gone after other professors as well. I took the risk to hide them. Still I had to do something. I had to do *something*! The students would have been killed otherwise. They came to me, because we were very close. They told me the government would kill them. They told me that they can't go to their homes. They can't go to their relatives' houses. So they asked if they could come to my house. I replied, "Yes, for sure you can come to my house." This is the reason. I knew I had to hide them. You won't believe it. My sister, my brother, my relatives, nobody knew I was hiding these students. In the mornings, I went into the basement, and told my students, "You can come over, take a shower and eat breakfast."

I had some relatives visit. They didn't know what was going on. It was not easy. I am happy when I look back. I think, "Thank God I did it!"

Q. What happened to the students after?

One of them was found. They arrested her and she was killed. The others went to other cities of Iran and were hiding. I couldn't get in touch with them; we could not have any connections. They weren't able to get in touch with me.

Q. Do you know if they are alive now?

Just one of them. She went to Argentina and married a man there. The others, I do not know about. I have some students who escaped from Iran. They find me, and call and email me. One of them lives in England, the other one lives in Canada. They couldn't escape legally. They had to escape illegally through Turkey or Pakistan. It was very hard for them to get out. This is a part of my life that I talk about. I am happy and sad. Why are there so many smart students here? They should have stayed in Iran. They should have done something there instead of escaping. If you look at students here in the United States, you see a lot of Persian people. They do not want to go back to Iran. Like my children, they do not want to go back to Iran. I still keep in touch with some of my students. After years and years, they find me. They remember me and we speak about the old days.

I still love Iran. Not the government. It's different. I still see myself as Iranian. After years and years of living here, I see myself as Iranian and American. I still love Iran, but I think I should be loyal to the United States because of the opportunity it has given my children and me. I am very happy.

I was always against the government. This is the reason I stopped teaching, in protest; I did not agree to teach social science their way! For example, they did not want to talk about a lot of things in Iranian politics that influenced the war. Just the Islamic religion was important for them. It is not the Republic of Iran but the *Islamic* Republic of Iran. This is the reason a lot of people, especially young people, do not accept it; they do not want to accept it. We have only the people who are still there, suffering there. You watch the news? If you look you can see that even the United Nations does not care that Iran doesn't honor human rights.

The current protests are huge. But the protesters didn't have anything when they were protesting. The soldiers had guns. You heard about the young lady who was killed? The revolutionary guard had guns! They shot them, the protestors. They could have done many other things but they decided to shoot them. The students did nothing but protest! In the December 1978 protest, they wanted freedom. They wanted just democracy and religious freedom, nothing else. Even right now, when they compare the Shah with our government, it is agreed that we made a huge mistake. People never thought a revolution for democracy would lead to the current repressive situation.

I believe in God. I grew up in an Islamic family, but I do not practice it like the Ayatollahs want. I think we have only one God. I respect all the religions. For me Jesus is as equal as Moses, as Muhammad. I believe in God. I think if you believe in one God, all the religions are the same. They ask you to be good. Don't kill the people in the name of God.

I do not believe the Islamic Republic government has faith in God. They regard it as a movement. Their God is different. The government tells the people that it is okay to kill people in the name of God. They say it is okay to go to extreme lengths for religious purposes. I do not want to talk about the details of what they do to the dissidents in Iran. It is horrible. I do not feel you can do these things. You should not kill people under the name of God.

Q. You are just opposed to this specific Islamic government, right? Are you opposed to Islam as a religion?

I'm not a religious person. I'm not. I do not practice religion but I respect all religions; the good things in them. Not the mass movements; not some of the leaders; not their interpretation of religion. You can see if you look at what happened in Iran right now. Religion is something between you and God. When it is mixed with politics, it creates bad things.

I left because I realized – maybe one year after Khomeini came back into power – I could not properly provide for my sons and daughter. I needed to give them education so their minds would not be washed. It was very bad for women. For example, if a lady wants to leave the country, she needs permission from her husband. She needs him to sign a paper saying, yes, she can leave. Do you know about the stoning of the women in Iran? Horrible!

The women at my daughter's school would lecture me on how to dress and bring up my daughter. Not only me; they would lecture the other parents as well. They would call us in and question us about why our daughters missed Friday prayer. I still have anger, as a woman. Why can a man have four wives? Right now Iran is a man's country. I admire the Iranian women because they stand up against the government. They will rebel with little things, not cover themselves completely. If they accepted everything they wouldn't be women. If you see a picture of a modern Iranian woman, they have on nice makeup. They are going to university. They are changing things little by little. It is gradual change. If you look at the protestors in the news, they are beautiful girls!

I keep up with events but 1997 was the last time I visited Iran. My relatives are gone. All my brothers and my sisters are gone from there. But everyone has someone they left behind, even if it's only a distant cousin or friends. All the people I care about who got left there are there because the government took their passports so they cannot leave the country. They want to leave the country but they cannot. A lot of people still can't leave the country, especially the students. But things are changing. I have hope for Iran.

Really, the only hope is the young people. Not my age or older, just the young people. I know a lot of young people. They left the country and go to Canada, Australia, and United States. Just last month one of my students finished her school and got accepted to USC because of her grades. But a lot of young people need to live in Iran, and the governmental authorities don't let them live when they arrest them in the street during a protest.

* * *

I have four sisters and three brothers. They are all very educated and all have graduated college with degrees. My parents were professionals. Two things were very important in our family: science and education. Especially my mother, she was a talented zoologist. When I was in England I wanted to visit her, as she was ill. But it was not easy to get permission to visit. Also, it was June and all my children had final exams. I could not leave them. Mother passed away, as did my father. Education was extremely important in my family. Your education is the most important thing. When I was leaving the country, I remember one night I told my children, "I am leaving everything here; I do not know what it is going to be like over there but I ask you to promise me that you will always put your education first. You must educate yourself."

If you have a luxury life, that is very nice and materialistic, it may not make you happy, and it may not last forever. The only thing that matters is everything you have here [points to her head]. You must invest in this. This is the most important thing in life. I tried to do something for my children, to teach them this. I tried to teach them you have to do everything you can to invest in your education. I think being spiritual is good, too. I talked to my children about this and how honesty is very important. They are very honest, and kind with their friends. The reason I go around as a volunteer to nursing homes, cancer society homes, and especially to homes where children suffer from leukemia is because I wanted to encourage something good in the world. Something for someone else. Something for my children. I want to help somebody. I taught my children that when you help somebody, you shouldn't necessarily talk about it. Not to show off but do it out of goodwill. It is natural.

As I told you, I believe in God. What we can do in this world is to be nice, honest, kind, and if you are educated you can help people. Even a lot of educated people, they cannot be honest or good. But if you are raised under the ideas of honesty and kindness, it helps you with your future.

Q. So it is more than education? Do you believe some people are born "good" and some born "bad"? Or is it something that you must develop?

It happens mostly through education. Your upbringing is important too. Family counts. I was very close to my mother. We talked about everything. She was a very good listener. When I was having problems, I would talk to her. My relationship with my sisters and brothers is still very close. We talk about the news. I think I am a very good listener; they talk to me and trust me about everything. I think it is very important how I grew up and how my parents raised me to be kind and to be nice and to have a good relationship with people. When I was living in Iran, I never talked about how I helped my students. I never talked about the kind of relationship I had with my students, even when I moved out of Iran to England. I felt it was something I shouldn't tell other people. I am now very friendly with my daughter and sons, but our relationship is more than just mother and children. It is a deep friendship. We talk about everything, just as I did with my mother.

Q. So your priorities are mainly with your children?

Yes, exactly.

The revolutionary guard weren't educated people. If they were educated people who were taught things like honesty and respect, then they would not shoot students protesting in the streets. They couldn't! They wouldn't have considered shooting them. And even doing that, they could not suppress the protests by force! They could not wash the minds of the educated people!

I have been back to visit. I still have a lot of friends who have stayed. They were scared; they were not happy, especially two or three years after the revolution occurred. The government fired a lot of professors. They wanted everything to be under the control of the government. They didn't want certain things being taught so they just fired professors. It's sad. But most important are the Iranian women who didn't leave the country. Some have professional jobs and support their families. In the United States they can define themselves not only as women but also as human beings. I admire the Iranian women who stayed in Iran. They have a tough life.

You should be very thankful for living in this country, especially you young people. You didn't experience what happened in other countries – not only in Iran – where they don't have the excellent educational institutions they have here. When you go to the university here, it's easy. Over there you have to pass a lot of tests to be accepted. It's good for you to be going to university so you can learn as much as you can. In countries like Iran, young people must struggle, living and learning in horrible universities. You do not have freedom to think.

Q. Regarding your experiences in Iran during the revolution, is there anything you regret doing? Is there anything you wish you would have done differently?

Everything I've done was right in my heart. I am happy because I did not accept the rule of my government. They tried to tell me what I should and should not teach, and I did not accept this. My students always respected me. I know they are all over the world but no matter where they are, they knew I was having trouble doing my job properly. I know that if I accepted everything the government wanted me to do and to teach, that it would be wrong. I have my values. After they tried to impose something on me that went against those values, I did not want to teach anymore, I knew it was done.[1]

NOTE

1. We have modified critical details of this interview to protect the privacy and safety of family and speaker.

PART FIVE

MY STORY, YOUR CHOICE HOW TO USE IT

When I tell this story it's not just because I heard it. I experienced it. I'm not just saying it to tell someone's story. I tell my story because I'm passing on my knowledge. I've been there. I've felt it. It's your choice to decide how to use it.

– Kimberly, Khmer Rouge survivor

20 THE FUNDAMENTAL THINGS APPLY

What lessons can we draw from the stories in this book? Are there shared patterns in wartime struggles for survival? Common themes in efforts to compose meaningful postwar lives? Can these stories help us think about the influences shaping our own abilities to retain humanity during times so searing they challenge our most basic values and underlying assumptions about what it means to flourish as human beings? The topic does not lend itself to facile answers, but insights are nonetheless discernible.

Simply put, we find the fundamental things apply. Those things that center us and provide meaning to our lives during peacetime – so unremarkable, yet precious once lost – prove critical in keeping our sanity, let alone our humanity, during war: love, friends, family, a sense of who we are, of belonging, of having value as a person. Beyond this, analysis underlines the importance of the human psychology, provides vital details concerning psychological mechanisms that contribute to emotional well-being, and suggests these can operate in ways that seem counterintuitive on first glance. (Table 20.1 summarizes our findings and links them with prior work in the field.)

RETAINING HUMANITY. First, what insight can we glean about the concept of humanity itself? Given the vague if widespread understanding of the term, part of our attention must focus on discovering what it meant to speakers to retain their humanity. Answers here came indirectly, as a theme underlying our conversations rather than as a topic confronted directly in interviews. What we found is nonetheless valuable. First, there is not widespread agreement among survivors on how they maintained their humanity during war, or even on what that

Table 20.1. *Summary of findings*

Hypothesis (Scholar advancing hypothesis)	Hypothesis Description	Confirmation/Rejection
Will to survive (Freud)	A universal and innate instinctual drive to survive exists and will work toward survival but also may work against people maintaining their humanity, reducing them to creatures who'll do anything to survive.	Survival drive confirmed; evidence on effect on humanity complex.
Repression (Freud, Becker)	Repressing difficult memories will inhibit constructing a happy life after war. Those who can emotionally engage their traumatic memories will fare better than those who do not.	Not confirmed, mixed effects of repressed memories.
Control over one's fate (Adler, Bettelheim, Maddi, Janoff-Bulman)	When environment, situational factors, and personality combine to provide a sense of control over one's destiny, surviving with one's humanity intact will be more likely. Relates closely to sense of agency.	Not confirmed. Counter effects often indicated. Fatalism often key.
Locus of control: agency (Maddi, Rotter, Bettelheim)	Those seeing themselves as weak and helpless will fare less well than those seeing themselves as able to take charge of their lives and effect change. An alternate interpretation: Those who lack strong sense of agency actually fare better, finding lack of control less a shock.	Not confirmed. Inordinate needs for control may work against survival. Counter-hypothesis may be stronger one.
Link with former selves (Bettelheim, Becker, Butler et al., Zimbardo)	Maintaining humanity will be facilitated by establishing a link between pre- and postwar selves.	Strongly confirmed.

Environment/situation/luck (Adler, Bettelheim, Zimbardo, Milgram)	In forging a link to prewar self, situational factors play as critical a factor as underlying personality strength; social environment exerts a crucial influence on moral action.	Mixed evidence.
Meaning in suffering (Frankl, Maddi)	Ability to find meaning in suffering will facilitate keeping humanity. Ability to feel a sense of control learned from new experiences – both hallmarks of the existential energy central to hardiness – may affect how one keeps in touch with one's humanity.	Confirmed. May be how control enters.
Self-esteem and continuity (Adler, Frankl, Bettelheim, Becker, post-traumatic stress disorder literature)	Retaining self-esteem increases the probability of surviving war. People w/ high self-esteem more likely to withstand and recover from shocks of war. Doing so may entail diverse psychological mechanisms, e.g., denial, focusing on family/friends, or establishing post-trauma routines to recreate sense of order and community felt in the prior life.	Strongly confirmed.
Blame (Post-traumatic stress disorder literature, e.g. Charuvastra and Cloitre)	Addressing survivor guilt helps people lead productive happy lives after the war.	Mixed but mostly confirmed.
Emotional support (Butler et al., post-traumatic stress disorder literature)	High levels of emotional support (from family, political, religious groups) helps cope with loss and reestablish or maintain humanity.	Strongly confirmed.

concept means. Most survivors thought of humanity as a three-part concept referring (1) to all human beings collectively; (2) to the quality or condition of being human; and (3) to the quality of being humane, of treating others with concern and care. This conceptualization suggests maintaining humanity thus includes the ability to retain the decency that is part of our human condition, to show respect and concern for others, and to demonstrate kindness and benevolence in our treatment of our fellow human beings, even during war.

Perhaps it should not be surprising that speakers did not concretely address what it meant to be humane. Most people do not ordinarily think in such terms, after all. If we listened carefully, however, we found that people would approach this topic by talking about what they wanted in life, about what it was that drove them to survive during the war. For some speakers, maintaining humanity involved sharing and effectively memorializing their wartime experiences and emotions.[1] Fabiola captures this quality in discussing the therapeutic healing of narrative, of telling her story:

> *Telling Andre and my daughter... about my experiences was not as difficult as I had originally thought it might be. They received it very well and were actually incredibly surprised I had never shared that information with them. So to be able to share that information now, so openly, and freely, to someone who isn't even my child means I've accepted it as part of who I am. I don't know when that happened but it must have happened sometime when I discovered who I truly was as a person.* (Fabiola, p. 222)

For others, a compartmentalized life worked better to protect their humanity. "We just didn't talk about it. It was one of those things you repress. That's how you cope.... To me it was a chapter and when the chapter was over you closed it and put it behind you" (Frank, p. 48). A Japanese-American interned during World War II echoed this idea.

> *Q. You and your siblings never talked about what went on in the camps?*
>
> *No, we didn't. Plus my brother was in Vietnam. I think that's where he went. He never talks about it. He never says anything about that war. He pushes it out of his mind, too. He doesn't mention anything. A lot of people don't talk about it. They never say anything.* (Grace, p. 128)

For some speakers, to stay human meant to forget. For others, maintaining humanity meant loving, being loved, and having loved ones around them. In a self-described agonizing search to understand why she survived when six million did not, Laura said: "Love. Love for my family. . . . Because they gave me the love, I was able to love others" (p. 67). In explaining how she fell in love with a young man who gave her extra food in the concentration camp, a man she later married, Laura provided insight on the importance of love during that horrible time. "My friends said, 'This is no place to love.'" But "those things helped me stay strong" (Laura, p. 58). Both Sara and Kimberly (Khmer Rouge survivors) echoed this thought: "It's love for family" (p. 152) that supplied them the ability to survive the Khmer Rouge. In explaining how he endured the pain of war and internment camp under the Vietnamese communists, Tuan said simply, "I stay alive for my family" (p. 141).

Most of the speakers, from Marie in Lebanon to Leyla in the Islamic Republic of Iran, mentioned their families. They wanted their loved ones to be safe, to have the basic needs of life: food, education, the opportunity for a good job, freedom, and people who recognize their specialness and love them because of that singularity. They were willing to risk death so sons will not be forced into wars (Leyla), so daughters will not suffer second-class status by a rigid Islamic theocracy (Leyla) or be condemned to poverty (Luis).[2] These things most of us crave, and they speak to an integral part of being human: knowing we are loved, and have loved ones, in turn, whose happiness is so precious it becomes entwined with our own sense of well-being. This love and the human connection it provides constitute an important part in survival during war and in the ability to find inner peace and reconstruct a good life in war's aftermath. "So the bottom line is to trust somebody, to love somebody that much. As you grow, you taste it, you feel it, and that sticks with you" (Kimberly, pp. 152–53). This theme runs like a *leitmotif*, in story after story.

WILL TO SURVIVE. Other common refrains also suggested what helped speakers stay alive and focused on what being human meant to them. One factor was the raw survival urge so famously noted by Freud. Tuan, a Vietnam Civil War and re-education camp survivor said: "I gotta do what I gotta do in order to survive. . . . I just had to do it. There was no question" (p. 141). A Lebanese Civil War survivor succinctly summarized: "I had to stay strong. I knew I just had to" (Marie, p. 228). A Khmer Rouge survivor fleshed out the physical drain this raw drive for survival entailed. "You try to cope and sleep, to just have enough energy to get up when they tell you to get up" (Kimberly, p. 154). Does this raw desire to live work to inhibit maintenance of humanity, reducing people to creatures who will do anything to survive? We found the survival instinct surfaced even when it jeopardized prior moral constraints. "If you didn't lie, then you would die....Everybody lied....I didn't want to die. You lied so you were able to survive" (Sara, p. 144). So the Freudian life force clearly exists, but its impact on the ability to maintain humanity is not clear. Would most of us consider it a moral transgression to lie to the Gestapo or the Khmer Rouge in order to protect one's self or others? Would stealing food to stay alive or give it to others constitute a violation of one's humanity? If we define morality and ethics as concerned with human well-being and the protection of human life rather than with a more deontological approach stressing moral rules such as the Ten Commandments, actions fostering such well-being clearly seem morally acceptable, even when entailing deeds – lying or theft – usually considered "wrong" in contemporary society.

But what if the will to survive involves us in murder? In taking another's life to protect one's own? Soldiers spoke of this. Tuan told how he might have met one of his relatives fighting for the North Vietnamese; in that case, Tuan knew he would have to kill his relative or be killed himself. "You don't shoot them, they shoot you!" (p. 140) Would such acts – taken in self-defense – lessen one's humanity? We can offer no adequate philosophical discussion of questions of this genre but we can ascertain how such acts shaped the humanity of our speakers. Tuan's narrative is not redolent of a man deprived of humanity. Instead, it evokes a picture of war that robs all combatants of the ability to make life-and-death moral choices. While some soldiers expressed remorse for being part of a war machine that kills people (Sebastian), most soldiers (Frank) echoed General Sherman's view of war as an all-encompassing moral abyss, void of moral compass: "War is hell. War is all hell."[3]

Where we find a difference is when we consider civilian deaths, massacres, and other acts that append to war. Another soldier, whose story is not included here, was involved in massacres of civilians during the Lebanese Civil War. "I killed love," he said of slaughtering civilians at Sabra and Shatila.[4] After the massacre, he said he lacked all ability to feel any emotion, even for his own family. But this was an annihilation of civilians, not a battle. A gray area concerns the "collateral damage" Doc described in explaining the loss of innocent civilians as a necessary part of a greater good. "It was a means to the bigger picture of Iraq: freedom from oppression....In any war...there will always be collateral damage" (p. 168). Causing collateral damage did not shake Doc's sense of his humanity; but he played a lot of video games to keep sane, and admitted video games desensitized him. "When I raise my gun and shoot at the enemy, I almost feel no remorse. It has built an almost inherent reaction to want to shoot at the enemy automatically." Doc suffered no PTSD, saying he "kept it light" and talked openly about the war with his wife. "Some people are not made for war.... It can be hard to escape memories and thoughts" (pp. 176–77). Doc took everything he learned in the war as a learning experience, arguing that his wartime experience prepared him for working in Homeland Security. But he also is quite honest about the war's impact on his psyche.

> *Q. You said you've killed people. How does that make you feel?*
>
> *That's a tough one so let's start from the beginning. Before entering Iraq I wanted to shoot everyone because in my mind, everyone was bad. I was somewhat excited; it was like a real-life video game. Then while I was in Iraq I became kind of numb. There are so many variables. I did what was appropriate protocol for the given situation. After the war, I realized if someone was shooting at me, then I must shoot back. I did not want to hurt civilians but that is a negative consequence of war. Regardless of where the war is located, collateral damage will occur.*
>
> *Q. You compare shooting on the field to video games. Would you still say that now?*
>
> *Yes. Training consists of playing video games. Shooting games depict a somewhat realistic scenario, in a setting that looks like the environment we were in. Also it trains the reflexes. But of course you don't die when you get hit in a game. You notice that difference in a live battle.*
>
> *Q. Do you still play games?*
>
> *I do. I play almost every day; you can almost say I am addicted.*
>
> *Q. Do you feel like the games you play remind you of the battlefield?*
>
> *Actually, no, which is kind of funny because the battlefield reminds me of the games. I have some of the best aim in real life and in games. A campaign through a city in Iraq is similar to a game because in the game there are these hidden shooters, both faceless and nameless enemies. It is kill or be killed. Traps, bombs, et cetera are set for us. You can say the same in a game.*
>
> *Q. Do you feel war desensitized you?*
>
> *In a sense. I still would be shocked if a tank was rolling down the block in front of my house but I can probably deal with blood better than an average American civilian.*

Q. Do you feel games desensitized you?

Yes, when I raise my gun and shoot at the enemy, I almost feel no remorse   *(pp. 175–76)*

Sebastian drew quite different lessons from the same Iraq war.

I actually have a cut on my back to remind me never to go back. I fundamentally disagree with everything going on there. It was easily the worst experience of my life. It's where the worst experiences of my life occurred. I had a profound sense of powerlessness and fear and pain. So it's still something I wrestle with and I don't know how well I would be able to manage. I don't think I could go through all those feelings again.   *(p. 187)*

How do we explain the strikingly divergent reactions to the same war? One answer may lie in the men's conflicting assessments of what the United States was doing in Iraq. Doc felt we liberated Iraq and brought democracy; Sebastian interpreted the war as having less to do with 9/11 than with oil. Beyond that, the immediate situations differed dramatically. While Sebastian found most soldiers decent people, "the military police battalion [I served with] were pretty fascist. Mean people. They were really out to get people. They just wanted to find people to pick on and I couldn't approve of that" (p. 183). Sebastian kept his humanity by giving most of his military pay to Iraqis he knew. He nonetheless claimed the war changed him from a "happy, outgoing, and trusting" person to someone "a lot more wary of people...a bit skeptical"

I became extremely closed off. I accept a lot less bullshit from people and the world around me. So I'm a little more demanding, a little colder. Probably a little more angry, too.... My trust of others has diminished greatly. My social interactions have also diminished because I won't talk to people.   *(pp. 184–85)*

Interestingly, both the interviewer – who knew Sebastian – and the coders reading his transcript found Sebastian possessed a heightened moral sensitivity and wondered if that made him harsher on himself.

Q. It's so weird to hear this from you because I know you as a friend and I know how you are socially. When I hear this, I try to imagine how you were before, because to me you're still a fun person to be around and a lot of people would agree with me in that sense. To me and to others you are a pleasant person, but when you talk about yourself you have a very pessimistic outlook on it.

It's hard; I have to force myself a lot (p. 186).

The assessment of Sebastian, then, from outside observers was that Sebastian had maintained more of his humanity than most soldiers. His severe, unforgiving view of himself points out the difficulties in assessing war's impact on humanity.

All the people quoted here are soldiers. What impact does war have on non-combatants? Gunther, the displaced person from Vienna, seemed badly damaged by World War II, both directly in terms of his immediate situation and because of the abuse he suffered at the hands of his stepfather, someone Gunther described as "damaged goods himself" because of the war (p. 84). Gunther describes his own U.S. Army experience as psychotic – "Kinda like *One Flew Over the Cuckoo's Nest*" (p. 87) – and crippled by events directly flowing from World War II, which Gunther claims left many people "damaged" (p. 92). In contrast, neither Japanese internee described herself as badly scarred. (Grace made light of her internment.) Both Khmer Rouge survivors claimed initially to be pleased, since under the Khmer Rouge they would not have to attend school anymore. ("I was happy because I thought to myself, 'No more school!'" [Kimberly, p. 144].) This was not at all the case for Laura (Holocaust survivor) or, eventually, for either of the young women surviving the Khmer Rouge. All three women described horrific wartime psychological scars. While none of these women speaks of having had their humanity destroyed by their experiences, they did mention guilt, and a continuing sense of sorrow constitutes *leitmotifs* in their narratives.

As is strikingly obvious in this analysis, finding general themes in the complexity of human life during war is challenging. Human beings are complex, and their reactions to war multiple and intertwined. Nonetheless, one verity stands out. The will to survive exists strongly in people. It relates closely to the desire to live for those they love. How is one's humanity affected when surviving necessitates committing acts ordinarily judged inhumane, such as killing others? This question is more difficult to answer, at least given the few cases analyzed here.

CONTROL OVER ONE'S FATE, LUCK, THE ENVIRONMENT, AND SITUA-
TIONAL FACTORS. Is surviving with humanity intact more likely when the environment provides a sense of control over one's destiny? If so, does that sense of control in turn facilitate keeping humanity intact? We found no one who spoke of control in this classic sense. Generally, people accepted that war wreaks havoc with their lives, making them scramble, both physically and emotionally, simply to endure. (Consider

Sebastian's "profound sense of powerlessness and fear and pain" in Iraq [p. 187] or Reza's discussion of the elaborate power game that engulfed his country, tossing people around like pawns.) Ngũgĩ did speak of the need "to dig deep in yourself and find a form of resistance that can keep you mentally and spiritually alive" (p. 204). But other than Ngũgĩ, no one linked emotional survival with a sense of control.[5]

In contrast to the striking lack of speakers who mentioned control, many speakers did signal the importance of luck. But luck was linked more to physical survival than to the survival of humanity. For example, in explaining why she survived, one of the Schindler's list Jews noted:

> *Students ask me, "How come you stayed alive when your family and the six million did not?" I could never give an answer to that. I didn't know myself. . . . It was a set of circumstances. It was luck. It was where I stood at a given time, and . . . what time of year it was.*   (*Laura, p. 55*)

Marie stressed luck's role in her family's treacherous exodus during Lebanon's civil war:

> *It was scary. My son-in-law arranged the driving. Sometimes we would drive down a road and right after we passed, it would get hit. Right after we passed the road! Sometimes even the road would get hit right in front of us as we were driving. A rocket would strike and the light would be so blinding. We always had to find detours. We arrived like a miracle.*
>
> (*p. 227*)

Herb judged himself "lucky" to have relatives sponsor his family's flight from the Nazis and Fabiola credits her physical survival to the luck of having a house with cinderblocks strong enough to withstand bombardment during Nicaragua's civil war. Even interviewees who did not explicitly mention luck nonetheless noted their good fortune in surviving the perils of war (Leyla).

FATALISM. If luck contrasts with control, it links closely to another fascinating phenomenon: fatalism. We initially expected fatalism to be a negative, hypothesizing that people who lose their sense of agency and believe the situation they are in is fatal would understandably then find little they can do to alter their fate. They subsequently would come to feel passive actors in the sequence of events. While we found some of this, the surprise was how frequently fatalism also worked as a positive force. "[T]he only way you can handle a major stressful thing like war is to become fatalistic. . . . It was the way to survive it. To get through it"

(Frank, p. 52). Frank continued, relating fatalism to luck, and asserting that each played a complex, nuanced role in retaining his humanity "It was fatalism. It was . . . if something's going to get you, it'll get you. If it's not, it will not. That was the basic thing" (p. 52). We interpreted fatalism's distinctly positive support for someone like Frank in the following manner. Fatalism meant the bad things afflicting the speaker resulted from random chance, and thus were not to be taken personally. Fatalism also reduced Frank's need to worry. If one has no control, and if one accepts that fact as a given, such acceptance can lead to a kind of serene acquiescence in whatever life brings. This protective aspect of fatalism was captured by Sebastian, American soldier fighting in Iraq.

> I was really afraid. . . . The way I managed dealing with that kind of stress was debilitating, sitting there thinking "I'm gonna die, I'm gonna die, I'm gonna die." So I was like, "Fuck it, I'm already dead." So I can just stop worrying about that and just worry about what I have to do.   (p. 186)

Civilians also voiced this view, as noted by Fabiola's comment on finding a strange sense of peace in accepting death's inevitability. Indeed, Fabiola credits fatalism with helping her survive.

> The coping mechanisms I used at the time, even being just eleven years old, was to tell myself that death would not be that bad after all. I saw death as perhaps a release from the turmoil around me. Saw that if my family and I were to die, then perhaps it would not be as bad.   (p. 222)

In another time and place, the young Grace expressed a similar view: if she couldn't change her situation, she might as well accept it as best she could.

> But what could we do? There wasn't anything we could do. . . . There wasn't much anybody could do. You just had to do what you had to do. What could we have done? There's nothing.   (pp. 123–28)

An Austrian Jewish refugee spoke thus of fatalism: "I knew we were being subject to totally arbitrary treatment. They could do anything they felt like" (Herb, p. 105). Likewise, Tuan's fatalism provided the expectation of oncoming calamity during Vietnam's civil war. Fatalism buffered the shock when the worst then happened.

> I wasn't afraid because when you fight together you don't know what happens. If it happens, it happens. You know it happens every day. Many

die any day. We hear bomb every day. Boom boom, every day. We know
someday it's your turn to die so we don't scare. I don't scare.   *(p. 134)*

For Tuan, knowing that you *couldn't* know what was to come somehow alleviated his fear from stress. Life is so chaotic, don't even try to
predict. Just expect any outcome and at least you get the peace that
arises from letting go of the need to predict and control events. "Every
day, when I was in the [Vietnam] war, I knew that each day could have
been the last. I knew what to expect" (Tuan, p. 139). We hypothesized
that the odd sense of peace accompanying fatalism was related to the
psychology of stress, in which anxiety and tension arise when one feels
responsible for things over which one has no control. We thus wondered
if those who emotionally accept their lack of control during war fare better psychologically than those who need the certainty associated with a
sense of control. The unusual role played by fatalism thus may explain
why so few people identified control as a factor in their psychological
survival.

CONTROL. Certainly luck and fatalism were mentioned far more frequently in discussing the trauma of war than was the need for control and power. Indeed, we found only one person who argued for
the value of gaining control. In underscoring the importance of writ-
ing/directing plays in his native Gĩkũyũ language as part of his fight
against neo-colonialism, Ngũgĩ used Adler's metaphor of power and
control to describe how his writing constituted an attempt to assert control over colonialism:

> *You are more empowered because not only do you know your own lan-*
> *guage very well but you are also a master of another language. In that*
> *sense you are more empowered.*   *(p. 204)*

Is it possible that people with strong needs for control have a tougher
time during war, and may be more likely to die as a result? One cannot interview people who do not survive a war, obviously, but examining letters from people who go through wars and write letters or journals
about their experiences might be one way to get at the issue of control.
It is also possible that discussions of luck and fatalism reflect an indirect
way to assert control. One might, for example, consider luck a supernat-
ural and deterministic concept reflecting the belief that external forces –
such as gods or spirits – prescribe certain events much as the laws of

physics prescribe the occurrence of certain events. Does this relate to control? Is the fatalism we found – which often played a positive role in alleviating stress emanating from the lack of control over one's very life during war – connected to the need for control Adler mentioned? Possibly. Our cautious conclusion on control's role in people's ability to retain their humanity during war is that control's psychology is complex and requires further study.

IMPORTANCE OF THE SELF AND CONTINUITY. If control's role was difficult to decipher, there was no ambiguity at all in recognizing how important it was for retaining humanity to establish a link between post- and prewar selves. Indeed, continuity of identity might constitute the single most essential factor in maintaining speakers' humanity. Certainly, preserving self-esteem and continuity was significant for most people we interviewed. Speakers' discussions of their sense of self provided essential clues and details concerning the psychological process that kept people emotionally whole.

How individuals saw themselves was tremendously important in maintaining the sense of self-esteem and self-worth necessary to feel their own humanity. Speakers who saw themselves not as victims but rather as survivors fared far better than those who felt beaten by wartime events. Viewing themselves as survivors, especially when in the midst of the traumatic experience, helped speakers protect and preserve their sense of agency. This provided speakers the ability to take action necessary to survive, whether by escaping Vietnam on a boat (Tuan) or enduring torture by the Gestapo (Mafalda). It allowed them to reclaim their humanity after their ordeals. In telling how she survived the Khmer Rouge reign of terror, Kimberly notes the importance of keeping undamaged her sense of self and self-worth, despite the degradations imposed on her by the regime. This lesson came from her parents, who insisted their identities remained intact, regardless of what was inflicted on them.

> *My parents said, "... We won't forget who we are, and we won't let anything take away from who we are. Even though we are living in the water or in a shack, we are still who we are."* (Kimberly, p. 156)

This resembles Leyla's story. Leyla was a college professor married to a highly placed official in the Shah of Iran's regime. After Khomeini returned, Leyla's teaching was censored. Her books were "edited" by having random pages ripped out. Her students and family threatened by an increasingly despotic Islamic regime, Leyla's sense of self was closely tied to her identity as a teacher and as a mother. Her decision to leave Iran was strongly driven by her desire to protect both these identities. "I know that if I accepted everything the government wanted me to do and to teach, that it would be wrong" (p. 258). Leyla's identity as a teacher meant she needed to teach honestly, even when forbidden to do so. Her love for her students was intimately linked to a broader identity, one that gave Leyla more than her own immediate and increasingly painful situation to think about. It empowered her to hide threatened students in her basement without her husband's knowledge or permission. "Everybody has a mission. It was the least I could do for my students. They were not just my students; they were my friends, and I love them" (p. 252). Leyla's other key identity is as a mother, and her decision to leave was driven by the desire to protect her sons from war and her daughter from the confinements of the Islamic theocracy.

Much of this psychological link between identity and humanity seemed a conscious self-evaluation, one reflected in speakers' ongoing efforts to craft narratives about the war that provided continuity and made sense of war's chaos. Survivors certainly did not characterize war as a good experience but many crafted narratives that showed how they had grown instead of being destroyed by the war. "As I look back I tell people: what I've gone through in life is an experience, and I thank God every day for this moment" (Kimberly, p. 160). The ability to construct such a narrative seemed a fundamental element in the ability to keep one's humanity.

SENSE OF BELONGING TO SOMETHING BIGGER THAN ONE'S SELF. Continuity of identity provided a key to another vital component in retaining humanity: one's sense of belonging to something larger than one's own self. Feeling linked into something important and lasting, bigger than one's own self, constituted an inner resistance to political oppression, as revealed both by Leyla and Ngũgĩ. With brothers fighting on different sides during the Mau Mau rebellion, Ngũgĩ himself was imprisoned for putting on plays in Gĩkũyũ. As a writer, Ngũgĩ's politics focused on language, and a critical part of his identity related to his refusal to write in the language of colonialism. His resistance reflected his connection with something beyond himself: both the Kenyan people and people everywhere who resist neo-colonialism. Just as Ngũgĩ found meaning, psychic protection, and the strength to survive by viewing himself as part of a worldwide resistance to colonialism so did Leyla draw solace and strength from conceptualizing herself as a teacher with responsibilities to her students. "The only thing that matters is everything you have here [points to her head]. You must invest in this. This is the most important thing in life" (p. 256). Similarly, Herb – a Jewish refugee who left Europe on the last boat before the ill-fated St. Louis – described how being a Zionist neutralized the sting of anti-Semitism.

> But this Zionist group was very important for all sorts of reasons. Perhaps most relevant to what we are talking about now, it buffered my self-esteem in such a way that the whole part of the experience, not the Holocaust at that time, not my whole Nazi experience, none of this threatened my self-esteem in any way. It threatened me, but not my self-esteem. (p. 108)

It is extraordinary that the fear, suffering, and human rights abuse these speakers experienced could be defused or even mitigated by the speakers' ability to frame this persecution as an event happening not only to them but also to a larger group of people with whom they could connect psychologically. In Herb's case, Zionism provided a practical antidote to the anti-Semitism that caused the persecution he experienced and which broke or killed so many others.

> It was not a good experience, I assure you. But it didn't really attack my sense of self. To begin with my sense of Jewish identity was strong. The youth group movement helped keep it very much in the foreground. The youth movement did that. I assume that if I were more assimilated into Austrian society, or came from a family that was highly assimilated... that would have been much more devastating for me because I would have had to ask myself, "What's wrong with me?" That's a question I don't think I'll ever have to ask myself. I knew the reason this was happening to me had nothing to do with me. It has to do with the fact that I am a Jew, and being a Jew is a good thing. It's not a bad thing. It's not something to be ashamed of; it's something you should be proud of. It's not something to be desperate about; it's something to be hopeful about. So I think it gave meaning to my experience but it also gave me a sense of worth, which I think made me less vulnerable. (p. 109)

The so-called Red Princess with the von Stauffenberg group during World War II suggested her commitment to a particular cause (anti-Fascism) took precedence over her own need to survive. She managed to get the Allies information on where to bomb the prison in which she was held, despite the obvious potential for her own death in doing so.

> *Even when I was in prison, I wasn't afraid of being killed. It doesn't matter somehow when it's one person against others. It's the idea that counts. So I tried to get them word, "You throw it exactly in that place," [Mafalda made a swooping gesture to imitate a bomb falling]. I knew the other side of the corridor where I was imprisoned . . . was where the Nazis had the list of resistance workers. That list needed to be destroyed, even if I died too.*
> (p. 98)

Some of the worst World War II wartime horrors – sadistic tortures, rapes, nighttime raids, and nonsensical beatings – have been explained as part of a carefully thought-out plan to break people's link with their prewar selves, and thus turn them into frightened, wartime wimps who would do anything to survive (Bettelheim 1985). We have no direct evidence on this. There is, however, support for the idea that linking one's wartime and prewar selves provides a sense of continuity that fosters maintaining humanity, especially if one's identity also links one's self to a broader cause or group that can ameliorate the sting of wartime persecution. Again, Herb articulated the importance of continuity and group identity in speaking of the Zionist group he joined.

> *I've been thinking through this period, particularly why I don't feel trauma, and I never felt the experience was a major traumatic experience. I'm trying to distinguish between being subjected to the experience and having the experience feel frightening and being dislocating. It was not a good experience, I assure you. But it didn't really attack my sense of self. . . . Not that I wasn't afraid of being hurt and of course even more afraid of my father being hurt or dragged away. Not that I didn't feel humiliation. I think it's a little different. You can feel humiliation without feeling it reflects something rotten about yourself. That's the part I was protected against.*
> (p. 109)

RELIGION. God, if not organized religion, was identified as a source of solace, often in the manner reflected in Herb's membership in a Zionist youth group, which seemed as much a social as a religious identity. Two other mentions of religion came from Holocaust survivor Laura and Leyla, who fled the Islamic Republic in Iran. In both cases religion was described as a faith providing principles but not an ultimate salve to the extreme circumstances faced. Leyla notes that religion and politics are not a good mix.

FAMILY. One influence that rings loudly throughout all the interviews is family, by far the most frequently mentioned group providing emotional solace. Indeed, family was critical for most speakers.

> *Your family is there no matter what's going to happen. . . . We don't sell our family out. I think that's the most valuable message to try to send; no matter what, or who you become, your family will be there for you.*
> (Kimberly, p. 152)

Later, she echoed this sentiment.

> *The thing that really gave me the ability to survive, to live through all of this, regardless of whether we had food or clothing, was to think there was somebody out there, especially a parent that loved me. That bond is strong. It is so strong that nobody can break it apart. Physically they can break you apart from each other but emotionally you can hear your dad's voice or your sister's voice and you think of the memories of the good times. Even though it was so devastating at the time, I could taste that little piece of salt [my mother gave me] like chocolate. It's all how you interpret it in your own mind and it gives you the inspiration and the strength to say, "Yes, I can live the next day."* (Kimberly, p. 162)

Even when separated from family, the lessons from and the strong ties to family lent strength. Separated from her family by the Khmer Rouge, Kimberly heard her father's voice in times of distress, "I keep that in my heart and say, 'I always have a family.' My father cannot be with me or talk with me, but I could hear the voice of my dad. He said, 'Listen. And follow'" (pp. 150–51).

Family ties drove amazing behavior. Safe in boarding school when she learned her mother and brothers were to be deported, Laura nonetheless wrote the Gestapo.

> *I knew what I had to do. I wrote a letter to the secret police and asked them to allow me to be deported with my mother and brothers. . . . If I had to do it all over again, I would do the very same because we were together for another few months.* (p. 58)

Rose was only six when forced to watch her grandfather beheaded for refusing to relinquish his Bible, which Rose saved, soaked with his blood. Unable to articulate thoughts about the Armenian genocide, partly because of her age but more – it appeared – because of the trauma it still induced in her, Rose did talk about how she recovered from this trauma and of the anguish surrounding the resultant separation from her mother. Rose made it clear that her family connections played a prominent role in her emotional recovery, acting as a strong support network. For Rose, enduring these ordeals was made easier because she went through them together with her family. Beyond this, many people (Luis, Leyla, Marie, Tuan) fled unspeakable conditions to make a better life for their children.

> **Leyla:** *"I could not properly provide for my sons and daughter. I needed to give them education so their minds would not be washed."*   (p. 255)

> **Tuan:** *"I had to stay alive. . . . I stay alive for my family."*   (p. 141)

> **Luis:** *(El Salvador Civil War; not included in this book):* *"My family was always in my concern. I wanted a better future for them, not in El Salvador, which was too dangerous for us to live in anymore."*

Perhaps Herb (an eminent social psychologist who devoted his professional life to understanding the psychology of conflict resolution) most succinctly captured the role of family in buffering the trauma of war: "Our nuclear family remained intact. That was probably the major factor in making this whole experience not a classically traumatic one" (p. 106).

MEANING IN SUFFERING. Can the mind's ability to shape the experience of war then craft a narrative that makes sense of harrowing wartime experiences? The search to find some meaning out of all the suffering played heavily on the minds of all our speakers. "Making sense of it all" was a need mentioned as much as the instinct to survive and far more than any desire for control and power. Further, numerous speakers linked their capacity to find meaning out of their suffering to their ability to maintain their sense of humanity. Indeed, many survivors – speakers such as Kimberly – alluded to the restorative aspect of trying to construct a narrative to explain their experiences to another person. Two survivors – both writers – expressed this most eloquently. Laura Hillman wrote a book about her Holocaust experiences, claiming she did not understand things herself until she had to write it all down. The process of writing helped her – forced her – to sort out events. This sorting process assisted Laura in finding a meaning out of her suffering and aided her in identifying factors that helped her survive. Bearing witness gave purpose to her survival.

> *Most of the time I don't want to talk about it. But it's my duty. It's my duty to speak until I no longer can so that we will be remembered. That's how the book started out. But then I always ask: Why did I survive? I survived and the book will tell you why.*   *(Laura, p. 69)*

Ngũgĩ also noted the extent to which the old adage about writing – that writing helps you find a point – had been incorporated into his life as a novelist. Ngũgĩ's heavily autobiographical writing reflects his own attempt to derive meaning out of the dreadful experiences he endured.

Writing was not the only way to create meaning out of wartime experiences. A refugee of Idi Amin's Uganda told how sending money to those left behind helped assuage his guilt at leaving. It was important, he told his daughter, to "help the people who are still left there, people who are still suffering" (Okello, p. 236).

Solders often experience difficulties finding meaning in their actions. American soldiers in both Iraq and Afghanistan told of wrestling with this problem. Doc decided his sacrifice was warranted because "we were doing a greater good in Iraq. We are helping the politically oppressed" (p. 171). Sebastian found no point in the Iraq War, judging it "easily the worst experience of my life. It's where the worst experiences of my life occurred. I had a profound sense of powerlessness and fear and pain. So it's still something I wrestle with" (p. 187).

Kimberly spoke of her three wars – "the war of your own people killing you. The war of the Vietnamese coming over. And the war of trying to escape from your own country looking for freedom, for a decent life again and something to call a family" (p. 160) – yet Kimberly captured a general view of how survivors search for meaning after a war.

> *Would I go back and change time? No. I accept this has given me the knowledge to understand we are all human. Some of us understand that better than others. Some can forgive better than others, and some people have more hatred than us. The war and living through a society like that [the Khmer Rouge], you learn how to end up on your feet so you have to find peace in yourself. If you don't have that, you cannot have peace. So no, there is nothing I want to change. I am blessed for what I have. I thank God for what he put me through; that I was able to feel it, see it, taste it, and now I know what life is all about.*   *(p. 164)*

HOPE. What other clues can we uncover about the mind's ability to shape the experience of war in a humane way? Certain psychological phenomena exert complicated, nuanced, and unexpected influences. Hope was one of these. One would expect retaining humanity during a war would be aided by believing there is something better at the end of the tunnel. This expectation might then influence and motivate individuals during the war, as they strive toward end goals that, at least in their minds, are achievable and justify the trauma, disruption, and horror of war. There is some systematic evidence supporting this view. In analyzing the overall perception that one's goals can be met, scholars find goal-directed thinking helps individuals utilize both pathways thinking (the perceived capacity to find routes to meet their desired goals) and agency thinking (the requisite motivations to use these routes).[6] Such findings would lead us to expect hope for a better future would be important in providing individuals with the goals, aspirations, and sense of agency that foster survival and flourishing. We did find some of this. Luis (El Salvador Civil War) said, "The hope, the hope for a better future always kept me going. If it was something that helped me recover, it was my own sanity." Leyla echoed this hope for the future of her former country, stating, "But things are changing. I have hope for Iran" (Leyla, p. 255). And Laura concluded her interview by saying, "Never give up for one thing. If you have an idea in your mind, what you want to do in your life and where you want to go, there's always hope even if there's a fork in the road" (Laura, p. 73).

Yet hope's influence was not always so straightforward. In particular, hope had an intricate link to loss. Tuan described having to fight a civil war he did not believe in, and in which he knew he would have to kill – or be killed by – relatives in the North. Worse than this for Tuan, however, was the postwar re-education camp in which he was not allowed to display any human emotion, even when his wife and baby visited him. Showing emotion meant Tuan risked longer incarceration for more "re-education." The hopelessness Tuan felt then led him to attempt the impossible: escaping from Vietnam on a boat. On the first attempt, Tuan took his wife and child. They were apprehended and, now feeling even more despairing than before, with no good solution in sight, Tuan agreed to sail alone on a boat with few provisions and no set destination. As the fuel was spent, the boat drifted for a week. With little food and water, one family with children lost one of them. Eventually, Tuan's boat was picked up by the Indonesians and he lived for years without his wife and child, who were left behind in Vietnam. Yet for Tuan, it was the lack of hope, and the sense of loss that accompanies this death of hope, that actually provided the freedom necessary to attempt the impossible escape.

In contrast, hopelessness engendered anger and bitterness in other speakers. The greater the loss, the angrier and more spitefully speakers reacted to the people who stole all they held dear. "How come [the war tribunal] doesn't get [the Khmer Rouge] and put them in the camp?

[Long pause.] Like how Khmer Rouge did with us." Sara's anger toward the Khmer Rouge remained palpable and was, Sara insisted, justified. "Yes, of course it's fair. They hurt me, so they need to be hurt too" (p. 147). Sara continued. "I hate [the Communists]. They take from me. They steal and kill. Communists! So bad" (p. 148). We can contrast Sara with the two Japanese internment camp victims interviewed for this project. Sara bitterly loathed and despised the communists for taking her family's wealth and freedom. The Japanese internees claimed not to mind the camps. Why? They had little to lose. With nothing to stay behind for, life could only get better. Their hopelessness facilitated their acceptance of internment. Hopelessness provided almost a peaceful-ness reminiscent of Frank's tranquility resulting from linking hope with fatalism.

COGNITIVE STRETCHING. Maintaining humanity was facilitated by the ability to grasp and assimilate a war's transformative power. By under-standing – and accepting – that the boundaries of the commonplace of political life had stretched and altered dramatically, speakers could incorporate this new reality into their worldviews. By expecting that something outside the normal parameters could happen, speakers were better able to prepare themselves mentally, and thus deal with the sit-uation more calmly if and when it happened to them. The capability to mentally prepare for and anticipate the worst – including death – greatly facilitated speakers' capacity to retain their humanity.

Initially, we thought perhaps this phenomenon was tapping into resilience, an individual's tendency to effectively cope with stress and adversity. Such resilience might result in a survivor "bouncing back" to his or her previous state of normal functioning. It might result in the speaker simply not showing negative effects. Or, as is suggested by recent work on PTSD, resilience could effectively constitute post-traumatic growth, in which wartime adversity provides a toughening that works much as an inoculation does to increase the capacity to deal well with future exposure to adversity. Instead, our interviews suggest that what we call cognitive stretching differs from resilience. Stretch-ing the parameters anticipated or accepted as normal for behavior seemed to provide wartime survivors the emotional flexibility necessary to accept certain situations and the circumstances surrounding them, thus preparing the speakers mentally for whatever was to come. Herb described his father's reaction to *Kristallnacht* as such a galvanizing force, impelling Herb's father to immediately request exit visas precisely because he recognized the Nazis had shifted the ground rules for acceptable political behavior.

Cognitive stretching thus seems related to hope's counterintuitive impact, as found in Frank's description of fatalism during World War II. Tuan also linked cognitive stretching to fatalism, not to a resilient "bouncing back," as he described fighting in the Vietnamese Civil War and preparing himself for death. For both men this cognitive preparation seemed to lessen the anxiety they might otherwise have felt. It was during the re-education camp experience, when Tuan lacked all knowledge of what was going to happen to him, that life became unbearable because of the lack of a frame of reference around which to organize his mind. The uncertainty of life in the camp prevented any shifting of cognitive expectations, leaving Tuan foundering, desperate to find new and consistent parameters for his life. "When I was in the war, I knew that each day could have been the last. The war, I knew what to expect. But in the camp I didn't" (p. 139).

A survivor of the Nicaraguan Civil War said much the same thing of that war, "I came to such a comfortable level with death. Once you accept that your death is inevitable, and that perhaps it is better than living, death does not scare you as much" (Fabiola, p. 222).

Acceptance, fatalism, and cognitive stretching seemed absent in the only one of our speakers whose humanity did *not* seem to have survived the war fully intact. "Before entering Iraq I wanted to shoot everyone because in my mind, everyone was bad. You can even say I was somewhat excited, a real life video game. Then while I was in Iraq you can say I became kind of numb" (Doc, p. 176). We did not probe too deeply when speakers raised the issue of their own behavior that they judged harshly and negatively. Instead, we listened, and occasionally someone would continue, as Frank did when he spoke about this dehumanizing aspect of war. "You learn to hate. . . . It led to the view that the only good Japanese was a dead one" (p. 47). Frank later told of learning Japanese and laying to rest this hatred some fifteen years after the war. While this aspect needs to be pursued more fully in later work, our tentative conclusion is that the ability to find a frame of reference for wartime events plays an important role for people who survive wars with their psyches emotionally intact.

LINK TO PREVIOUS LIFE. Emotional well-being was closely connected to both the recognition and the acceptance of a new reality. Its relation to self-esteem also was related to the ability to link one's wartime experience with one's previous life. Often, contact with nuclear family members provided speakers with this element of stability. Two Japanese internees told how living with their families provided important psychic continuity. Both girls shared the barracks with their families; this made their internment less traumatizing. Indeed, both girls felt such a strong element of stability that their core was not shaken by the experience and they spoke of leading lives relatively similar to their lives back home. (Both women spoke of the importance of being able to run, play, and come home to their families.)[7] A world apart, London children who remained in London with their parents during World War II fared better emotionally than did children who were evacuated to safety during the blitz of World War II (Myra, Blitz survivor; not included in this book).[8] Herb captures this phenomenon succinctly, noting that staying with his family "was probably the major factor in making this whole experience not a classically traumatic one" (p. 106).

Occasionally, psychic stability was provided by something from their old life that endured or – in Laura's case – was replaced. The man Laura met in camp – and later married – promised he would plant a lilac tree to take the place of the one lost at her childhood home. The emotional significance of this promise is evident in the title of Laura's autobiography: *I Will Plant You a Lilac Tree*. Forging links to a prior, happier life made it easier to retain humanity.

COPING MECHANISMS. Individual speakers coped differently with the trauma of war. Some internalized what happened. Others talked openly – occasionally even obsessively – about the events experienced. Many felt sharing their pasts constituted a valuable passing of knowledge so other people could be aware of what happened, and could learn from it. This reflected their efforts to discern meaning out of their suffering. But many simply closed a door and moved on. We did not find that speakers who chose to internalize their experience were necessarily repressing their emotions; we simply have no evidence on this, one way or the other. Sometimes, when we asked them about this, speakers told us they could cope with the memories of the war themselves, without talking about their experiences. Often, we found people needed time to assimilate and integrate what had happened to them. Closing a door until they were ready to deal with the emotional fallout of their experiences constituted a protective, useful defense. Focusing on the future felt positive to them; looking back at their loss was painful and felt negative. The magnitude of war often necessitated time to heal.

"It never crossed my mind something would happen in Cambodia. Unfortunately, it did happen, and I was devastated. I was lost" (Kimberly, p. 149).

A wide variety of experiences were described as helpful in dealing with wartime losses. Luis (El Salvador Civil War) said, "I do not want to think about such things anymore. I left El Salvador in the past and I am now in California. I only think about California now." Luis continued, "I saw horrible things happen in my country; but . . . I am putting everything that happened in the past. I try not to think about what had happened." Grace reflected this view, held by many survivors:

> *I don't have to be worrying about it at my age now. Not with everything else going on in the world today. It was something nobody should have to go through.*   *(Grace, p. 127)*

The student who interviewed her great grandmother about the Armenian genocide noted: "An aspect of Rose I picked up on very quickly was her strong suppression of the event I was interviewing her about. . . . Rose has found a way to deal with these atrocities committed to her, and that is by not talking about them" (private correspondence). The student interviewer – Rose's great granddaughter – felt a critical part of Rose's maintaining her humanity came by presenting a front of being strong. This persona helped Rose move on, maintain a normal life, and not dwell on the atrocities she encountered.

Forgetting the war thus constituted a central part of recovery for many speakers. "I do my best to forget about Vietnam" (John, U.S. soldier in the Vietnam War, story not included in this book). Forgetting was a common theme throughout the interviews. "What do you want to know? It's bad. You don't want to hear [it]," Sara said (p. 146). When asked if she discussed the massacres committed during the Armenian genocide, Rose replied, "What good would it do?" (p. 198). Had Marie wanted to escape Lebanon during the Civil War? "Yes. I had nothing to lose. . . . I didn't want to remember anything anymore. There was no moving on. Too much was seen" (p. 231). Frank captured this sentiment for many speakers. "We just didn't talk about it [the war]. It was one of those things you repress. That's how you cope with it" (p. 48). Children of survivors often echoed this refrain, stating that their parents never spoke of the war, with them or with anyone as far as they knew.

FINDING HAPPINESS. Coping was closely related to the deep-seated need to find happiness. Each speaker's concept of happiness influenced what the speaker considered humane and not humane. For example, young Japanese internees claimed that because they were with their families they felt protected and free of worries. "I was young and kids have fun....I didn't have anybody tell me anything" (Grace, p. 126). Another young internee echoed this view: "I thought of it like an adventure or something. I was happy and I was not worried....It was like a picnic. Because when you are young, you do not worry. You are carefree" (Kimi, Japanese internee; full transcript not included here). If it seems surreal to have internment described as one that included "fun times," it is even stranger to hear similar descriptions from a Khmer Rouge survivor:

> *When we got there, as a young child I said, "Hey, no more school. Freedom. No Mom and Dad to tell us what to do" and we were free....Slowly, only a few months later, we realized what's happening. We knew we were not going to be able to have a family anymore. Your family is who they told you would be your family.*
>
> *Q. You said your family was really close; how was it when you realized you weren't going to be able to have a family anymore?*
>
> *I was devastated. In shock.*   *(Kimberly, p. 150)*

Jewish children hidden with their parents also sometimes described their time in hiding with their parents as one of emotional closeness, in which ordinary rules of conduct were suspended. One woman related how before the war, whenever guests came, her parents made her wait for the tasty treats, and urged her to study hard to succeed in school. Not so during the war. In hiding, parents – at least in their children's eyes – went the extra distance to make it up to children by relaxing the ordinary rules of childhood. In particular, parents gave their children the best of what little food there was; they were especially gentle with the children, relaxing requirements of etiquette, homework, and so on. This seemed an age-related phenomenon; the older the speaker, the greater the worry and the consciousness of what truly was happening. But even older speakers who survived concentration camps mentioned the importance of being able to find moments of fun and happiness, and claimed such frivolity helped them stay human. (A Czech survivor named Otto described parties in a concentration camp.)[9]

Approaching happiness elliptically during war is one thing. Finding happiness after war is another, more important task. Happiness was arrived at via different avenues. Iranian Islamic Revolution survivor

Leyla related her deeply held belief that education is ultimately the most important possession contributing to success in life. She found this critical not only for herself but also for her children:

> *The only thing that matters is everything you have here [points to her head]. You must invest in this. This is the most important thing in life. I tried to do something for my children, to teach them this. I tried to teach them that you have to do everything you can to invest in your education.*
>
> *(p. 256)*

SURVIVOR GUILT. No matter how young when they went through their ordeal, most speakers felt survivor guilt. Losing a member of one's nuclear family was especially important in inducing guilt. "The guilt for staying alive, most of us had guilt feelings. Why didn't my parents live? Why did I live?" (Laura, p. 64). Others described guilt at leaving their homeland. "Leaving behind a country of my people who did not have the option of freedom led to guilt" (Fabiola, p. 221). Other times it was simply seeing someone die that triggered remorse. Luis described how a friend was killed while standing right next to Luis. "I could only think about how I might have been able to save Roberto. If I had only pulled him with me one minute before, he would have still been alive" (El Salvador Civil War). To assuage his guilt, Luis later brought his friend's family to the United States. An American soldier in Iraq gave the citizens of Iraq his paycheck, food, and books because of the guilt he experienced.

> *We were supposed to be making their lives better by coming and being liberators but it was just as bad as before, if not worse. But I did make a connection with them. I did what I could to help them as individuals. I gave them most of my paychecks. I gave them things that were sent from home, like food and books for the children. Things like that.*
>
> *(Sebastian, p. 183)*

BLAME. Guilt is closely related to blame, and the assignment of blame was tough to analyze. While blame was rarely directed at specific individuals, speakers frequently attributed the wrongs that befell them to the government's inability to deal with the situation. Such blame was expressed as hate for their government. For example, in speaking of the Salvadoran Civil War, Luis blamed both the civilians for their revolutionary actions and the Salvadoran government for not giving people what they needed.

It wasn't right for the workers to riot because they didn't work for it, to have a higher position. It wasn't right. People who specialized in a certain occupation should just do the best they can do in their job. At the same time, the government should have made sure more people were educated so they would be able to get better jobs, so the people would have a better life.

How individuals blamed people for wartime cruelty seemed related to their ability to move on and find peace, if not happiness. Glimpses of this are evident in the narratives of the two Khmer Rouge survivors. Sara remains angry and bitter at the Khmer Rouge; Kimberly seems to have found forgiveness and peace, and notes that she was saved because someone else took blame for not reporting Kimberly when she was ill.

"A person who owed a great deal to my grandparent because she was raised by my grandparent, this person told the leader that it was her fault. She took the blame. They ended up punishing her. They killed her. So I got to live because of her. At the time, as a thirteen year old it didn't make sense." (Kimberly, p. 154)

Shortly after relating this story, in response to our last question, Kimberly told what she took away from the Khmer Rouge experience.

Q. Is there anything you left out you still want to share?

I know that a lot of people will ask "If you could go back and change things, what would you change?" I would not change anything, to be honest with you. Everything happened for a reason. For who I am today, what happened to me made me stronger, a person with a kinder heart. To see the world and find peace in a different way, a way that people don't normally see; to see what life is all about. Yes, I do hate that time. Yes, I lost my brother, my grandmother, and my uncle. But an eye for an eye? There were those who said, "You kill my brother, so I'm going to kill you back." With revenge, what does that make us? We're no better than that person who killed in the first place. It's hard. It's hard to say it now. But then I wouldn't have become who I am today. I know who the leader was that killed my brother. He stayed at our house. I told my mom, "It wouldn't take a lot to kill this guy. Just get the cleaver and kill him."

She said, "Does that bring your brother back? No. Does it make you feel better? Or will you have to live with that for the rest of your life?" You don't need to go to school to learn that. (Kimberly, p. 164)

CONCLUSION

Despite its importance, the subject of how people retain humanity during war has produced surprisingly little systematic academic work. Yet
retaining humanity during war involves us in issues central for politics, ethics, and moral psychology. Studying what helps people survive
these traumas thus is vital insofar as it furthers understanding of how the
human mind copes with life and death situations, suggests what people
turn to in their darkest hours, and yields insight on the psychological
mechanisms that foster human well-being.

Our study began by reviewing biographies and memoirs, plus
scholarly literature on general psychoanalytic theories and on coping
with emotional traumas and with PTSD more particularly. This review
yielded several propositions to test, propositions stressing the raw
drive to survive, the importance of both situational and personality
factors in this survival, and how people find meaning out of suffering
and cope with the dislocations and loss of war. These propositions
were examined using a dataset that included more than fifty in-depth
narrative interviews with individuals who experienced a broad range
of wars, genocides, and other brutalizing political conflicts, from the
Armenian genocide in the early twentieth century through World War II
and Vietnam and ending with current soldiers in Iraq. Our narratives
included all wartime participants, from soldiers to civilians and victims
of oppression and war. We had no independent measures indicating
which individuals did retain their humanity during war and relied on
the speakers' own self-reports.

Our findings confirm the importance of psychological mechanisms,
reaffirm parts of the major theoretical approaches, and fill in important
details on how these general theories may work, often in ways that are
counterintuitive. In terms of our general theories about what drives people while they are undergoing wars, we found support for the Freudian
view that a raw drive to live impels most of us. Indeed, one question
to explore in future work is whether many of the coping mechanisms
we found critical for humane survival are simply reflections of the basic
Freudian desire to survive. This possibility seems a bit reductionist, however, so we explored other explanations as well. In doing so, we found
strong support for Frankl's claim that people need to be able to find
meaning in their suffering but little evidence supporting Adler's emphasis on the human need for power and control; indeed, our findings lead
us to ask if people with inordinate need for control may fare worse in

surviving wars' chaos. In contrast, however, we did find strong support for the importance of the environment's influence, one both Adler and Bettelheim emphasize. Luck plays a critical role during war, not just in physical survival but also in surviving with one's humanity intact.

What about more specific psychological mechanisms that might help preserve humanity? Here, we found the fundamental things apply when we ask about the critical aspects of what we might call a humane self that survives war. These include a sense of self and a sense of belonging to something broader than one's self, forging links between wartime experiences and one's prior life, and an odd mixture of fatalism, hope, and the ability to stretch one's mental map to encompass the new shifts in the political and personal world. People spoke often of the importance of their ability to maintain their sense of self and self-esteem while undergoing the trauma of war; especially critical was the ability to find a linkage between their pre- and postwar selves. Such continuity of self signified in emotional resilience.

An interesting observation was how closely intertwined some of these psychological coping mechanisms were. For example, hope was closely related to fatalism, acceptance closely related to happiness. Speakers who lost hope for a better future became fatalistic, but this fatalism was not necessarily a negative thing. Fatalism seemed to alleviate a sense of guilt at surviving when others did not. Fatalism and acceptance helped speakers recognize they had no control over their lives and this, in turn, seemed to free them to lead happy lives later. Fatalism also provided an escape from the stress associated with feeling responsible for events over which one had no control. This finding relates to the conspicuous lack of discussion about being alarmed at losing control over one's life and made us wonder if people with inordinate needs for control may not fare as well in war as do those who can adjust and adapt to not having such control. This possibility remains to be checked in future work. Finally, we found fatalism related to hope and forgiveness. Lack of hope often was a positive factor that helped speakers to stretch cognitively and find new ways to survive and flourish. The capacity to adjust cognitively to the new realities of war and the changed world after war seemed critical to speakers' ability to build a happy postwar life and to assimilate their memories of the war into a narrative that allowed them to flourish emotionally, if not to find forgiveness and meaning out of the suffering they had endured.

Let us now try to step back and put our empirical findings in a broader context.

NOTES

1. This book features stories of eighteen speakers. In this chapter, however, we also include excerpts from stories not able to be printed here for reasons of space. We are grateful to all those interviewed.
2. Luis is a survivor of the El Salvadoran Civil War. His full interview is not included in this book.
3. The Sherman quote appears in many different forms but all signifiy Sherman's view that all war is immoral. See Langer 1991 for a discussion of whether having no choice removes moral responsibility.
4. In September 1982, between 762 and 3,500 Palestinian and Lebanese Shia civilians were slaughtered at the Sabra and Shatila Palestinian refugee camps in Beirut, Lebanon.
5. The closest person was Herb, whose Zionism provided a sense of belonging that helped him survive. We find this a different phenomenon, however, one discussed later.
6. See Snyder 1994, 2000.
7. Only Grace's full story is included here.
8. While many children were saved by being evacuated from London during the Blitz of World War II, children separated from their parents because they were being taken to safety in the countryside surprisingly showed more adverse psychological reactions than their counterparts who stayed behind in London with their parents during World War II. See Bowlby 1951.
9. Monroe 2004, chapter 2.

CONCLUSION
The enormity of it all

War is a horrifying, brutal thing, so ferocious, dark, and foul it lies beyond words, perhaps beyond human comprehension.[1] In the last century alone, war claimed more than 160 million lives and touched countless others.[2] The statistics stagger and overpower, leaving us struggling to fathom the experiences of loved ones who were soldiers or civilians trapped in wars. How can we expect to help our children and students understand the reality of war, when we ourselves remain overwhelmed, simply by the numbers and the contemplation of war's devastation? Even those who live through war find it difficult to grasp fully what they endured and the extent of its effect on them.

As I write this, I think of my own father, a young man just out of law school and newly married when he enlisted in World War II. Daddy wore glasses so thick he was the last person you would want to turn loose in combat with a gun. The army had little idea what to do with lawyers anyway in those days, so my father was assigned desk jobs, spared the worst of the war. But he was kept on after the war to hear war crimes in the Far East. He lived through air raids in China and recorded legal testimony on both civilian and military atrocities. After being assigned as the American member of the British Commission of War Crimes in the Pacific, Daddy heard far too many stories of abuse in prisoner-of-war camps in Formosa,[3] of American soldiers getting drunk and raping civilians,[4] of random violence, and of bombs falling from the skies. My father died in 1973, when he was only 55, before he reached the age where people tend to step back and try to make sense of their lives and before I became interested in war as a topic of research. He never talked about the war with me or my brother. At the time, I did not think much of this silence. Kids can be remarkably cavalier and blasé about their parents' lives, and I was certainly no different. But after speaking with so many others about their wartime experiences, I now wonder if this distancing signifies something deeper.

Frank never wrote home about the war, never once told people back home what it was really like. "You just talked about the scenery and how beautiful it was in the South Pacific, or you joked about things you did with your buddies, kind of made your parents feel you were on some kind of pleasure trip to an exotic place with friends. You didn't want them to know how bad it really was." Another American soldier wrote his fiancée just one letter saying this would tell her what war really was like. After that, he insisted, they must agree not to talk about the war, since sharing it with her would only make it more real for him and would upset her. Others – Rose and Mafalda in this book – still refuse to speak of their wartime experiences.

Trauma isolates. Some find healing in talking; for others, distancing offers protection, putting time and space between the wartime terror and the speaker's present life.[5] Not talking about the war – putting a "do not disturb" sign on one's memory, in one Polish World War II survivor's recounting – creates an emotional buffer, protecting both survivors and family members, providing a safe haven for wounds to heal in their own time. Beyond this curative aspect of silence lies another reality. What people see and experience during war simply overwhelms them. Not speaking of it may signal respect and awe for the event and for those who perished in the war. The enormity of it all demands a kind of reverential silence.[6]

Considering the magnitude of the unique, incommunicable shock and pain accompanying war, can social science expect to reveal anything significant about the human experience of war? Can we presume to convey more than factual lists of battles, casualties, strategies, and shifts in the geopolitical map? Should we attempt to chart the terrain of the human psyche and how it fares during war? Is it enough only to fill in little pieces in the puzzle, to get one tiny bit to fit into the right spot, and then trust the poets and the literary giants to provide a glimpse of the whole frightening picture?

I wish I had answers to these questions. I recognize the limitations in comprehending another's reality even as I trust insight can be gained if we combine our best analytical tools with the emotional sensitivity that must accompany genuine attempts to understand others as they talk about their lives. But given the importance of grasping even a glimmer of war's psychological impact, social scientists must tackle this topic. Ascertaining the psychological aftermath of war is essential for policy-making and for understanding the ethical dilemmas surround-ing moral choices – individual and collective – in international affairs. Studying what helps people survive wartime traumas is further vital insofar as it enhances understanding of how the human mind copes with life and death situations, suggests what people turn to in their dark nights of the soul, and yields insight into the psychological mechanisms that foster human well-being. Connecting even a few dots in a much larger and complicated picture can sharpen and focus a more compre-hensive understanding of what helps people preserve or reclaim their humanity after a war. Social scientists can attempt to do this, with both humility toward the limitations of our analytical tools and an apprecia-tion for the unique skills we bring to the topic.

So, stepping back, what does our social science analysis tell us about how people pick up the pieces, try to make connections, and weave a pattern that lends meaning to the appalling, unexpected events that shook their worlds and threatened their spirits? Can the stories of peo-ple whose existing lives were shattered by war teach us about our own human capacity to process trauma, heal wounds, reclaim lost spirits, and derive meaning and purpose from the most horrific of personal events?

As we began our study, we found insights from biographies, mem-oirs, and scholarly literature on coping with emotional traumas and PTSD. Distilling these insights produced propositions we then analyzed using a dataset of over fifty in-depth narrative interviews with survivors from a broad range of wars, genocides, and other brutalizing political conflicts. Eighteen of these narratives – from the early twentieth-century Armenian genocide through World War II and Vietnam and ending with current soldiers in Iraq and civilians in Afghanistan – formed the focus of our analysis. Narratives were not limited to soldiers, and included civilians and victims of oppression in a wide variety of wars. We utilized no independent measures to indicate which individuals did retain their humanity, but instead relied on speakers' own self-reporting, allowing the individuals to weigh for themselves their raw drive to survive, their assessment of both situational and personality factors in this survival, and how they created meaning out of suffering and coped with dislo-cations and loss. Within these constraints, we pinpointed a few critical factors future analysts can build upon as – we hope – later scholars use our work to develop more refined, systematic tools of analysis.

Overall, our findings confirm the importance of psychological mechanisms, reaffirm parts of the major theoretical approaches to understanding human behavior, and fill in important details concerning how people actually operate, often in ways that are counterintuitive. First, Freud was right. A raw drive to live impels most of us. Indeed, many of the coping mechanisms we found critical for humane survival may be reflecting this basic desire to survive. The reductionism of this formulation, however, encouraged us to explore further clarification.

Doing so revealed a second striking finding: the ability to unearth meaning out of suffering helped people find peace. Third, neither physical nor emotional survival correlated with the human need for power and control. In contrast, the environment's influence on surviving was frequently mentioned.[7] Luck plays a critical role during war, not just in survival, but also in determining how much of one's humanity continues intact. When we considered particular psychological mechanisms that help preserve humanity, we found several factors related to the enduring existence of a humane self. These included (1) a sense of self-worth; (2) a sense of belonging to something broader than one's self; (3) forging a link between wartime experiences and one's prior life; and (4) an odd mixture of fatalism, hope, and the ability to stretch one's mental map to encompass shifts in the political and personal world. Further, in noting the importance of a sense of self and self-esteem while undergoing the trauma of war, the ability to find a linkage between one's pre- and postwar selves seemed especially important. Such continuity of self signified emotional hardiness and strength.[8]

Beyond this, we found another interesting observation. People's psychological coping mechanisms are remarkably intertwined. For example, hope was closely related to fatalism, and acceptance closely related to happiness. Speakers who lost hope for a better future became fatalistic, but this fatalism was not necessarily a negative. Fatalism could alleviate guilt at surviving when others did not. Fatalism and acceptance helped people recognize they had little control over their lives. This acceptance – ironically – freed them to lead happy lives later. This may be because such fatalism provided an escape from the stress associated with feeling responsible for events over which one truly had no control.[9] We linked this finding to the fact that we found little or no discussion of being alarmed at losing control over one's life. (We wonder: Do people with inordinate needs for control not fare as well in war as those who can adjust and adapt to not having such control?[10]) Finally, fatalism was related to hope. Paradoxically, lack of hope could prove a positive factor insofar as it forced speakers to stretch cognitively and devise new possibilities to survive and flourish. The capacity to adjust cognitively to the shifting political and personal realities of war critically impacted survivors' capabilities to build a happy life, find meaning in their suffering, and craft a narrative that allowed them to find a sense of peace in their post-war lives.

In addition to the conclusions presented here, analysis points to several important avenues for future research. As a teaching tool, incorporating interviews with people who survived wars proved an invaluable pedagogical instrument, one that can alert young people to the importance of political psychology and help them recognize their own ability to conduct moving oral histories. As a Khmer Rouge survivor told us, people tell their stories to pass on their knowledge. How we decide to use this information is our choice. Ideally, wartime stories teach students that everyone has a story to tell; learning how to listen can heighten respect for the "ordinary" people they meet each day. Life stories put us in touch with deep eternal themes that students need to think about. They increase students' sensitivity to the suffering and wisdom of others.

In thinking about how best to teach about war, I am reminded of *Brideshead Revisited,* a novel that begins during World War II and returns the hero to memories of a happier time during his college years. The protagonist is Charles Ryder, who goes up to Oxford in the 1920s and meets the Flytes, a charismatic if ill-fated aristocratic family, through their son, Sebastian. Ryder's has been a loveless life; his mother was killed during World War I and his reserved father gives new meaning to the term "repressed Englishman." Charles is drawn to Sebastian's *joie de vivre* and neglects his studies as a result. Ryder's older cousin berates Charles, trying to steer him back onto the straight and narrow and away from the sybaritic world of what the cousin judges Sebastian's hedonistic, self-indulgent, bad set. Charles replies:

> *"I like this bad set and I like getting drunk at luncheon"; that was enough then. Is more needed now? Looking back, now, after twenty years, there is little I would have left undone or done otherwise. I could match my cousin Jasper's game-cock maturity with a sturdier fowl. I could tell him that all the wickedness of that time was like the spirit they mix with the pure grape of the Douro, heady stuff full of dark ingredients; it at once enriched and retarded the whole process of adolescence as the spirit checks the fermentation of the wine, renders it undrinkable, so that it must lie in the dark, year in, year out, until it is brought up at last fit for the table. I could tell him, too, that to know and love one other human being is the root of all wisdom.*[11]

Rereading these stories, thinking about my students and how I so casu-
ally suggested they interview someone they knew personally, I wonder
how much of what they learned originated in the emotional impact of
stories told by a speaker with whom they shared a particular bond, a
human connection: a friend, parent, grandparent, or relative. How much
of social science needs to be infused with affection for us to understand
others? What are the limits of dry, objective, analytical rigor for comprehending another's reality? Need we – can we – combine both the rigor
of analysis with our empathy and love for other human beings, especially when attempting to understand soldiers returning home after a
tour of duty in a faraway place, or civilians whose lives were upended
by war? Again, I have no answers, just the mundane encouragement
to other scholars to adopt this technique and add their own interviews
to an archival data base from which others can draw.[12] Broadening the
number of cases will prove invaluable in identifying the critical factors
constituting a typology of humanitarian survival.

From a scholarly point of view, future work needs to clarify what it
means to retain humanity. More important, what does it mean to survivors to feel their humanity continues intact? Should we conceptualize
humanity as a dichotomous phenomenon, or as a scale? Our interviews
were conducted in the United States; how sensitive does this make our
findings to national or cultural influences on post-war recovery? Would
collecting a larger data archive of interviews help isolate the potential
import of such cultural and national differences? Would including material from journals and letters of those who perished reveal a significantly
different picture? From a policy point of view, the value of understanding critical factors that aid in post-war adjustment cannot be overesti-
mated and social scientists should draw on all the possible materials at
hand for our analysis. We have offered only a beginning sketch, a skele-
tal framework of the psychology of keeping humanity during war. Future
work should explore the finer details of our outline, asking what the stories of people whose lives were scarred by war can teach us about our
own human ability to process traumatic ordeals, heal wounds, restore
lost spirits, and derive meaning and purpose from the most horrific of
personal events.

These questions raise a deeper, more philosophically challenging
and profound issue: Can systematic work in social science yield the
insight we need, as scholars and as human beings, to deal with the
emotional consequences of war? Asking students to conduct the kind of
interviews my class did for this project seems far more useful a way for

them to gain a sense of what war really is like than merely reading traditional social science texts, and I recommend this hands-on teaching technique, which provides an immediacy and a personal impact that is inestimable. For years scholars separated reason and emotion, thinking the former far superior in helping people reach moral choices. Cognitive scientists now tell us emotion enters and influences the reasoning process at so many points that trying to separate the two may well be futile. Maybe that is as it should be. Perhaps emotional jolts shock us out of traditional ways of thinking.

Since I began using narrative analysis, the technique has become more widely accepted in political science. One aspect of narrative, however, continually unsettles social scientists: interpreting silences. I argued in earlier work that people do not comment on the ordinary, on the commonplace.[13] Silences capture what is unremarkable. The trick for analysts lies in interpreting the silences correctly.

In reviewing the stories in this book, we find little of the swashbuckling jingoism that so frequently accompanies justifications and beginnings of wars. No scenes out of *Gone with the Wind,* of wild enthusiasm, of a rush to combat before the war is over and the chance for battlefield glory eludes young patriots. No rousing calls to exaltation from inspirational leaders speaking of the need to avenge "a day of infamy." Instead, we find people stuck in the mud in the middle of a civil war. Wars that easily constitute the worst experiences of a lifetime. People who saw too much, who carry bad memories and bad feelings, and live the rest of their lives as damaged goods, not happy heroes. At best, collateral damage is justified – and then only rarely – by a greater good.

Perhaps these insights give social science a unique edge over poetry or fiction. Fiction gives the author voice. Social science attempts to give voice to others. We endeavor to do so free of our own preconceptions, devoid of literary agendas, striving for objectivity, a detached and fair neutrality we recognize we may never fully achieve.

Stepping back and listening to these stories, gathered so randomly, we are struck by their contrast with the many books on war written by the policy makers, the old men who start wars. Such books frequently entail a justification for the wars the protagonists began, or at least ratified or colluded in. With the exception of Doc – himself now involved in homeland security – we find none of this here. Virtually every other person in this book emphasizes only the negatives of wars. The forest they show us is dark, primordial, and dangerous, in which no soldiers cheer, no crowds exalt. Our speakers – ordinary people all – reach out to us, exuding revulsion and the desire to suppress the memory of their war, searching to make sense of their experience, yearning to close the chapter and move on, back to the blessed mundane of the everyday, away from an experience so searing that the enormity of it tends to reduce the rest of life to a blessed footnote in which – they hope – we can all now permanently reside.

NOTES

1. The title of this chapter is a paraphrase of a quote by a soldier from the Battle of the Bulge, who said the enormity of it all tended to reduce everything else in life to a kind of footnote.
2. See Chapter 1, note 1 for a discussion of actual numbers.
3. Formosa is the historic name for Taiwan.
4. Two American soldiers got drunk, stole a jeep, and barged into a Taiwanese family home. They raped the mother, sodomized the young daughter, beat the father, and killed the grandmother. My father prosecuted them and they received life imprisonment. Later my father learned, the sentence was commuted to six months.
5. Psychiatrists speak of patients at "talk stage" and suggest people reach that stage – if at all – in their own time.
6. A survivor of the Battle of the Bulge said the enormity of war tended to reduce everything else in life to a kind of footnote. The idea that war's intensity makes the later life recede in significance is the dominant theme in "Plenty" by David Hare. It echoes in "The Last of the Blonde Bombshells," a movie that depicts war's ability to create a community of those who lived through it together.
7. Both Adler and Bettelheim emphasize this.
8. Such extreme experiences can also help bond people who underwent them together, providing a sense of solidarity. See Ahmed 2004 for a controversial discussion of the relations among emotions, language, communities, rhetoric, and culture.
9. The complex relationship of fatalism, hope, and survival is discussed in a wide variety of fields, from Spinoza's philosophical treatise on ethics (1677) to contemporary work on stress in the workplace.
10. This is a hypothesis to be checked in future work.
11. Charles Ryder, in Evelyn Waugh (1946), Book I, Chapter Two.
12. The Ethics Center at UCI, www.ethicscenter.uci.edu, will store such transcripts, and make them available for others.
13. See Appendix A in Monroe 2004 for how narrative helps us understand moral choices made by people during war.

BIBLIOGRAPHY

Adler, A. (1927a/1955.) *The Practice and Theory of Individual Psychology*. New York: Routledge and Kegan Paul.

Adorno, T. W., Frenkel-Brunswik, E., Levinson, D. J., and Sanford, R. N. 1950. *The Authoritarian Personality*. New York: Harper and Row.

———. (1927b/1998.) *Understanding Human Nature*. Center City, MN: The Hazeldon Foundation.

———. (1931/1980.) *What Life Should Mean to You*. New York: G. P. Putnam Sons.

———. Alfred Adler Institutes of San Francisco and Northwestern University. *The Collected Clinical Works of Alfred Adler. 1898–1937*. Volumes 1–12. Bellingham, WA: The Classical Adlerian Translation Project.

Ahmed, Sarah. 2004. *Cultural Politics of Emotion*. New York: Routledge.

Andrews, M. 2007. *Shaping History: Narratives of Political Change*. New York: Cambridge University Press.

Anouilh, J. 1943. *Antigone*. London: Methuene.

Banks, Arthur S. 2004. *Political Handbook of the World*. 5th ed. Binghamton, NY: CQ Press.

Bar-On, D., Eland, J., Kleber, R., Krell, R., Moore, Y., Sagi, A., Soriano, E., Suedfeld, P., van der Velden, P., and van Ijzendoorn, M. 1998. "Multigenerational perspectives on coping with the Holocaust experience: An attachment perspective for understanding the developmental sequelae of trauma across generations." *International Journal of Behavioral Development*, 22: 315–38.

Bartone, P. 1999. "Hardiness protects against war-related stress in Army Reserve forces." Educational Publishing Foundation and the Division of Consulting Psychology, 1061–4087/99/S3.00, *Consulting Psychology Journal: Practice and Research*, 51(2): 72–82.

Becker, G. 1997. *Disrupted Lives: How People Create Meaning in a Chaotic World*. Berkeley: University of California Press.

Bettelheim, B. 1943. "Individual and mass behavior in extreme situations." *Journal of Abnormal and Social Psychology*, 38: 417–52.

———. 1950. *Love Is Not Enough: The Treatment of Emotionally Disturbed Children*. Glencoe, IL: Free Press.

———. 1983. *Freud and Man's Soul: An Important Re-Interpretation of Freudian Theory*. New York: Knopf.

———. 1985. *The Informed Heart: Autonomy in a Mass Age*. First published 1960. Glencoe, IL: Free Press.

Bielenberg, C. 1971. *When I Was a German, 1934–1945: An Englishwoman in Nazi Germany*. New York: Norton.

Blass, T. 1993. "Psychological perspectives on the perpetrators of the Holocaust: The role of situational pressures, dispositions and their interactions." *Holocaust and Genocide Studies*, 7(1): Spring 1993: 30–52.

Blass, T., ed. 1999. *Obedience to Authority: Current Perspectives on the Milgram Paradigm*. Mahwah, NJ: Erlbaum.

Bock, D. C., and Warren, N. C. 1972. "Religious belief as a factor in obedience to destructive demands." *Review of Religious Research*, 13: 185–91.

Bowlby, J. 1951. *Maternal Care and Mental Health: Bulletin of the World Health Organization*, 3: 355–534.

Burger, N., Charness, G., and Lynham, J. 2011. "Field and online experiments on self-control." *Journal of Economic Behavior and Organization*, 77: 393–404.

Butler, L. D., Koopman, C., Azarow, J., Blasey, C. M., Magdalene, J. C., DiMiceli, S., Seagraves, D. A., Hastings, T. A., Chen, X. H., Garlan, R. W., Kraemer, H. C., and Spiegel, D. 2009. "Psychosocial predictors of resilience after the September 11, 2001 terrorist attacks." *Journal of Nervous and Mental Disease*, 197(4): 266–73.

Butler, J. 1997. *Excitable Speech: The Politics of the Performative*. New York: Routledge.

Carll, E., ed. 2007. *Trauma Psychology: Issues in Violence, Disaster, Health, and Illness*. Vol 2. Westport, CT: Praeger.

Charuvastra, A., and Cloitre, M. 2008. "Social bonds and posttraumatic stress disorder." *Annual Review of Psychology*, 59: 301–28.

Clark, A. 1997. *Being There: Putting Brain, Body, and World Together Again*. Cambridge, MA: MIT Press.

Connell, Raewyn. 2012. "Transsexual women and feminist thought: Toward new understanding and new politics." *Signs: Journal of Women in Culture and Society*, 37(4): 857–81.

Dambrun, Michael, and Vatine, Elise. 2010. "Reopening the study of extreme social behaviors: Obedience to authority within an immersive video environment." *European Journal of Social Psychology*, 40(5): 760–73.

Delahanty, D. L., Herberman, H. B., Craig, K. J., Hayward, M. C., Fullerton, C. S., and Ursano, R. J. 1997. "Acute and chronic distress and posttraumatic stress disorder as a function of responsibility for serious motor vehicle accidents." *Journal of Consulting and Clinical Psychology*, 65: 560–67.

Dwyer, S. 2005. "'Enter Here' – At Your Own Risk: The Moral Dangers of Cyberporn." In R. Cavalier, ed., *The Impact of the Internet on Our Moral Lives*. Albany: State University of New York Press, pp. 69–94.

Ehlers, A., and Clark, D. M. 2000. "A cognitive model of posttraumatic stress disorder." *Behaviour, Research and Therapy*, 38(4): 319–45.

Eliot, Stephen. 2003. *Not the Thing I Was: Thirteen Years at Bruno Bettelheim's Orthogenics School*. New York: St. Martin's Press.

Elms, A., and Milgram, S. 1966. "Personality characteristics associated with obedience and defiance toward authoritative commands." *Journal of Experimental Research in Personality*, 2: 292–89.

Fiske, S. T., and Taylor, S. E. 1991. *Social Cognition*. 2nd ed. New York: McGraw-Hill.

Foa, E. B. 1997. "Psychological processes related to recovery from a trauma and an effective treatment for PTSD." *Annals of the New York Academy of Sciences*, 821: 410–24.

Foa, E. B., and Kozak, M. J. 1986. "Emotional processing of fear: Exposure to corrective information." *Psychological Bulletin*, 99: 20–3.

Foa, E. B., Molnar, C., and Cashman, L. 1995. "Change in rape narratives during exposure therapy for PTSD." *Journal of Traumatic Stress*, 8: 675–90.

Foa, E. B., Rothbaum, B. O., Riggs, D. S., and Murdock, T. B. 1991. "Treatment of posttraumatic stress disorder in rape victims: A comparison between cognitive-behavioral procedures and counseling." *Journal of Consulting and Clinical Psychology*, 59: 715–23.

Frankl, V. 1977. *The Will to Meaning: Foundations and Applications of Logotherapy.* New York: New American Library.

———. 2004. *Man's Search for Meaning: An Introduction to Logotherapy.* Boston: Beacon and London: Random House/Rider.

Freud, Sigmund. 1999. *The Standard Edition of the Complete Psychological Works of Sigmund Freud.* Translated from the German under the General Editorship of James Strachey. In collaboration with Anna Freud. Assisted by Alix Strachey and Alan Tyson. 24 vols. First published 1953–1974. London: Hogarth Press.

Frye, J. S., and Stockton, R. A. 1982. "Discriminant analysis of post-traumatic stress disorder among a group of Vietnam veterans." *American Journal of Psychiatry*, 139: 52–56.

Galloway, S. 2008. *The Cellist of Sarajevo.* New York: Riverhead/Penguin.

Goldhagen, Daniel. 1996. *Hitler's Willing Executioners.* London: Abacus.

Haas, D. C. 1966. "Chronic post-traumatic headaches classified and compared with natural headaches." *Cephalalgia*, 16(7): 486–93.

Haney, C., and Zimbardo, P. 1973. "The past and future of U.S. prison policy: Twenty-five years after the Stanford prison experiment." *American Psychologist*, 53(7): 709–27.

Hillman, L. 2005. *I Will Plant You a Lilac Tree: A Memoir of a Schindler's List Survivor.* New York: Atheneum of Simon and Schuster.

Holmes, D., Alpers, G. W., Ismailji, T., Classen, C., Wales, T., Cheasty, V., Miller, A., and Koopman, C. 2007. "Cognitive and emotional processing in narratives of women abused by intimate partners." *Violence Against Women*, 13(11): 1192–205.

Homer. 1813. *The Odyssey and the Iliad.* Georgetown, D.C.: Richards and Mallory.

Janoff-Bulman, R. 1992. *Shattered Assumptions: Towards a New Psychology of Trauma.* New York: Free Press.

Joseph, S., and Linley, P. A. 2008. *Trauma, Recovery, and Growth: Positive Psychological Perspectives on Post-Traumatic Stress.* Hoboken, NJ: John Wiley.

Kelman, H. C. 1999. "The interdependence of Israeli and Palestinian national identities: The role of the Other in existential conflicts." *Journal of Social Issues*, 55(3): 581–600.

Keneally, T. 1982. *Schindler's List.* New York: Simon and Schuster.

Kobasa, S. C. 1979. "Stressful life events, personality, and health: Inquiry into hardiness." *Journal of Personality and Social Psychology*, 37(1): 1–11.

Koestler, A. 1943. *Arrival and Departure.* New York: The Macmillan Company.

Kohn, George C. 1999. *Dictionary of War.* New York: Facts On File Publications.

Koopman, C. 1997. "Political psychology as a lens for viewing traumatic events." *Political Psychology*, 18(4): 831–47.

Kross, E., and Ayduk, O. 2011. "Enhancing the pace of recovery: Self-distanced analysis of negative experiences reduces blood pressure reactivity: Short report." *Psychological Science*, 19(3): 229–31.

Langer, Ellen J. 1975. "The illusion of control." *Journal of Personality and Social Psychology*, 32: 311–28.

Langer, Lawrence. 1991. *Holocaust Testimonies: The Ruins of Memory*. New Haven, CT: Yale University Press.

Lyons, Tom. 1983. *The Pelican and After*. New York: Prescott, Durrell.

Maddi, S. R. 2007. "Hardiness: An operationalization of existential courage." *Journal of Humanistic Psychology*, 44(3): 279–98.

Maddi, S., and Kobassa, S. 1984. *The Hardy Executive*. New York: Dow Jones-Irwin.

Marley, D. D. 2002. *Wars of the Americas: A Chronology of Armed Conflict in the New World, 1492 to the Present*. Santa Barbara, CA: ABC-CLIO.

McDermott, R., Wernimont, N., and Koopman, C. 2011. "Applying psychology to international studies: Challenges and opportunities in examining traumatic stress." *International Studies*, 12: 19–135.

Milgram, S. 1974. *Obedience to Authority: An Experimental View*. New York: Harper and Row.

Monroe, K. R. 2004. *The Hand of Compassion: Moral Choice During the Holocaust*. Princeton, NJ: Princeton University Press.

———. 2012. *Ethics in an Age of Terror and Genocide: Identity and Moral Choice*. Princeton, NJ: Princeton University Press.

Neria, Y., Galea, S., and Norris, F. 2009. *Mental Health and Disasters*. New York: Cambridge University Press.

Nicholls, Brendon. 2010. *Ngugi wa Thiong'o, Gender, and the Ethics of Postcolonial Reading*. Farnham, Surrey, UK: Ashgate Publishing.

Regehr, C., Cadell, S., and Jansen, K. 1999. "Perceptions of control and long-term recovery from rape." *American Journal of Orthopsychiatry*, 69(1): 110–15.

Reicher, S. D., and Haslam, S. A. 2006. "Rethinking the psychology of tyranny: The BBC Prison Study." *British Journal of Social Psychology*, 45: 1–40.

Rotter, J. B. 1966. "Generalized expectancies of internal versus external control of reinforcements." *Psychological Monographs*, 80(609): 1–28.

Scaruffi, Piero. 2009. *Wars and Casualties of the 20th and 21st Centuries*. Website Copyright Piero Scaruffi 2009. http://www.scaruffi.com/politics/massacre.html.

Seidner, Stanley S. 2009. "A Trojan horse: Logotherapeutic transcendence and its secular implications for theology." Mater Dei Institute. Working Paper.

Sereny, G. 1995. *Albert Speer: His Battle with Truth*. London: Macmillan.

Snyder, C. R. 1994. *The Psychology of Hope*. New York: Free Press.

———. 2000. *Handbook of Hope: Theory, Measures, and Applications*. New York: Academic Press.

Sophocles. 1899. *Antigone*. Translated by G. H. Palmer. Boston: Houghton and Mifflin.

Speer, A. 1997. *Inside the Third Reich: Memoirs*. First published 1970. New York: Macmillan.

Staub, E., Pearlman, L. A., Gubin, A., and Hagengimana, A. 2005. "Healing, reconciliation, forgiving and the prevention of violence after genocide or mass killings:

An intervention and its experimental evaluation in Rwanda." *Journal of Social and Clinical Psychology*, 24(3): 297–334.

Steinbeck, J. 1942. *The Moon is Down*. New York: Viking Press.

Suedfeld, P. 1997a. "Homo Invictus: The indomitable species." *Canadian Psychology*, 38: 164–73.

———. 1997b. "Reactions to societal trauma: Distress and/or eustress." *Political Psychology*, 18: 849–61.

Suedfeld, P., Fell, C., and Krell, R. 1998. "Structural aspects of survivors' thinking about the Holocaust." *Journal of Traumatic Stress*, 11: 323–36.

Tedeschi, R. G., and Calhoun, L. G. 1995. *Post-Traumatic Growth: Positive Changes in the Aftermath of Crisis*. Mahwah, NJ: Erlbaum.

Tolstoy, L. 1869. *War and Peace*. New York: Alfred A. Knopf.

Turner, R. H., and Killian, L. M. 1972. *Collective Behavior*. Englewood Cliffs, NJ: Prentice-Hall.

Waugh, Evelyn (1973) [1946]. *Brideshead Revisited*. Boston: Little, Brown and Company.

Wiesel, E. 2006. *Night*. First published 1958/1960. New York: Hill and Wang; Farrar and Strauss and Giroux.

Zahava, Solomon. 1988. "The effect of combat-related posttraumatic stress disorder on the family." *Psychiatry*, 51: 323–29t.

Zimbardo, P. G. 2007. *The Lucifer Effect: Understanding How Good People Turn Evil*. New York: Random House.

Zimbardo, P. G., Maslach, C., and Haney, C. 1999. "Reflections on the Stanford Prison Experiment: Genesis, transformations, consequences." In T. Blass, ed., *Obedience to Authority: Current Perspectives on the Milgram Paradigm*. Mahwah, NJ: Erlbaum, 193–237.

ACKNOWLEDGMENTS BY THE SENIOR AUTHOR

Our first thanks must go to the people who were kind enough to share their life stories with us. Unless speakers specifically asked us to use their real names, we have given them pseudonyms, and modified those parts of their stories that might identify them to strangers. Hence our thanks can only be private. Second, I thank the students in Political Science 149, Fall 2010, for the incredible interviews they collected and for reminding us all why teaching is such a pleasure. These interviews are available for other scholars via the Vaughen Archives at the UCI Ethics Center. Two students, Sif Heide-Ottosen and Shant Setrak Meguerditchian deserve special thanks for their work with me on this project, presented as a co-authored conference paper at the American Political Science Association in 2011. Third, my gratitude to the usual cast of characters: my friends and colleagues whose friendship and counsel is a constant encouragement and support: Fred Alford, Tony Broh, Barbara Dosher, David Easton, Jim Glass, Jennifer Hochschild, Cecelia Lynch, Rose McDermott, Sandra Morton, Phyllis Osaben, Kamal Sadiq, Kay Schlozman, Joanna Scott, Etel Solingen, and Edna Mejia. This book was completed during a 2012–2013 fellowship at the Radcliffe Institute for Advanced Study at Harvard University. My thanks to the staff of the Radcliffe and to Judy Vichniac, Associate Director, and to Dean Elizabeth Cohen who, along with the other Fellows and friends, provided a warm and nurturing intellectual environment in which to write and think about difficult and complex topics. In addition, Helen Haste and her colleagues at Harvard's Civic and Moral Education Initiative provided valuable feedback at a seminar presentation on the book manuscript, as did participants on panels at the International Society of Political Psychology and the American Political Science Association. Anonymous readers at Cambridge University Press provided helpful comments and Elaine

McDevitt and Nicholas Lampros kindly offered editorial advice. Conversations with Alexander Lampros provided insight into the psychology of war and Gertrude Renwick Monroe offered both editorial assistance and her usual encouragement. Finally, my two young co-authors put this on a faster track than it otherwise would have been and reinforced my joy in working with young people. To all of these people, and to the staff and my editor – Robert Dreesen – at Cambridge University Press, I am most grateful.

INDEX